8-24-87

C0-DAN-399

TALK THRU
THE NEW
TESTAMENT

TALK THRU the NEW TESTAMENT

from
WALK THRU THE BIBLE

by
Kenneth Boa

Tyndale House Publishers, Inc.
Wheaton, Illinois

Charts on pages 42-47, 55-60, 148, 149, 213, 214, and
227-229 are from the *Walk Thru the New Testament*
seminar notebook, copyrighted by Walk Thru the Bible
Ministries, © 1975, 1977, 1979. These charts may not
be reproduced without written permission.

First printing, August 1981

Scripture quotations are from
the New American Standard Bible.
© The Lockman Foundation
1960, 1962, 1963, 1968, 1971, 1973, 1975.
Used by permission.
Library of Congress Catalog Card Number 81-52011
ISBN 0-8423-6912-0, cloth
Copyright © 1981 by Walk Thru the Bible Ministries, Inc.
Published by Tyndale House Publishers, Inc.
All rights reserved.
Printed in the United States of America.

To my father
KENNETH BOA
who shared his name with me
and much more.

Contents

Introduction to the New Testament

The historians, poets, and prophets who wrote the 39 books of the Old Testament were men who passionately anticipated the fulfillment of Yahweh's redemptive program and the coming of His Anointed One. Their inspired predictions were gloriously realized in the coming of Jesus the Messiah. Thus, the New Testament completes the cosmic story begun in the Old Testament of God's plan to bring salvation upon the earth.

He Kaine Diatheke (Latin, *Novum Testamentum*) literally means "The New Covenant." The Greek word *diatheke* speaks of a last will and testament that came into effect upon the death of the testator. The New Covenant was ratified with the blood of Christ, and a person enters into that covenant relationship when he comes to God on *His* terms. This redemptive covenant is a unifying theme that binds the books of the New Testament together (see Luke 22:20; 1 Cor. 11:25; Heb. 8:7-13; 9:15-17).

Like the Old Testament, the New Testament is not one book but an anthology of books that ranged in length from a single sheet of papyrus to a full scroll. The 27 books of the New Testament reflect a wide diversity of themes, personalities, literary forms and achievement, backgrounds, and purposes, so that each book has a unique contribution to make. The New Testament, less than one-third the length of the Old Testament, was written from about A.D. 45-95 in *Koine* ("common") Greek, the international language of the people. This language was not only widely used, but it was clear, precise, and flexible.

The New Testament books were separately circulated and gradually collected together. Their inspiration and apostolic authority guaranteed them a place in the canon of Scripture as they were set apart from other writings in the early church. As these books were copied and distributed throughout the Roman Empire, they were eventually placed in a standard order (more logical than chronological).

Of the nine New Testament authors, only Luke was a Gentile. Paul wrote 13 books, John wrote five, Luke and Peter wrote two, and Matthew, Mark, James, Jude, and the author of Hebrews each wrote one. Sometimes these books are arranged into three periods: (1) the lifetime of Christ, 4 B.C.—A.D. 33 (Matthew, Mark, Luke, John); (2) the expansion of the church in Acts, A.D. 33-62 (Acts, Romans, 1 and 2 Corinthians, Galatians, Ephesians, Philippians, Colossians, 1 and 2 Thessalonians, Philemon, James); (3) the post-Acts consolidation of the church, A.D. 62-95 (1 and 2 Timothy, Titus, Hebrews, 1 and 2 Peter, 1, 2, and 3 John, Jude, Revelation). A more common classification is the threefold division into the Historical Books, the Pauline Epistles, and the Non-Pauline Epistles and Revelation. This can be modified into the following chart:

The Structure of the New Testament

Pauline Epistles: Churches	Pauline Epistles: Individuals				Non-Pauline Epistles and Revelation
	1 Timothy	2 Timothy	Titus	Philemon	
	2 Thessalonians			Hebrews	
	1 Thessalonians			James	
	Colossians			1 Peter	
	Philippians			2 Peter	
	Ephesians			1 John	
	Galatians			2 John	
	2 Corinthians			3 John	
	1 Corinthians			Jude	
	Romans			Revelation	
Acts					
Matthew	Mark		Luke	John	
Historical Books					

Historical Books: These five books depict key events in the life of Christ, the foundation of the church, and the early spread of Christianity. The Old Testament anticipated the person and work of the Lord Jesus in manifold ways, and the hope of the prophets was incarnated in the form of the God-man, the Word who became flesh (John 1:1,14). After His resurrection, He empowered His apostles to spread the glad tidings of salvation beginning in Jerusalem and reaching to Rome and beyond.

Pauline Epistles: The epistles as a whole develop the seed doctrines in the gospels and show how they can transform the lives of believers. Paul wrote nine letters to churches and four to individuals as he sought to instruct, correct, and encourage believers throughout the Roman Empire. Paul wanted Christians to base their practice upon the reality of their position in Christ.

Non-Pauline Epistles and Revelation: Peter, John, James, and the author of Hebrews dealt frankly and firmly with a multitude of problems that were creeping into the churches. They pointed to the person and power of the resurrected Christ as the believer's source of life and godliness. Revelation is a fitting conclusion to the New Testament as it looks ahead to the hope of Christ's return, the vindication of God's righteousness, and the culmination of His eternal plan in the new heavens and new earth.

Introduction to the Historical Books

The four gospels comprise about 46% of the New Testament, and when the book of Acts is added, the figure goes up to 60%. The early church placed the gospels at the beginning of the New Testament canon, not because they were the first books to be written, but because they are the foundation upon which Acts and the epistles are built. The gospels are at once rooted in and the fulfillment of the Old Testament, and they provide the historical and theological backdrop for the rest of the New Testament.

The Greek word *euaggelion* refers to the "glad tidings" or "good news" about Jesus Christ that was orally proclaimed. It later came to be applied to the written accounts as well. The English word "gospel" is a derivative of the Anglo-Saxon *godspell* which can mean "God story" or "good story." Although later gospels were written, the early church regarded only the four gospels as we know them to be authoritative and divinely inspired. They were distinguished from one another by the Greek preposition *kata* ("according to") followed by the name of the writer. The present order of the four gospels goes back at least to the late second century, and it was thought to be the order in which they were written. Although there are some who have theorized that the gospels were originally written in Aramaic, there is no real evidence for this position. The inhabitants of Palestine were primarily bilingual (Aramaic and Greek), and many were trilingual (Hebrew or Latin). But Greek was the common language of the whole empire, and thus the most suitable vehicle for the gospel accounts.

The literary form of the gospels had no counterpart in Hellenistic literature. Although they are full of biographical material, they are really thematic portraits that almost entirely overlook the 30-plus years of preparation for Christ's relatively brief public ministry. Even this portion of His life is presented in a highly skewed fashion with the emphasis on His last week. In all, only about 50 days of Jesus' ministry are touched upon in the combined gospels.

The four complementary accounts provide a composite picture of the person and work of the Savior, working together to give depth and clarity to our understanding of the most unique figure in human history. In them He is seen as divine and human, the sovereign Servant, the God-man. Each gospel has a distinctive dimension to add, so that the total is greater than the sum of the parts.

Topics	Matthew	Mark	Luke	John
Probable Date	A.D. 58-68	A.D. 55-65	A.D. 60-68	A.D. 80-90
Place of Writing	Syrian Antioch or Palestine	Rome	Rome/ Greece	Ephesus
Original Audience	Jewish Mind (Religious)	Roman Mind (Pragmatic)	Greek Mind (Idealistic)	Universal
Theme	Messiah-King	Servant-Redeemer	Perfect Man	Son of God
Traditional Picture of Christ (cf. Ezek. 1:10; Rev. 4:6-8)	The Lion (strength, authority)	The Bull (service, power)	The Man (wisdom, character)	The Eagle (deity, person)

The gospels were written to awaken and strengthen faith in Christ and to answer objections and misconceptions about Him. They were also designed to guide believers into a fuller understanding of His person and power. As Christianity spread beyond Palestine, the oral testimony of the apostles was no longer adequate. Their message was multiplied and preserved through the medium of the written word.

Matthew, Mark, and Luke are known as the *synoptic gospels*. The Greek word *synoptikos* means "seeing together," and it is an appropriate description of these gospels because of their common viewpoint and similar characteristics, especially in contrast to John, the *supplemental gospel*.

Topics	Synoptics (Matt., Mark, Luke)	John
Portrait of Christ	God-*man*	God-*man*
Perspective	Historical	Theological
Unique Material	Less unique (Matt., 42%; Mark, 7%; Luke 59%)	More unique (92%)
Chronology	Only one Passover mentioned	Three or four Passovers mentioned
Geography	Concentrate on Galilean ministry	Concentrates on Judean ministry
Discourse Material	More Public	More Private
Teaching Method	Parables	Allegories
Teaching Emphasis	More on ethical, practical teachings	More on the person of Christ
Relationship to Other Gospels	Complementary	Supplementary

The agreements and differences among the synoptics have led to the "synoptic problem" of determining their literary relationship. The agreements include selection of materials, broad chronological outline, and literary structure. The differences include unique material, differences in some parallel accounts, and different historical contexts for some episodes. There are many proposed solutions to this problem, but most are variations on three basic suggestions: (1) oral tradition, (2) interdependence, and (3) documentary sources. The two-document theory proposes that Mark and an unknown source document named Q were the basis for Matthew and Luke. Multiple-document theories propose additional hypothetical source documents. The most satisfactory approach involves four elements: (1) direct knowledge, (2) oral tradition, (3) use of documents, and (4) the superintending ministry of the Holy Spirit (cf. John 14:26).

Christ indeed came in "the fulness of the time" (Gal. 4:4). Politically, the Roman Empire provided universal peace, improved travel (Roman roads), and a common language (Greek) that would facilitate the spread of the gospel. Economically, conditions of high taxation, poverty, and unrest put most people in a state of need. Spiritually, Judaism had lost its vitality and the Roman gods were dead or dying. It was in this context that Christianity flourished in its crucial beginning years.

Matthew: The first gospel presents Jesus as the Christ, Israel's Messianic King. Jesus' genealogy, fulfillment of Old Testament prophecy, authority, and power are emphasized as His Messianic credentials. In spite of His unique words and works, gradually mounting opposition culminates in His crucifixion. But the King left an empty tomb and will come again.

Mark: The second gospel presents Jesus as the Servant who came to "give His life a ransom for many." In the beginning of His ministry He was a servant to the multitudes, but as His departure grew near, Jesus concentrated on teaching and ministering to His disciples. A full 37% of this gospel is devoted to the events of His last and most important week.

Luke: The third gospel presents Jesus as the perfect Son of Man whose mission was "to seek and to save that which was lost." This lucid historical portrait of Christ traces His advent, activities, admonitions, affliction, and authentication to demonstrate His perfect character and redemptive work.

John: The fourth gospel presents Jesus as the eternal Son of God who offered eternal life to all who would believe in Him. John uses a carefully chosen series of seven signs to demonstrate that Jesus is the Christ. Five chapters of this gospel record Jesus' parting discourse to His disciples only a few hours before His death. After His victorious resurrection, Christ further instructed His men in a number of appearances.

Acts: There are four gospel accounts, but only one canonical book of Acts. Thus, this book provides the only historical portrait of the period from the ascension to the travels and trials of Paul. Acts chronicles some of the key events in the spread of the gospel from Judea to Samaria, Syria, and the rest of the Roman Empire.

Matthew

"Say to the daughter of Zion, 'Behold your King is coming to you, gentle, and mounted upon a donkey, even on a colt, the foal of a beast of burden.' "

Matthew 21:5

"Pilate said to them, 'Then what shall I do with Jesus who is called Christ?' They all said, 'Let Him be crucified!' "

Matthew 27:22 (Also see 1:1; 4:17.)

Focus	Credentials			Pattern			Preaching		Culmination	
	1 4			5 16:12			16:13 25		26 28	
D i v i s i o n s	Birth of the King	Baptism of the King	Temptation of the King	Sermon on the Mount	Series of Miracles	Spread of Opposition	Many Discourses	One Discourse	Death of the King	Resurrection of the King
	1 2	3	4	5 7	8 9	10 16:12	16:13 23	24 25	26 27	28
T o p i c s	Person			Pre-cepts	Power	Pro-gram	Preach-ing	Predic-tions	Pas-sion	Power
	Chronological			Thematic			Chronological			
	Growing Reception						Growing Rejection			
	Teaching the Throngs						Teaching the Twelve			
Loca-tions	Bethlehem and Nazareth			Ministry in Galilee			Ministry in Judea			
	1 4:12			4:13 18			19 28			
Time	4 B.C. — A.D. 33									

Talk Thru—The Old Testament prophets predicted and longed for the coming of the Anointed One who would enter history to bring redemption and deliverance. The first verse of Matthew succinctly announces the fulfillment of Israel's hope in the coming of the Christ: "The book of the genealogy of Jesus Christ, the son of David, the son of Abraham." Matthew was placed first in the canon of New Testament books by the early church because it is the natural bridge between the testaments. This gospel describes the person and work of Israel's Messianic King. An important part of Matthew's structure is revealed in the phrase "when Jesus had finished" (7:28; 11:1; 13:53; 19:1; 26:1), which is used to conclude the five key discourses of the book: the Sermon on the Mount (5:3-7:27), instruction of the disciples (10:5-42), parables of the kingdom (13:3-52), terms of discipleship (18:3-35), and the Olivet Discourse (24:4-25:46). A broader approach to this book is: Credentials (1-4), Pattern (5-16:12), Preaching (16:13-25:46), and Culmination (26-28).

Credentials (1-4): The promise to Abraham was that "in you all the families of the earth shall be blessed" (Gen. 12:3). Jesus Christ, the Savior of the world, is "the son of Abraham" (1:1). But He is also "the son of David," and as David's direct descendant, He is qualified to be Israel's King. The magi knew that the "King of the Jews" (2:2) had been born and came to worship Him. John the Baptist, the Messianic forerunner who broke the 400-year prophetic silence, also bore witness of Him (cf. Mal. 3:1). The sinlessness of the King was proved when He overcame the Satanic temptations to disobey the will of the Father.

Pattern (5-16:12): In this section, Matthew uses a topical rather than a chronological arrangement of his material in order to develop a crucial pattern in Christ's ministry. The *words* of the Lord are found in the Sermon on the Mount (5-7). This discourse requires less than 15 minutes to read, but it has profoundly influenced the world. In it the King presents new laws and standards for His people. The *works* of the Lord are presented in a series of 10 miracles (8-9) which reveal His authority over every realm (disease, demons, death, and nature). Thus, the words of the Lord are supported by His works; His claims are verified by His credentials. The third part of the pattern is found in 10-16:12, which lists a series of *reactions* to

18

Christ's words and works. Because of increasing opposition, Jesus began to spend proportionately more time with His disciples as He prepared them for His coming death and departure.

Preaching (16:13-25:46): In a series of discourses, Jesus communicated the significance of the reactions of accepting or rejecting His offer of righteousness. His teaching in 16:13-21:11 was primarily directed to those who accepted Him, while 21:12-25:46 was aimed at those who rejected their King. The Lord predicted the terrible judgment that would fall on Jerusalem and the dispersion of the Jewish people. Looking beyond these events (fulfilled in A.D. 70), He also described His second coming as the Judge and Lord of the earth.

Culmination (26-28): Christ's final ministry in Judea (beginning in 19:1) reached a climax at the cross as the King willingly gave up His life to redeem sinful men. Jesus endured awesome human hatred in this greatest demonstration of divine love (cf. Rom. 5:7,8). His perfect sacrifice was acceptable, and this gospel closes with His glorious resurrection.

Title—At an early date this gospel was given the superscription *Kata Matthaion*, "According to Matthew." As this title suggests, other gospel accounts were known as well (the word "gospel" was added to the superscription at a later time). Matthew ("gift of the Lord") was also surnamed Levi (Mark 2:14; Luke 5:27).

Author—Modern scholars often deny the apostolic origin of this gospel because it does not have as many lifelike touches as the other gospels and because an apostle like Matthew would not have depended so heavily on a non-apostolic writer like Mark. While there are problems, the first argument is more a matter of stylistic approach, and the second argument overlooks the apostolic origin of Mark's gospel (Peter) and Matthew's critical use of Mark (if he used it at all). The arguments against Matthean authorship are much weaker than the external and internal evidence for the traditional view. The early church uniformly attributed this gospel to Matthew, and no contrary tradition ever developed. This book was known early and quickly accepted.

In his *Ecclesiastical History* (323), Eusebius quoted a statement by Papias (c. 140) that Matthew wrote *logia* ("sayings") in Aramaic. No Aramaic gospel of Matthew has been found, and it is evident that Matthew is not a Greek translation of an Aramaic original. Some believe that Papias was in error, but it is possible that Matthew wrote an abbreviated version of Jesus' sayings in Aramaic before writing his gospel in Greek for a larger circle of readers.

Matthew, the son of Alphaeus (Mark 2:14) occupied the unpopular post of tax collector in Capernaum for the Roman government. As a publican he was no doubt disliked by his Jewish countrymen. When Jesus called him to discipleship (9:9-13; Mark 2:14; Luke 5:27,28), his quick response probably meant that he had already been stirred by Jesus' public preaching. He gave a big reception for Jesus in his house so that his associates could meet Jesus. He was chosen as one of the 12 apostles, and the last appearance of his name is in Acts 1:13. His life from that point on is veiled in exaggerated tradition.

Date and Setting—Like all the gospels, Matthew is not
easy to date—suggestions have ranged from A.D. 40-140. The two appearances of "to this day" (27:8; 28:15) indicate that a substantial period of time had passed since the events described in the book, but they also point to a date prior to the A.D. 70 destruction of Jerusalem. The Olivet Discourse (24-25) also anticipates this event (unless predictive prophecy is denied). The strong Jewish emphasis of this gospel is another argument for a date prior to A.D. 70. If Matthew depended on Mark's gospel as a source, the date of Mark would determine the earliest date for Matthew. The likely range for this book is A.D. 58-68. It may have been written in Palestine or Syrian Antioch.

Theme and Purpose—Although Matthew has no purpose statement, it was clearly written to proclaim the words and works of Jesus Christ so that the reader could make an intelligent decision about Him. The opening genealogy reaches back into the Old Testament, and the many references to Christ's fulfillment of specific prophecies show that Israel's long-awaited Messiah had come. Matthew was no doubt used by Jewish believers as an evangelistic tool to reach other Jews.

It is evident that Matthew also had an instructional purpose in writing his gospel. It systematically presents the claims, credentials, authority, ethical teachings, and theological teachings of the Lord Jesus. As such, it has been used as a teaching manual since the early years of the church.

Contribution to the Bible—The most striking feature of the first gospel is its Jewish emphasis. Matthew traces the genealogy of Jesus back to Abraham and frequently calls Him the son of David. He strongly stresses the fulfillment of Messianic prophecies in the life of Christ. Also prominent are Jewish customs and traditions (without explanations), the place of the Mosaic law in Jesus' teaching, the "lost sheep of the house of Israel," and the scribes and Pharisees. Matthew develops the theme of the kingdom because the Jewish reader would wonder why Jesus did not establish the promised kingdom if He was indeed Messiah.

The good news of this book reaches beyond the Jews to the rest of the world as well. Gentile women are found in Christ's genealogy; Gentiles worshiped Him after His birth, "the field is the world" (13:38); and the great commission is to "make disciples of all the nations" (28:19; also see 8:11,12; 21:33-43).

Fully 60% of Matthew's 1,071 verses contain the spoken words of Jesus. Matthew paints a broad picture of Christ's life without going into the fine details that are often seen in the other gospels. The highly organized content of this gospel (discourses, miracles, parables, questions) is thematically arranged to stress the combined thrust of the Savior's words and works. Matthew builds his themes in such a way that they all join together in the climax of the book.

Christ in Matthew—Matthew presents Jesus as Israel's promised Messianic King (1:23; 2:2,6; 3:17; 4:15-17; 21:5,9; 22:44,45; 26:64; 27:11,27-37). The phrase "the kingdom of heaven" appears 32 times in Matthew but nowhere else in the New Testament. Matthew uses more Old Testament quotations and allusions than any other book (almost 130) to show that Jesus fulfills the qualifications for Messiah. Characteristic of this gospel is the telling phrase "that what was spoken through the prophet might be fulfilled," appearing nine times

in Matthew but in no other gospel. Jesus is the climax of the prophets (12:39,40; 13:13-15,35; 17:5-13), the Son of Man (24:30ff.), the servant of the Lord (8:17; 11:5,6; 12:17-21), and the "son of David" (nine times in Matthew, but only six times in the rest of the gospels).

Mark

"For even the Son of Man did not come to be served, but to serve, and to give His life a ransom for many."

Mark 10:45

Focus	Servant to the Multitudes 1 7		Servant to the Disciples 8 10			Sacrifice for the World 11 16		
D i v i s i o n s	Words of Jesus 1 4	Works of Jesus 5 7	Testimony of Peter 8	Transfiguration of Jesus 9	Teaching of Jesus 10	Ministry in Jerusalem 11 13	Ministry on the Cross 14 15	Ministry after the Tomb 16
T o p i c s	Sayings and Signs of the Servant					Suffering of the Servant		
	"For even the Son of Man did not come to be served, but to serve..."					"and to give His life a ransom for many"		
	Proclamation		Rejection				Exaltation	
	Three Years		Six Months			Eight Days		
Loca- tions	Wilder- ness 1:1-13	Galilee 1:14 9			Perea 10	Judea (Bethany and Jerusalem) 11 16		
Time	A.D. 29-33							

Talk Thru—Mark, the shortest and simplest of the four gospels, gives a crisp and fast-moving look at the life of Christ. With few comments, Mark lets the narrative speak for itself as it tells the story of the Servant who constantly ministered to others through preaching, healing, teaching, and ultimately, His own death. Mark traces the steady building of hostility and opposition to Jesus as He resolutely moved toward the fulfillment of His earthly mission. Almost 40% of this gospel is devoted to a detailed account of the last eight days of His life, climaxing in the resurrection (11-16). The Lord is portrayed in this vivid book as a Servant to the multitudes (1-7), a Servant to the disciples (8-10), and the Sacrifice for the world (11-16).

Servant to the Multitudes (1-7): Mark passes over the birth and early years of Jesus' life and begins with the events that immediately preceded the inauguration of His public ministry—His baptism by John and His temptation by Satan (1:1-13). The first four chapters emphasize the words of the Servant while chapters 5-7 accent His works. But in both sections there is a frequent alternation between Christ's messages and miracles in order to reveal His person and power. Though He came to serve others, Jesus' authority prevailed over many realms.

Servant to the Disciples (8-10): Although Jesus has already been teaching and testing His disciples (see chapter 4), His ministry with them becomes more intense from this point on as He begins to prepare them for His departure. The religious leaders were growing more antagonistic, and Christ's "hour" was only about six months away. Mark 8:31 marks the pivotal point in the gospel as the Son of Man spoke clearly to His disciples about His coming death and resurrection. The disciples struggled with this difficult revelation, but Jesus' steps were heading inexorably to Jerusalem.

Sacrifice for the World (11-16): Mark allots a disproportionate space to the denouement of the Servant's redemptive ministry. During His last week in Jerusalem, hostility from the chief priests, scribes, elders, Pharisees, Herodians, and Sadducees reached crisis proportions as the Lord publicly refuted their arguments in the temple. After His last supper with the disciples, Jesus offered no resistance to His arrest, abuse, and agonizing crucifixion. His willingness to bear countless human sins was the epitome of servanthood. This gospel closes with

His resurrection, but the "long ending" of 16:9-20 has been the subject of considerable debate. Manuscript evidence suggests that Mark may have abruptly ended his gospel at 16:8.

Title—The ancient superscription to this gospel was *Kata Markon*, "According to Mark." The author is best known by his Latin name *Marcus,* but in Jewish circles he was called by his Hebrew name *John*. Acts 12:12,25; 15:37 refer to him as "John who was also called Mark."

Author—According to Acts 12:12, Mark's mother Mary had a large house that was used as a meeting place for believers in Jerusalem. Peter evidently went to this house often because the servant girl recognized his voice at the gate (Acts 12:13-16). Barnabas was Mark's cousin (Col. 4:10), but Peter may have been the person who led him to Christ (Peter called him "my son, Mark" in 1 Peter 5:13). It was this close association with Peter that lent apostolic authority to Mark's gospel, since Peter was evidently Mark's primary source of information. It has been suggested that Mark was referring to himself in his account of "a certain young man" in Gethsemane (14:51,52). Since all the disciples had abandoned Jesus (14:50), this little incident may have been a firsthand account.

Barnabas and Saul took Mark along with them when they returned from Jerusalem to Antioch (Acts 12:25) and again when they left on the first missionary journey (Acts 13:5). For some reason, Mark left early and returned to Jerusalem (Acts 13:13). When Barnabas wanted to bring Mark on the second missionary journey, Paul's refusal led to a disagreement. The result was that Barnabas took Mark to Cyprus and Paul took Silas through Syria and Cilicia (Acts 15:36-41). Nevertheless, Paul wrote that Mark was with him during his first Roman imprisonment (Col. 4:10; Philem. 24) about 12 years later, so there must have been a reconciliation. In fact, at the end of his life Paul sent for Mark, saying "he is useful to me for service" (2 Tim. 4:11).

The early church uniformly attested that Mark wrote this gospel. Papias, Irenaeus, Clement of Alexandria, and Origen are among the church fathers who affirmed Marcan authorship.

Date and Setting—Many scholars believe that Mark was the first of the four gospels, but there is uncertainty over its date. Because of the prophecy about the destruction of the temple (13:2), it should be dated before A.D. 70, but early traditions disagree as to whether it was written before or after the martyrdom of Peter (c. 64). The probable range for this book is A.D. 55-65.

Mark was evidently directed to a Roman readership and early tradition indicates that it originated in Rome. This is why Mark omitted a number of things that would not be meaningful to Gentiles, such as the genealogy of Christ, fulfilled prophecy, references to the law, and certain Jewish customs that are found in other gospels. Mark interpreted Aramaic words (3:17; 5:41; 7:34; 15:22) and used a number of Latin terms in place of their Greek equivalents (4:21; 6:27; 12:14,42; 15:15,16,39).

Theme and Purpose—Even in the first verse it is obvious that this gospel centers on the person and mission of the Son of God. Mark's theme is captured well in 10:45 because Jesus is portrayed in this book as a Servant and as the Redeemer of men (cf. Phil. 2:5-11). Like the other gospels, Mark is not a biography but a topical narrative. Mark juxtaposes Christ's teachings and works to show how they authenticate each other. Miracles are predominant in this book (there are 18), and they are used to demonstrate not only the power of Christ but also His compassion. Mark shows his Gentile readers how the Son of God was rejected by His own people, achieving ultimate victory through apparent defeat. There was no doubt an evangelistic purpose behind this gospel as Mark directed his words to a Gentile audience that knew little about Old Testament theology. This book may also have been used to instruct and encourage Roman believers.

Contribution to the Bible—Mark uses a simple and unvarnished style that is brisk and clear. The narrative moves vigorously and efficiently, very appropriate for a gospel that depicts the divine Servant at work. The quick pace and brevity of this book (it has only two extended discourses: 4:1-34; 13:3-37) reflect Mark's emphasis on action more than words, making it suitable to the practical orientation of the Roman mind.

Only 18 out of Christ's 70 parables are found in Mark—and some of these are only one sentence in length—but he lists over half of Christ's 35 miracles, the highest proportion in the gospels. Mark's language is characterized by broken sentence structure, colloquialisms, and extra expressions that may reproduce Peter's style of speaking. He uses the historic present tense 151 times to depict action in progress. The vivid descriptions in this book are often more detailed than the parallel accounts in Matthew and Luke. Mark records a wide range of emotional reactions: "they were all amazed" (1:27), "they became very much afraid" (4:41), "they began laughing at Him" (5:40), "they took offense at Him" (6:3), "they were utterly astonished" (7:37). Jesus' own reactions of compassion, anger, grief, sorrow, warmth, distress, sympathy, and indignation are also very evident.

Christ in Mark—The Lord is presented as an active, compassionate, and obedient Servant who constantly ministered to the physical and spiritual needs of others. Because this is the story of a Servant, Mark omits His ancestry and birth and moves right into His busy public ministry. The distinctive word of this book is *euthus*, translated "immediately" or "straightway," and it appears more often in this compact gospel (42 times) than in the rest of the New Testament. Christ was constantly moving toward a goal which was hidden to almost all. Mark clearly shows the power and authority of this unique Servant, identifying Him as no less than the Son of God (1:1,11; 3:11; 5:7; 9:7; 13:32; 14:61; 15:39).

Luke

"For the Son of Man has come to seek and to save that which was lost."

Luke 19:10

Focus	Advent		Activities		Antagonism and Admonitions		Afflic-tion	Authenti-cation
	1 4:13		4:14 9:50		9:51 19:27		19:28 23	24
Divisions	Identification of the Son of Man	Presentation of the Son of Man	Authority of the Son of Man	Ministry of the Son of Man	Rejection of the Son of Man	Teaching of the Son of Man	Suffering of the Son of Man	Resurrection of the Son of Man
	1 2	3:1-4:13	4:14 6	7 9:50	9:51 11	12 19:27	19:28 23	24
Topics	Seeking the Lost						Saving the Lost	
	Miracles Prominent			Parables and Teaching Prominent				
	Presentation			Preaching			Passion	
Locations	Nazareth, Wilderness	Galilee		On the Way to Jerusalem			Jerusalem	
Time	5 B.C. — A.D. 33							

Talk Thru—Luke builds the gospel narrative on the platform of historical reliability. His emphasis on chronological and historical accuracy makes this the most comprehensive of the four gospels. This is also the longest and most literary gospel, and it presents Jesus Christ as the Perfect Man who came to seek and save sinful men. This book can be divided into five sections: Advent (1:1-4:13), Activities (4:14-9:50), Antagonism and Admonitions (9:51-19:27), Affliction (19:28-23:56), and Authentication (24).

Advent (1:1-4:13): Luke places a strong emphasis on the ancestry, birth, and early years of the Perfect Man and of His forerunner John the Baptist. Their infancy stories are intertwined as Luke records their birth announcements, advents, and temple presentations. Jesus prepared over 30 years (summarized in one verse, 2:52) for a public ministry of only three years. The ancestry of the Son of Man is traced back to the first man Adam, and His ministry commenced after His baptism and temptation.

Activities (4:14-9:50): The authority of the Son of Man over every realm is demonstrated in 4:14-6:49. In this section His authority over demons, disease, nature, the effects of sin, tradition, and men is presented as a prelude to His many-faceted ministry of preaching, healing, and discipling (7:1-9:50).

Antagonism and Admonitions (9:51-19:27): The dual response of growing belief and growing rejection has already been introduced in the gospel (compare 4:14 and 6:11), but from this point on the level of opposition to the ministry of the Son of Man becomes intense. When the religious leaders accuse Him of being demonized, Jesus pronounces a series of divine woes upon them (11). Knowing that He is on His last journey to Jerusalem, Jesus instructs His disciples on a number of practical matters including prayer, covetousness, faithfulness, repentance, humility, discipleship, evangelism, money, forgiveness, service, thankfulness, the second advent, and salvation (12:1-19:27).

Affliction (19:28-23:56): After His triumphal entry into Jerusalem, Jesus encountered the opposition of the priests, Sadducees, and scribes and predicted the overthrow of Jerusalem (19:28-21:38). The Son of Man instructed His disciples for the last time before His betrayal in Gethsemane. A grueling series of three religious and three civil trials culminated in His crucifixion.

Authentication (24): The glory and foundation of the Christian message is the historical resurrection of Jesus Christ. The Lord conquered the grave as He promised, and appeared on a number of occasions to His disciples before His ascension to the Father.

Title—*Kata Loukon*, "According to Luke," is the ancient superscription that was added to this gospel at a very early date. The Greek name Luke appears only three times in the New Testament (Col. 4:14; 2 Tim. 4:11; Philem. 24).

Author—It is evident from the prologues to Luke and Acts (Luke 1:1-4; Acts 1:1-5) that both books were addressed to Theophilus as a two-volume work (Luke is called "the first account"). Acts begins with a summary of Luke and picks up the story where the gospel left off, and the style and language of both books are quite similar. The "we"-sections of Acts (Acts 16:10-17; 20:5-21:18; 27:1-28:16) reveal that the author was a close associate and traveling companion of Paul. Because all but two of Paul's associates are named in the third person, the list can be narrowed to Titus and Luke. Titus has never been seriously regarded as a possible author of Acts, and Luke best fits the requirements. He was with Paul during his first Roman imprisonment, and Paul referred to him as "Luke, the beloved physician" (Col. 4:14; cf. Philem. 24). During his second Roman imprisonment, Paul wrote "Only Luke is with me" (2 Tim. 4:11), an evidence of Luke's loyalty to the apostle in the face of profound danger.

Luke may have been a Hellenistic Jew, but it is more likely that he was a Gentile (this would make him the only Gentile contributor to the New Testament). In Colossians 4:10-14, Paul lists three fellow workers who are "from the circumcision" (vss. 10,11) and then includes Luke's name with two Gentiles (vss. 12-14). His obvious skill with the Greek language and his phrase "their own language" in Acts 1:19 also imply that he was not Jewish. It has been suggested that Luke may have been a Greek physician to a Roman family who at some point was set free and given Roman citizenship. Another guess is that he was the "brother" of 2 Corinthians 8:18,19. Ancient tradition strongly supports Luke as the author of Luke-Acts (including the Muratorian Fragment, Irenaeus, Tertullian, Clement of Alexandria, Origen, Eusebius, and Jerome), and no alternative was ever suggested. Tradition also says that Luke was from Syrian Antioch, remained unmarried, and died at the age of 84.

Date and Setting—Luke was not an eyewitness of the events in his gospel, but he relied on the testimony of eyewitnesses and written sources (1:1-4). He carefully investigated and arranged his material and presented it to Theophilus ("friend of God"). The title "most excellent" (see Acts 23:26; 24:3; 26:25) indicates that Theophilus was a man of high social standing. He probably assumed responsibility for publishing Luke and Acts so that they would be available to Gentile readers. Luke translates Aramaic terms with Greek words and explains Jewish customs and geography to make his gospel more intelligible to his original Greek readership. During Paul's two-year Caesarean imprisonment, Luke may have traveled in Palestine to gather information from eyewitnesses of Jesus' ministry. The date of this gospel depends on that of Acts since this was the first volume (see Acts, Date and Setting). If Luke was written during Paul's first imprisonment in Rome it would be dated in the early 60's. It may, however, have been given final form in Greece. In all probability, its publication preceded the A.D. 70 destruction of Jerusalem.

Theme and Purpose—Luke clearly states his purpose in the prologue of his gospel: ". . . to write it out for you in consecutive order, . . . so that you might know the exact truth about the things you have been taught" (1:3,4). Luke wanted to create an accurate, chronological, and comprehensive account of the unique life of Jesus the Christ to strengthen the faith of Gentile believers and stimulate saving faith among nonbelievers. Luke may also have had a secondary purpose of showing that Christianity was not a politically subversive sect. He records Pilate's acknowledgment of Christ's innocence three times (23:4,14,22). The theme of this gospel is the perfect Son of Man who came "to seek and to save that which was lost" (19:10).

Contribution to the Bible—Luke, the longest book in the New Testament, is the most comprehensive and precise of the gospels. The combined books of Luke and Acts constitute 28% of the New Testament, making Luke the most prolific of its contributors (2,138 verses; Paul wrote 2,033). Not only was this gospel carefully recorded and documented, but it was also written in the most refined Greek in the New Testament—only the Epistle to the Hebrews is comparable. Luke's large vocabulary and great breadth of expressions and constructions give his work a literary richness and beauty that makes his gospel the favorite of many. Luke alone contains the four beautiful hymns commonly known as the *Magnificat* of Mary (1:46-55), the *Benedictus* of Zacharias (1:67-79), the *Gloria in Excelsis* of the heavenly host (2:14), and the *Nunc Dimittis* of Simeon (2:28-32).

Luke's strong interest in people is evident from his portraits of Zacharias, the good Samaritan, the prodigal son, the repentant tax-gatherer, Zaccheus, and the two disciples on the Emmaus road. He also gives a special place to women (e.g., Elizabeth, Mary, Anna, Martha, Mary of Bethany) and children (e.g., the childhoods of John and Jesus). Other themes that are developed in Luke include prayer, the work of the Holy Spirit, poverty and wealth, medical topics, praise and thanksgiving, and domestic life. Luke's gospel shows the universality of the Christian message, describing the Son of Man as the Savior for all men: Jews, Samaritans, Gentiles; poor and rich; respectable and despised; publicans and religious leaders.

Christ in Luke—The humanity and compassion of Jesus are repeatedly stressed in this gospel. Luke gives the most complete account of His ancestry, birth, and development. He is the ideal Son of Man who identified with the sorrow and plight of sinful men in order to carry our sorrows and offer us the priceless gift of salvation. Jesus alone fulfills the Greek ideal of human perfection.

John

"Many other signs therefore Jesus also performed in the presence of the disciples, which are not written in this book; but these have been written that you may believe that Jesus is the Christ, the Son of God; and that believing you may have life in His name."

John 20:30,31 (Also see 1:11,12.)

Focus	Seven Miracles			Upper Room		Supreme Miracle		
	1 ———— 12			13 ———— 17		18 ———— 21		
Divisions	Manifestation of the Son of God	Presentation of the Son of God	Rejection of the Son of God	Instructions by the Son of God	Intercession of the Son of God	Sufferings of the Son of God	Resurrection of the Son of God	Appearances of the Son of God
	1:1-18	1:19 — 4	5 — 12	13 — 16	17	18 — 19	20	21
Topics	Pro-logue	Public Ministry		Private Ministry		Paschal Ministry		Epi-logue
	Revelation		Rejec-tion	Reception		Reject-tion	Reception	
	Coming		Con-fron-tation	Comfort		Cruci-fixion	Climax	
	"that you may believe"			"that you may have life"				
Locations	Wilder-ness	Galilee, Judea, Sama-ria	Judea, Galilee	Judea				Galilee
	1	2 — 4	5 — 6	7 ———————— 20				21
Time	A Few Years			A Few Hours		A Few Weeks		

Talk Thru—This most unusual gospel, with its distinct content and style, serves as a supplement to the three synoptics. It is easily the simplest and yet the most profound of the gospels, and for many people it is the greatest and most powerful. A tremendous amount of literature has been built around the gospel of John, and the controversies over the origin and content of this book often cloud its spiritual brilliance. John wrote his gospel for the specific purpose of bringing people to spiritual life through belief in the person and work of Jesus Christ. The three basic sections of this gospel are Seven Miracles (1-12), Upper Room (13-17), and Supreme Miracle (18-21).

Seven Miracles (1-12): This section could be called the Book of the Seven Signs because John carefully selected seven miracles out of the many that Christ accomplished (cf. John 21:25) in order to build a concise case for His deity. They are called signs because they symbolize the life-changing results of belief in Jesus: (1) water to wine: the ritual of law is replaced by the reality of grace (2:1-11); (2) healing the nobleman's son: the gospel brings spiritual restoration (4:46-54); (3) healing the paralytic: weakness is replaced by strength (5:1-18); (4) feeding the multitude: Christ satisfies spiritual hunger (6:1-13); (5) walking on water: the Lord transforms fear to faith (6:16-21); (6) sight to the man born blind: Jesus overcomes darkness and brings in light (9:1-7); (7) raising of Lazarus: the gospel brings people from death to life (11:1-44). These signs combine together to show that Jesus is indeed the Son of God. John's usual pattern in these chapters is to record the reactions of belief and disbelief after a miracle before moving to the next. In effect, this forces the reader to think about his own reaction to the words and works of Christ.

The Incarnate Word "came to His own, and those who were His own did not receive Him" (1:11). In a series of growing confrontations (5-12), John portrays the intense opposition that will culminate in the Lord's final rejection on the cross. Even though many people received Him, the inevitable crucifixion is foreshadowed in several places (2:4,21,22; 7:6,39; 11:51,52; 12:16).

Upper Room (13-17): John surveyed the incarnation and public ministry of Jesus in 12 chapters, but radically changed the pace in the next five chapters to give a detailed account of a few crucial hours. In this clear and vivid recollection of Jesus' last discourse to His intimate disciples, John captured the Lord's words of comfort and assurance to a group of fearful and confused followers. He knew that in less than 24 hours He would be on the cross. Therefore, His last words spoke of all the resources that would be at their disposal after His departure. They will be indwelled and empowered by the Triune Godhead. The Upper Room Discourse has the message of the epistles in capsule form as it reveals God's pattern for Christian living. In it, the key themes of servanthood, the Holy Spirit, and abiding in Christ are developed.

Supreme Miracle (18-21): After recording Christ's high priestly prayer on behalf of His disciples and all who believe in Him through their word (17), John immediately launches into a dramatic description of Christ's arrest and trials before Annas, Caiaphas, and Pilate. In His crucifixion, Jesus willingly fulfilled John the Baptist's prophetic words: "Behold, the Lamb of God who takes away the sin of the world!" (1:29). John closes his profound gospel with a particularly detailed account of the post-resurrection appearances of the Lord. The resurrection is the ultimate sign that points to Jesus as the Son of God.

Title—The title of the fourth gospel follows the same format as the titles of the synoptic gospels: *Kata Ioannen,* "According to John." Like the others, the word "Gospel" was later added. *Ioannes* is derived from the Hebrew name *Johanan,* "Yahweh has been gracious."

Author—Jesus nicknamed John and his brother James "Sons of Thunder" (Mark 3:17). Their father was Zebedee, and their mother Salome served Jesus in Galilee and was present at the crucifixion (Mark 15:40,41). John was evidently among the Galileans who followed John the Baptist until they were called to follow Jesus at the outset of His public ministry (1:19-51). These Galileans were later called to become full-time disciples of the Lord (Luke 5:1-11), and John was among the 12 who were selected to be apostles (Luke 6:12-16). After the ascension, John became one of the "pillars" of the church in Jerusalem along with James and Peter (Gal. 2:9). He is mentioned three times by name in Acts (3:1; 4:13; 8:14), each time in association with

Peter. Tradition says that John later went to Ephesus (perhaps just before the destruction of Jerusalem). He was eventually exiled by the Romans to the island of Patmos for a time (Rev. 1:9).

The author of this gospel is identified only as "the disciple whom Jesus loved" (13:23; 19:26; 20:2, 21:7,20). His knowledge of Palestinian geography and Jewish customs makes it clear that He was a Palestinian Jew, and his meticulous attention to numbers (2:6; 6:13,19; 21:8,11) and names (1:45; 3:1; 11:1; 18:10) indicates that he was an eyewitness. This fits his own claims to be a witness of the events he described (1:14; 19:35; 21:24,25). The "disciple whom Jesus loved" was part of the inner circle of disciples and closely associated with Peter. The synoptic gospels name this inner circle as Peter, James, and John. Since Peter is separate from the beloved disciple, only James and John are left. James was martyred too early to be the author (Acts 12:1,2), so the apostle John was the author of this gospel. This conclusion from internal evidence is consistent with the external testimony of the early church. Irenaeus (c. 185) was a disciple of Polycarp who was in turn a disciple of the apostle John. In his *Against Heresies*, he bore witness to Johannine authorship of this gospel and noted that John lived until the time of the emperor Trajan (98-117). Clement of Alexandria, Theophilus of Antioch, Origen, and others also ascribe this book to John. Eusebius in his *Ecclesiastical History* (323) interpreted a statement of Papias (c. 125) to mean that there were two Johns, the apostle John and the elder John, and this idea was picked up by modern critics. A closer examination of Papias' words shows that John the elder and John the apostle were probably the same person.

Date and Setting—In spite of the strong internal and external testimony to the apostle John, theological assumptions have motivated a number of critics to deny Johannine authorship of this gospel. Until recently it was popular to claim a second-century date for this book. The discovery of the John Rylands Papyrus 52 containing portions of John 18:31-33,37,38 has overthrown this conjecture. This fragment has been dated at c. A.D. 135, and a considerable period of time must have been required for John's gospel to be copied and circulated until it reached Egypt where this papyrus was found.

On the other hand, John was written after the last of the synoptic gospels (c. 66-68). His familiarity with the pre-holocaust topography of Jerusalem (e.g., 5:2; 19:13) does not require a date before A.D. 70. Since John's three epistles and Revelation were written after his gospel, the probable range for this work is A.D. 80-90. By this time, John would have been one of the last surviving eyewitnesses of the Lord. According to tradition, John wrote this gospel in Ephesus.

Theme and Purpose—The fourth gospel has the clearest purpose statement in the Bible: "but these have been written that you may believe that Jesus is the Christ, the Son of God; and that believing you may have life in His name" (20:31). John selected the signs he used with the apologetic purpose of creating intellectual ("that you may believe") and spiritual ("that believing you may have life") conviction about the Son of God. The key verb in John is "believe," and requires both knowledge (8:32; 10:38) and volition (1:12; 3:19; 7:17).

The predominant theme of this gospel is the dual response of faith and unbelief in the person of Jesus Christ. Those who place their faith in the Son of God have eternal life, but those who reject Him are under the condemnation of God (3:36; 5:24-29; 10:27-29)—this is the basic issue. John 1:11,12 summarizes the reactions of reception and rejection that are traced through the rest of the book. His rejection by His own people can be seen over and over from chapters 2 to 19 (". . . those who were His own did not receive Him"), but John also lists a number of men and women who believed in Him ("But as many as received Him . . .").

Some of the key words in this thematic presentation of portions of Jesus' life are truth, light, darkness, word, knowledge, belief, abide, love, world, witness, and judgment. This gospel is not only evangelistic, but it is also designed to build believers in their faith and understanding of spiritual principles. John was no doubt familiar with the synoptic gospels and created this fourth gospel as a spiritual supplement to the others. While the other gospels focus on the Galilean ministry, John practically avoids it and concentrates on the Judean ministry.

Contribution to the Bible—John is the most selective, topical, and theological of the gospels. Its simple style and vocabulary somehow capture the most profound theological concepts, making the book itself reminiscent of the teaching techniques of Jesus. John uses simple linguistic constructions and avoids the complex sentence structure characteristic of the Pauline epistles. He is particularly adept at parallelism (e.g., light versus darkness), which is an important feature in Hebrew poetry. Unlike the synoptics, John contains no parables; he uses allegories instead (e.g., the good shepherd in 10:1-18, and the true vine in 15:1-6).

Although John is more fragmentary and selective in his use of material (21:25), the structure of his narratives and discourses is tighter and more coherent than that of the other gospels. The discourses in John are logical units that develop unified themes, and the frequent sprinkling of questions and objections help to develop these themes. These discourses are interwoven with the narrative sections and John uses them to explain the spiritual significance of the "signs." In this way the narratives of this gospel become symbolic. Of the eight miracles in 1-12 and 21, only the feeding of the multitudes and the walking on the water are found in the synoptics.

One of the most unique features of John's gospel is the highly theological prologue. It gives a matchless portrayal of the incarnation of the truth, life, and glory of the eternal God. John shows the relevance of the Living Word to all men (3:16; 10:16; 12:32).

Christ in John—This book presents the most powerful case in all the Bible for the deity and humanity of the incarnate Son of God. "The man who is called Jesus" (9:11) is also "the Holy One of God" (6:69). The deity of Christ can be seen in His seven "I am . . ." statements: "I am the bread of life" (6:35,48); "I am the light of the world" (8:12, 9:5); "I am the door" (10:7,9); "I am the good shepherd" (10:11,14); "I am the resurrection and the life" (11:25); "I am the way, and the truth, and the life" (14:6); "I am the true vine" (15:1,5). The seven signs (1-12) and the five witnesses (5:30-40) also point to His divine character. On certain occasions, Jesus equated Himself with the Old Testament I AM (Yahweh)—see 4:25,26; 8:24,28,58;

13:19; 18:5,6,8. Some of the most crucial affirmations of His deity are in 1:1; 8:58; 10:30; 14:9; 20:28.

The Word was God (1:1), but the Word also became flesh (1:14). The humanity of Jesus can be seen in His weariness (4:6), thirst (4:7), dependence (5:19), grief (11:35), troubled soul (12:27), and His anguish and death (19).

Geography of the Gospels

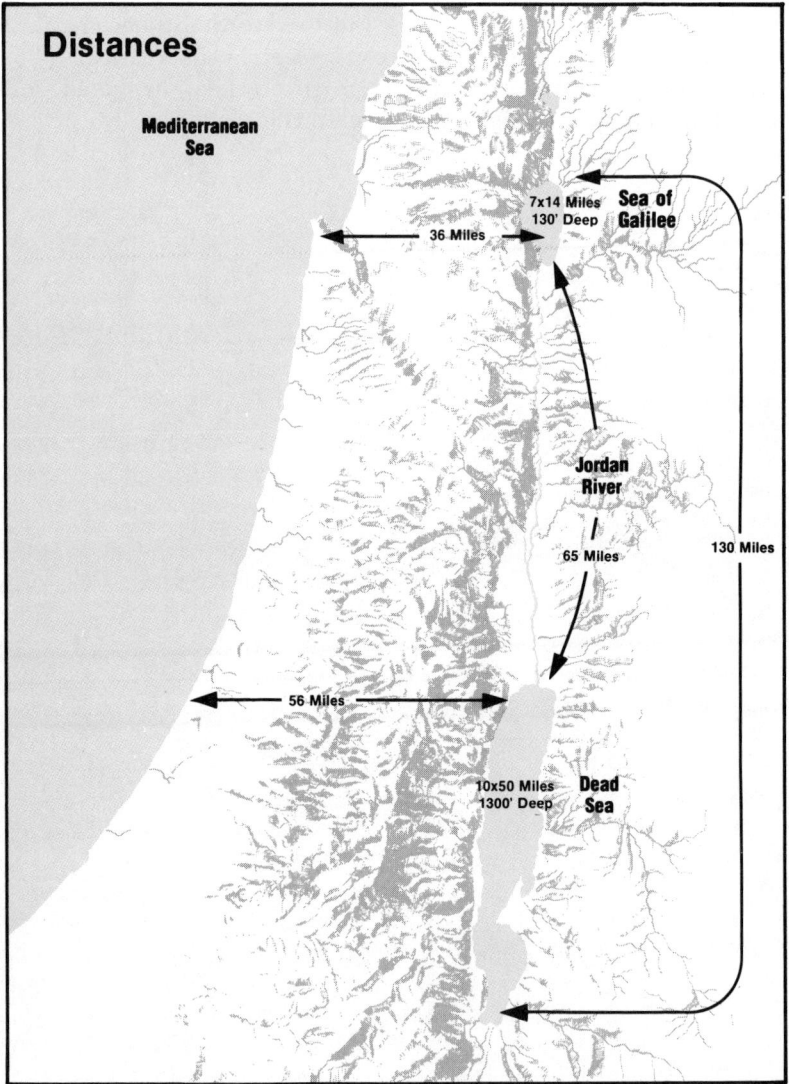

42

Every Geographical Location in the Gospels

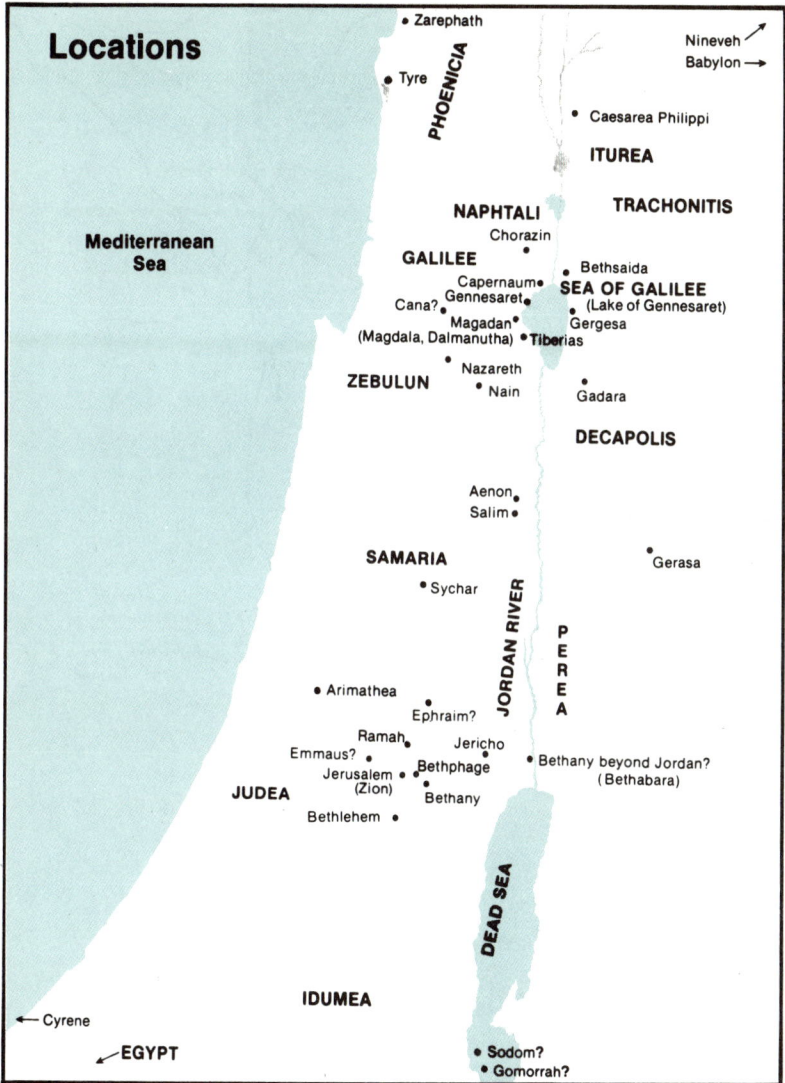

Locations

- Zarephath
- Tyre

PHOENICIA

Nineveh →
Babylon →

- Caesarea Philippi

ITUREA

TRACHONITIS

NAPHTALI

- Chorazin

Mediterranean
Sea

GALILEE

- Bethsaida

Capernaum •
Gennesaret •

SEA OF GALILEE
(Lake of Gennesaret)

Cana? •
Magadan •
(Magdala, Dalmanutha) • Tiberias

Gergesa

- Nazareth

ZEBULUN

- Nain

Gadara

DECAPOLIS

Aenon •
Salim •

SAMARIA

Gerasa

- Sychar

JORDAN RIVER

P
E
R
E
A

- Arimathea

Ephraim? •

Ramah •

Jericho

Emmaus? •
Jerusalem •
(Zion)

Bethphage •
Bethany •

• Bethany beyond Jordan?
(Bethabara)

JUDEA

Bethlehem •

DEAD SEA

IDUMEA

← Cyrene

↙ EGYPT

• Sodom?
• Gomorrah?

Geography of the Gospels: Travel Routes/Economy

Travel Routes

Damascus
Kefr-Bir'im
Gischala
Meiron
Achzib
Hazor
Acco
Bethsaida
Sykaminos
Capernaum
Hippos
Gaba
Philoteria
Dora
Gadara
Legio
Caesarea
Scythopelis
Ginnaia
Pella
Zaphon
Amathas
Succoth
Apollonia
Nabartha
Anti Patris
Joppa
Tyrus
Lydda
Rabbath-Ammon
Bethel
Ekron
Jerico
Beth-Harim
Azotus
Jerusalem
Heshbon
Ascalon
Bethany
Bethlehem
Gaza
Hebron
Engedi
Masada
Arad
Beersheba
Kir Moab
Zoara

Chronology of the Life of Christ

DATE OF BIRTH: ca. December 5 B.C./January 4 B.C.

Jesus Christ was born between the following two dates:

(Luke 2:1-5)
CENSUS OF
QUIRINIUS
(CYRENIUS)

6 B.C.

(Matt. 2:1, Lk. 1:5)
DEATH OF
HEROD THE GREAT

Mar. 29 - Apr. 11
4 B.C.

COMMENCEMENT OF MINISTRY: ca. Autumn A.D. 29

Jesus Christ probably began his ministry between the following two dates:

15th YEAR OF THE REIGN OF TIBERIUS*
(Luke 3:1-3)

August 19, A.D. 28

December 31, A.D. 29

Reckoned from either the Julian Calendar or Tiberius Regnal Year

DURATION OF MINISTRY: Autumn A.D. 29 — April 14, A.D. 33 (3½ YEARS)

Commencement
of Christ's
Ministry

Autumn
A.D. 29

Passover #1
April 7,
A.D. 30

John 2:13.23

Passover #2

Unstated
Mark 2:23-28
Luke 6:1-5
Matthew 12:1-8

Passover #3
April 25,
A.D. 32

John 6:4

Passover #4
April 14,
A.D. 33

John 11:55-12:1

*Basic Dating: Harold W. Hoehner, "Chronological Aspects of the Life of Christ," Bibliotheca Sacra, vol. 130, 131.

Four Gospel Glimpses of Christ

	Matthew	Mark	Luke	John
Christ Portrayed as	Prophesied King	Obedient Servant	Perfect Man	Son of God
Original Audience	Jews	Romans	Greeks	All Men
Key Word	"fulfilled"	"immediately"	"Son of Man"	"believe"
Key Verse	21:5	10:45	19:10	20:31
Outstanding Feature	Sermons	Miracles	Parables	Allegories
Arrangement of Material	Topical	Chronological	Chronological	Topical
Tone	Prophetic	Practical	Historical	Spiritual
Percent Spoken by Christ	60%	42%	50%	50%
Quotations from Old Testament	53	36	25	20
Allusions to Old Testament	76	27	42	105
Unique Material	42%	59%	7%	92%
Broad Division		Synoptic Gospels (humanity of Christ)		Supplemental Gospel (deity of Christ)

Major Themes in the Life of Christ

1. WHO IS HE?

OFFICE	PROPHESIED	FULFILLED	ROLE
Prophet	Deuteronomy 18:15-18	John 6:14	Standard Bearer
Priest	Psalm 110:4	Hebrews 5:5-10	Sacrifice
King	Isaiah 9:6-7	John 12:13	Sovereign

2. WHAT DID HE SAY?

MESSAGE	THEME
Sermon on the Mount (Matthew 5-7)	Requirements of Righteousness
Upper Room Discourse (John 13-17)	Resources of Righteousness
Olivet Discourse (Matthew 24-25)	Results of Rejecting Righteousness

3. WHAT DID HE DO?

MESSAGE VALIDATED	MIRACLE	SCRIPTURE
"I am the resurrection and the life"	Raising Lazarus	John 11
"I am the bread of life"	Feeding Five Thousand	John 6
"Authority to forgive sins"	Healing Paralytic	Luke 5
"Authority of Jesus"	Various Miracles	Matthew 5-9

4. HOW DID THE PEOPLE RESPOND?

	ACCEPTANCE	REJECTION
LEADERS	Few Believed	Because: 1. Claims to deity (John 5:18) 2. Company He kept (Mark 2:16) 3. Challenge to their traditions (Mark 7:1-13)
MULTITUDES	Many Believed	Because: 1. Lack of conformity to their expectations (John 6:15) 2. Refusal to accept moral demands (John 3:19-21) 3. Mob psychology (Mark 15:11-13)

Acts

"But you shall receive power when the Holy Spirit has come upon you; and you shall be My witnesses both in Jerusalem, and in all Judea and Samaria, and even to the remotest part of the earth."

Acts 1:8

Focus	Triumph		Transition		Travels			Trials		
	1 8:3		8:4 12		13 21:26			21:27 28		
D i v i s i o n s	Power of the Church	Progress of the Church	Persecution of the Church	Propagation of the Church	Paul's First Missionary Journey	Paul's Second Missionary Journey	Paul's Third Missionary Journey	Paul's Arrest in Jerusalem	Paul's Trials in Caesarea	Paul's Arrival in Rome
	1 2|3 8:3		8:4 9|10 12		13 15:35	15:36 18:22	18:23 21:26	21:27 23	24 26	27 28
T o p i c s	Establishment		Extension		Expansion			Explanation		
	Witnessing in the City		Witnessing in the Provinces		Witnessing in the World					
	Jews		Jews and Samaritans		Gentiles					
	Peter		Philip		Paul					
Loca-tions	Jeru-salem		Judea and Samaria		Uttermost Part					
Time	2 Years (A.D.33-35)		13 Years (A.D.35-48)		14 Years (A.D.48-62)					

Talk Thru—Luke begins the book of Acts where he left off in his gospel. Acts records the initial fulfillment of the great commission of Matthew 28:19,20 as it traces the beginning and growth of the New Testament church (this growth pattern can be seen in 1:15; 2:41,47; 4:4; 5:14; 6:7; 9:31; 12:24; 13:49; 16:5; 19:20). Christ's last words before His ascension were so perfectly realized in the book of Acts that they effectively outline its contents: "but you shall receive power when the Holy Spirit has come upon you; and you shall be My witnesses both in *Jerusalem,* and in all *Judea and Samaria,* and even to the *remotest part* of the earth" (1:8). Acts traces important events in the early history of Christianity from the ascension of Christ to the outpouring of the Holy Spirit to the rapid progress of the gospel, beginning in Jerusalem and spreading throughout the Roman Empire.

Acts is a pivotal book of transitions: from the gospels to the epistles (history), from Judaism to Christianity (religion), from law to grace (divine dealing), from Jews to Jews and Gentiles (people of God), and from kingdom to church (program of God). The profound changes that took place on the cross required about a generation (Acts covers about 30 years) to be effected in time. As a book of transitional history, the patterns in Acts are not as normative as the teachings in the epistles. Four basic themes in Acts are: Triumph (1:1-8:3); Transition (8:4-12:25); Travels (13:1-21:26); and Trials (21:27-28:31).

Triumph (1:1-8:3): After appearing to His disciples "over a period of forty days" (1:3), the Lord told them to wait in Jerusalem for the fulfillment of His promise concerning the Holy Spirit. Ten days after His ascension, this promise was significantly fulfilled as the disciples were suddenly empowered and filled with the Holy Spirit. This took place on the Feast of Weeks (Pentecost), 50 days after First Fruits (the resurrection). Because every Jewish male was required to appear at the sanctuary for this feast (Exod. 23:14-17; Deut. 16:16), Jerusalem was swelled with Jews and proselytes from all over the Roman Empire. On this day the disciples were transformed and filled with courage to proclaim the brand new message of the resurrected Savior. Peter's powerful sermon, like all the sermons in Acts, was built upon the resurrection, and 3,000 people responded with saving faith. After dramatically healing a man who was lame from birth, Peter delivered a second crucial message to the people of Israel that resulted in thousands of additional responses. The religious leaders arrested the apostles, but this only gave Peter an opportunity to preach a special sermon to them.

The enthusiasm and joy of the infant church was marred by internal and external problems. Ananias and Sapphira received the ultimate form of discipline because of their treachery, and the apostles were imprisoned and persecuted because of their witness. Seven men were selected to assist the apostles, among whom were Stephen and Philip. Stephen was brought before the Sanhedrin, and in his defense he surveyed the Scriptures to prove that the Man they condemned was the Messiah Himself. They were so convicted by his words that they dragged him out of the city and made him the first Christian martyr.

Transition (8:4-12:25): Philip went to the province of Samaria and successfully proclaimed the new message to these people who were hated by the Jews. Peter and John confirmed his work and exercised their apostolic authority by imparting the Holy Spirit to these new members of the body of Christ. God sovereignly transformed Saul the persecutor into Paul the apostle to the Gentiles, but He used Peter to introduce the gospel to the Gentiles. It required a special vision for Peter to realize that Christ had broken down the barrier between Jews and Gentiles. After Cornelius and other Gentiles came to Christ through his preaching, Peter had to convince the Jewish believers in Jerusalem that "the Gentiles also had received the word of God" (11:1). As persecution continued to increase, so the church continued to increase and spread all over the Roman Empire.

Travels (13:1-21:26): Beginning with chapter 13, Luke switches the focus of Acts from Peter to Paul. Antioch in Syria gradually replaced Jerusalem as the headquarters of the church, and all three of Paul's missionary journeys originated from that city. The first journey (48-49) concentrated on the Galatian cities of Pisidian Antioch, Iconium, Lystra, and Derbe. After this journey, a council was held among the apostles and elders of the church in Jerusalem to determine whether the Gentile converts had to submit to the law of Moses. The second missionary journey (50-52) brought Paul once again to the Galatian churches, but then beyond for the first time to

Macedonia and Greece. Paul spent much of his time in the cities of Philippi, Thessalonica, and Corinth and later returned to Jerusalem and Antioch. In his third missionary journey (53-57), Paul spent almost three years in the Asian city of Ephesus before visiting Macedonia and Greece for the second time. Although he was warned not to go to Jerusalem, Paul would not be dissuaded.

Trials (21:27-28:31): It was not long before Paul was falsely accused of bringing Gentiles into the temple. He would have been killed by the mob if the Roman commander had not intervened. Paul's defense before the people and before the Sanhedrin led to violent reactions, and when the commander learned of a conspiracy to assassinate Paul, he sent his prisoner to governor Felix in Caesarea. During his two-year Caesarean imprisonment (57-59), Paul defended the Christian faith before Felix, Festus, and Agrippa. His appeal to Caesar meant a long voyage to Rome where he was placed under house arrest until his trial before Caesar.

Title—As the second volume in a two-part work by Luke, this book probably had no separate title. But all available Greek manuscripts designate it by the title *Praxeis,* "Acts," or by an expanded title like "The Acts of the Apostles." *Praxeis* was commonly used in Greek literature to summarize the accomplishments of outstanding men. While the apostles are mentioned collectively at several points, this book really records the acts of Peter (chapters 1-12) and of Paul (chapters 13-28).

Author—Acts 1:1 refers Theophilus to "the first account," that is, the gospel of Luke. See Luke, Author for the internal and external support for Lucan authorship of Luke-Acts. Luke's source for the "we"-sections in this book (16:10-17; 20:5-21:18; 27:1-28:16) was his own memory if not some kind of diary. For the remainder of this book Luke no doubt followed the same careful investigative procedures that he used in writing his gospel (Luke 1:1-4). As a close traveling companion of Paul, Luke had access to the principal eyewitness for chapters 13-28. It is also likely that he had opportunities to interview key witnesses in Jerusalem like Peter and John for the information in chapters 1-12. Acts 15:23-29 and 23:26-30 indicate that Luke may have used written documents as well.

Date and Setting—Suggested dates for the writing of Acts range from A.D. 62 to the middle of the second century. Twentieth-century archaeological discoveries have strikingly confirmed the trustworthiness and precision of Luke as a historian, and show that his work should be dated in the first century. Luke's perplexingly abrupt ending with Paul awaiting trial in Rome has led many to believe that Acts was completed prior to Paul's trial (62). If it was written after this crucial event, why didn't Luke mention the outcome? Luke may have had a reason, but the simplest explanation of his silence is that Paul had not yet stood before Caesar. Acts gives no hint of the persecution under Nero (64), Paul's death (68), or the destruction of Jerusalem (70).

On the other hand, Acts was written after Luke, and Luke was written after Mark *if* he used that gospel. This would require a date for Mark in the 50's—a problem for some scholars but not for all.

Theme and Purpose—While there are four accounts of the life of Jesus, this is the only book that carries on the story from the ascension to the period of the New Testament epistles. Thus, Acts is the historical link between the gospels and the epistles. Because of Luke's strong emphasis on the ministry of the Holy Spirit, this book should really be regarded as the Acts of the Spirit of Christ working in and through the apostles. As a missionary himself, Luke's interest in the progressive spread of the gospel is obviously reflected in this apostolic history. Luke was personally involved in the process of this story, so it was not written from a detached point of view. But this does not detract from the authority and coherence of this primary historical document.

From a theological standpoint, Acts was written to trace the development of the body of Christ over the one-generation transition from a primarily Jewish to a predominantly Gentile membership. This apologetic work presents Christianity as distinct from Judaism but also as its fulfillment.

Contribution to the Bible—Acts is highly selective in its content, and it does not attempt to be a comprehensive survey of the first 30 years of the Christian church. Nevertheless, it is invaluable as the background history for most of the epistles. Without it the epistles would be quite difficult to understand, and the history of the early church would be a vague patchwork. There are certain problems in harmonizing the events in Acts with the information about Paul in his epistles, but these events generally fit well together.

When Luke and Acts are joined together, they offer a monumental account of the foundation and initial development of Christianity. Their style and literary quality are unsurpassed in the New Testament. Luke uses over 700 words not found in the other 25 New Testament books—he must have been steeped in the Septuagint, because nine-tenths of these words were used in it.

Luke includes about 80 geographical references and mentions over 100 people by name in Acts. His precision in citing locations (e.g., provinces, cities, specific sites) and titles (e.g., consul, tetrarch, proconsul, Asiarch) was once challenged by critics but is now verified by archaeological evidence. Another prominent feature of this book is the amount of space given to speeches and sermons; no less than 24 messages are found in its 28 chapters.

Christ in Acts—The resurrected Savior is the central theme of the sermons and defenses in Acts. The Old Testament Scriptures, the historical resurrection, the apostolic testimony, and the convicting power of the Holy Spirit all bear witness that Jesus is both Lord and Christ (see Peter's sermons in 2:22-36 and 10:34-43). "Of Him all the prophets bear witness that through His name everyone who believes in Him receives forgiveness of sins. . . . And there is salvation in no one else; for there is no other name under heaven that has been given among men by which we must be saved" (10:43; 4:12).

Every Geographical Location in Acts/Epistles

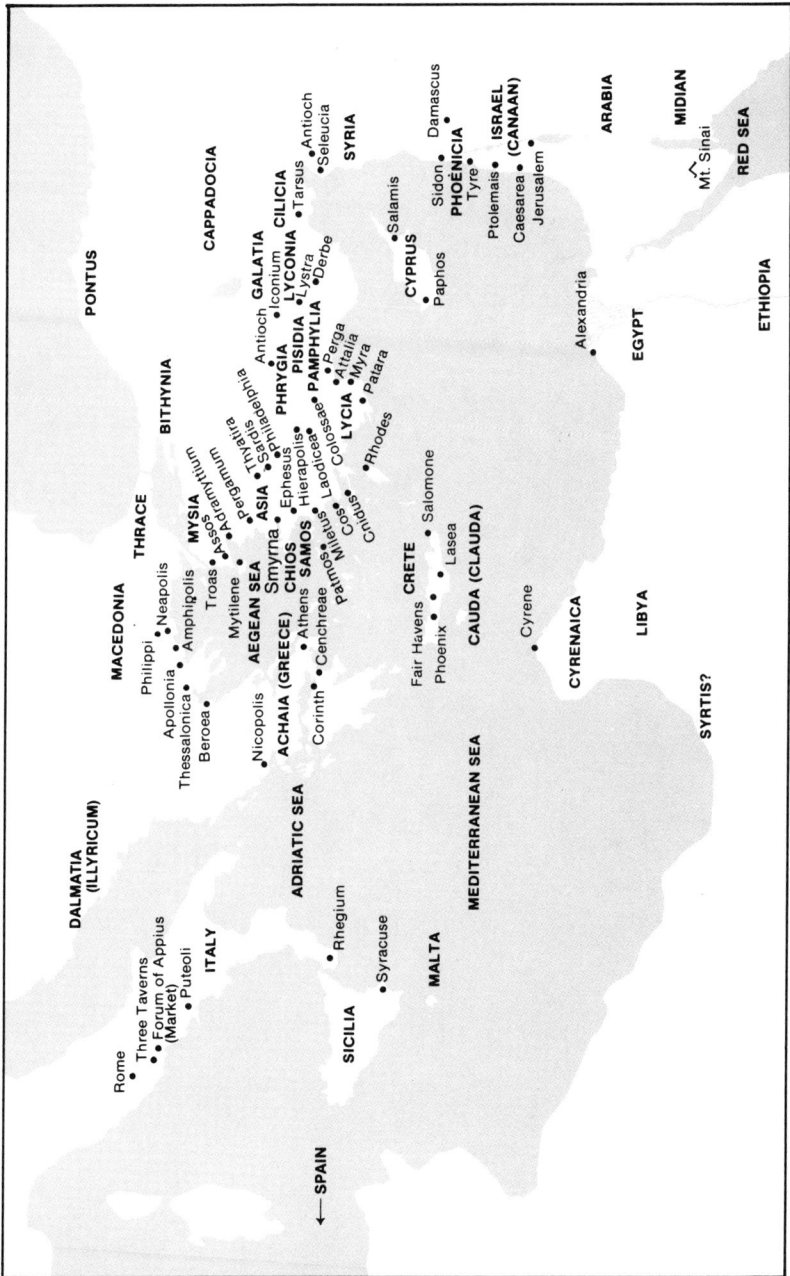

Geography of the Book of Acts: Travel Routes

Paul's First Missionary Journey

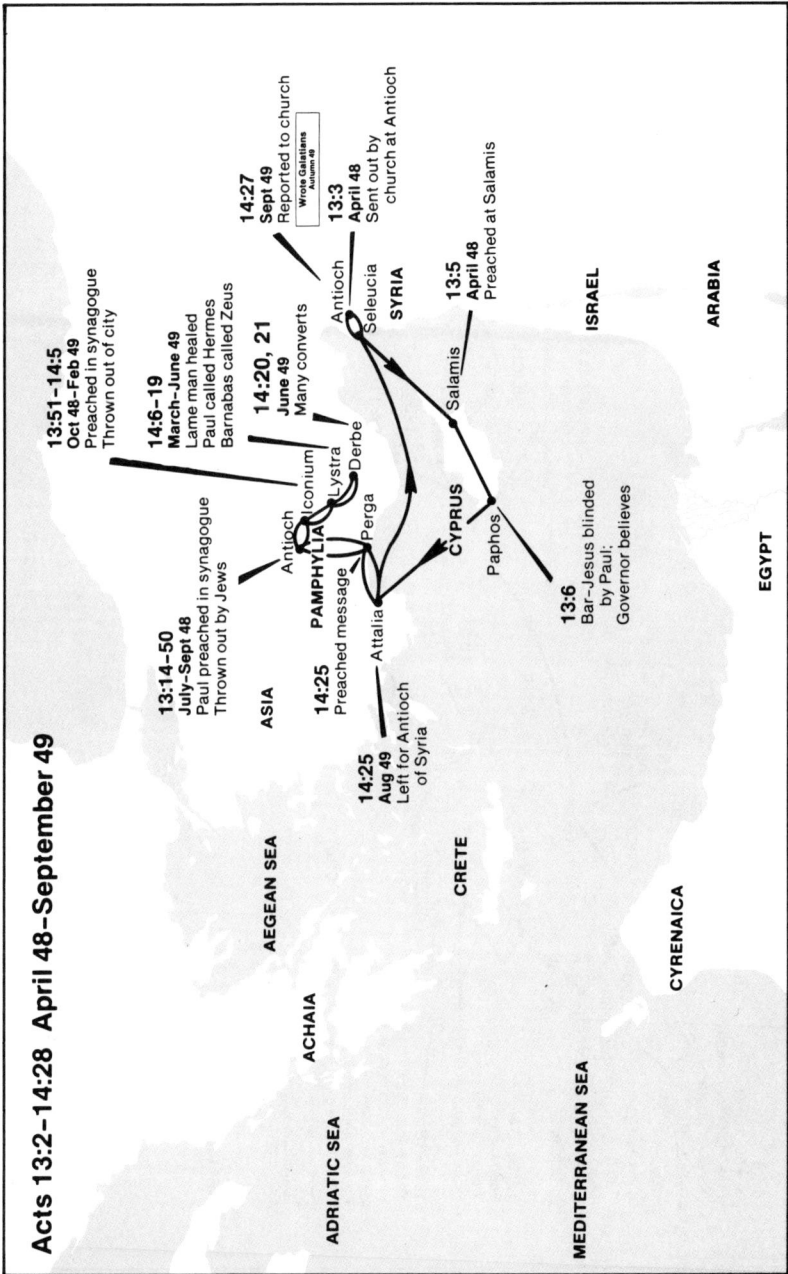

Acts 13:2–14:28 April 48–September 49

13:51–14:5
Oct 48–Feb 49
Preached in synagogue
Thrown out of city

14:6–19
March–June 49
Lame man healed
Paul called Hermes
Barnabas called Zeus

14:20, 21
June 49
Many converts

14:27
Sept 49
Reported to church

Wrote Galatians
Autumn 49

13:3
April 48
Sent out by
church at Antioch

13:5
April 48
Preached at Salamis

13:6
Bar–Jesus blinded
by Paul;
Governor believes

13:14–50
July–Sept 48
Paul preached in synagogue
Thrown out by Jews

14:25
Preached message

14:25
Aug 49
Left for Antioch
of Syria

Antioch
Seleucia
SYRIA
Salamis
CYPRUS
Paphos
ISRAEL
ARABIA
EGYPT
Iconium
Lystra
Derbe
Antioch
PAMPHYLIA
Perga
Attalia
ASIA
AEGEAN SEA
CRETE
ACHAIA
ADRIATIC SEA
CYRENAICA
MEDITERRANEAN SEA

Paul's Second Missionary Journey

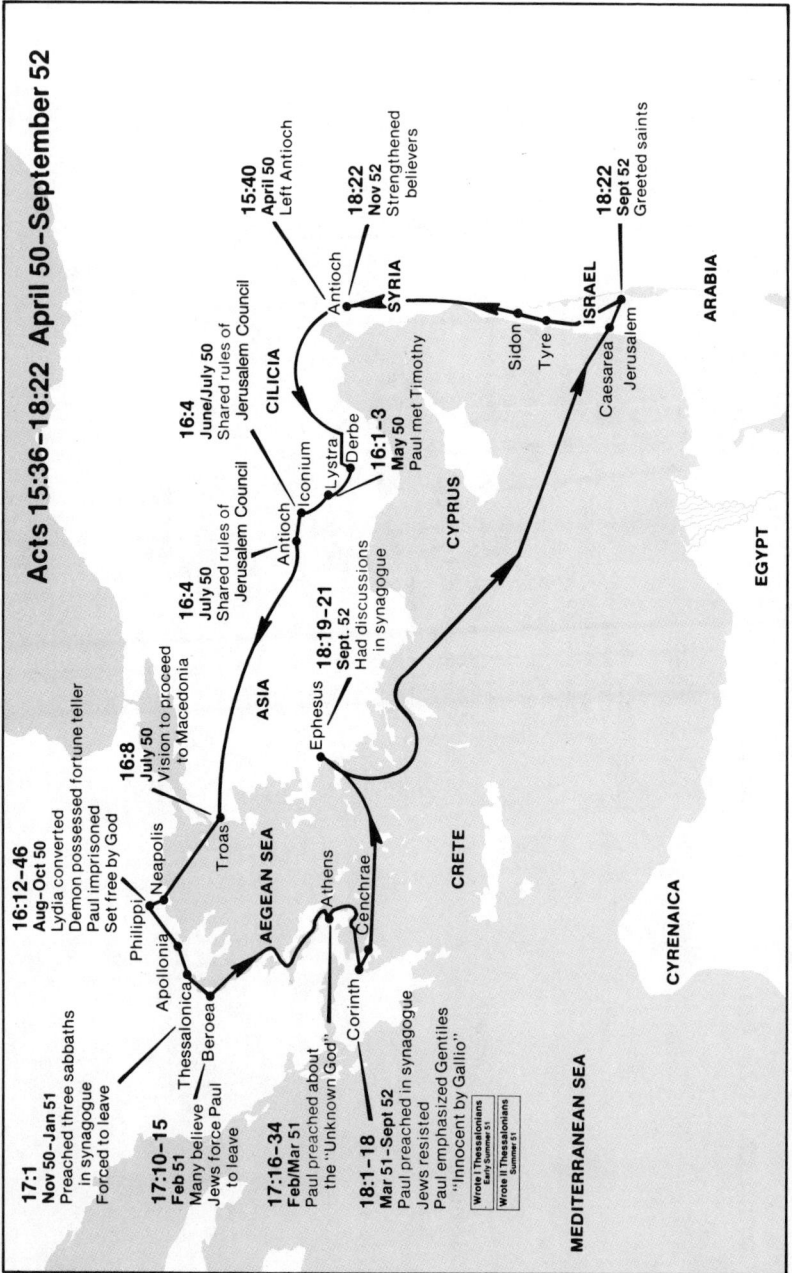

Paul's Second Missionary Journey
Acts 15:36–18:22 April 50–September 52

15:40
April 50
Left Antioch

18:22
Nov 52
Strengthened believers

18:22
Sept 52
Greeted saints

16:4
June/July 50
Shared rules of Jerusalem Council

16:1–3
May 50
Paul met Timothy

16:4
July 50
Shared rules of Jerusalem Council

18:19–21
Sept. 52
Had discussions in synagogue

16:4
July 50
Shared rules of Jerusalem Council

16:8
July 50
Vision to proceed to Macedonia

16:12–46
Aug–Oct 50
Lydia converted
Demon possessed fortune teller
Paul imprisoned
Set free by God

17:1
Nov 50–Jan 51
Preached three sabbaths in synagogue
Forced to leave

17:10–15
Feb 51
Many believe
Jews force Paul to leave

17:16–34
Feb/Mar 51
Paul preached about the "Unknown God"

18:1–18
Mar 51–Sept 52
Paul preached in synagogue
Jews resisted
Paul emphasized Gentiles
"Innocent by Gallio"

Wrote I Thessalonians
Early Summer 51

Wrote II Thessalonians
Summer 51

SYRIA
CILICIA
ASIA
CYPRUS
CRETE
ISRAEL
ARABIA
EGYPT
CYRENAICA
AEGEAN SEA
MEDITERRANEAN SEA

Antioch
Derbe
Lystra
Iconium
Antioch
Ephesus
Troas
Neapolis
Philippi
Apollonia
Thessalonica
Beroea
Athens
Corinth
Cenchrae
Sidon
Tyre
Caesarea
Jerusalem

Paul's Third Missionary Journey

Acts 18:23–21:16 Spring 53–May 57

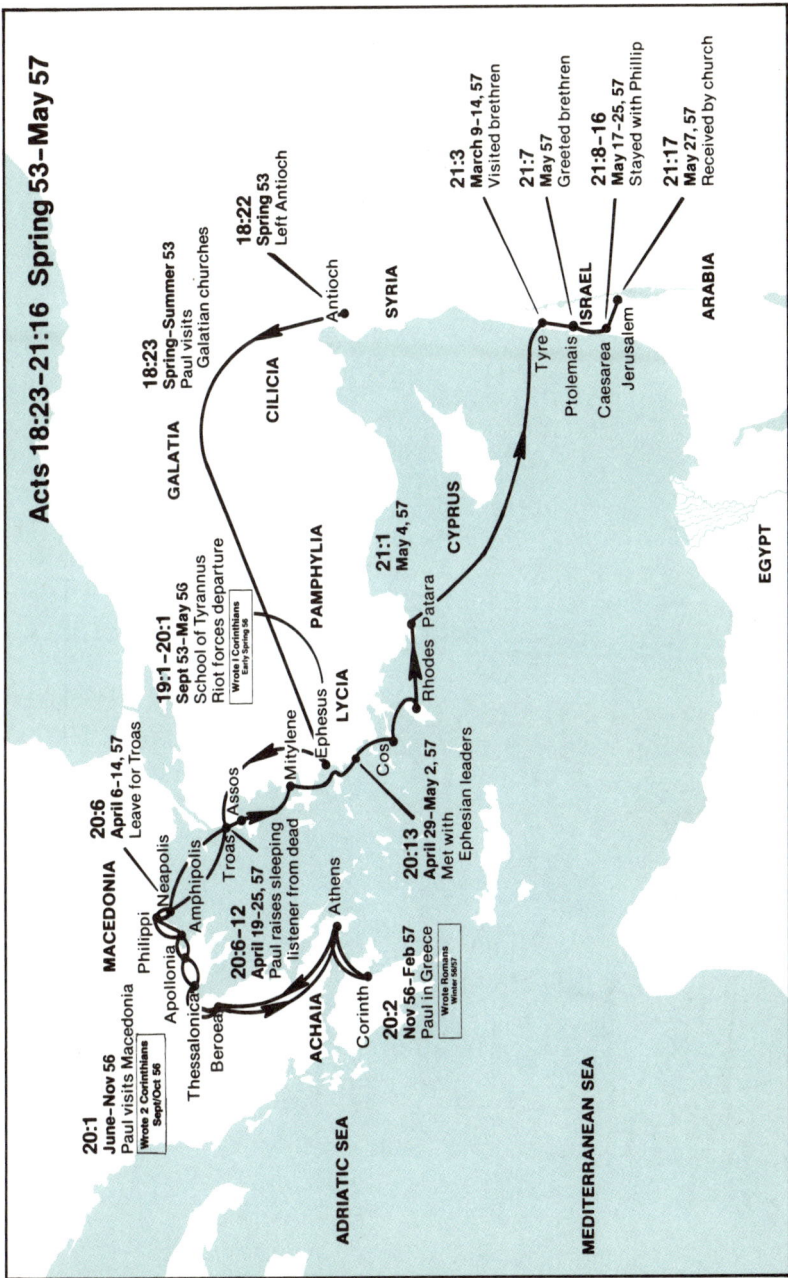

21:3
March 9–14, 57
Visited brethren

21:7
May 57
Greeted brethren

21:8–16
May 17–25, 57
Stayed with Phillip

21:17
May 27, 57
Received by church

18:22
Spring 53
Left Antioch

18:23
Spring–Summer 53
Paul visits
Galatian churches

Antioch

SYRIA

CILICIA

GALATIA

ARABIA

ISRAEL

Tyre

Ptolemais

Caesarea

Jerusalem

21:1
May 4, 57

PAMPHYLIA

CYPRUS

LYCIA

Rhodes Patara

EGYPT

19:1–20:1
Sept 53–May 56
School of Tyrannus
Riot forces departure

Wrote I Corinthians
Early Spring 56

Ephesus

Mitylene

Cos

20:13
April 29–May 2, 57
Met with
Ephesian leaders

20:6
April 6–14, 57
Leave for Troas

Assos

Troas

Neapolis

Philippi

MACEDONIA

Amphipolis

Apollonia

Thessalonica

Beroea

20:6–12
April 19–25, 57
Paul raises sleeping
listener from dead

Athens

ACHAIA

Corinth

20:2
Nov 56–Feb 57
Paul in Greece

Wrote Romans
Winter 56/57

20:1
June–Nov 56
Paul visits Macedonia

Wrote 2 Corinthians
Sept/Oct 56

ADRIATIC SEA

MEDITERRANEAN SEA

Paul's Trials and Imprisonments

Acts 21:26–28:29 May 57 – February 60

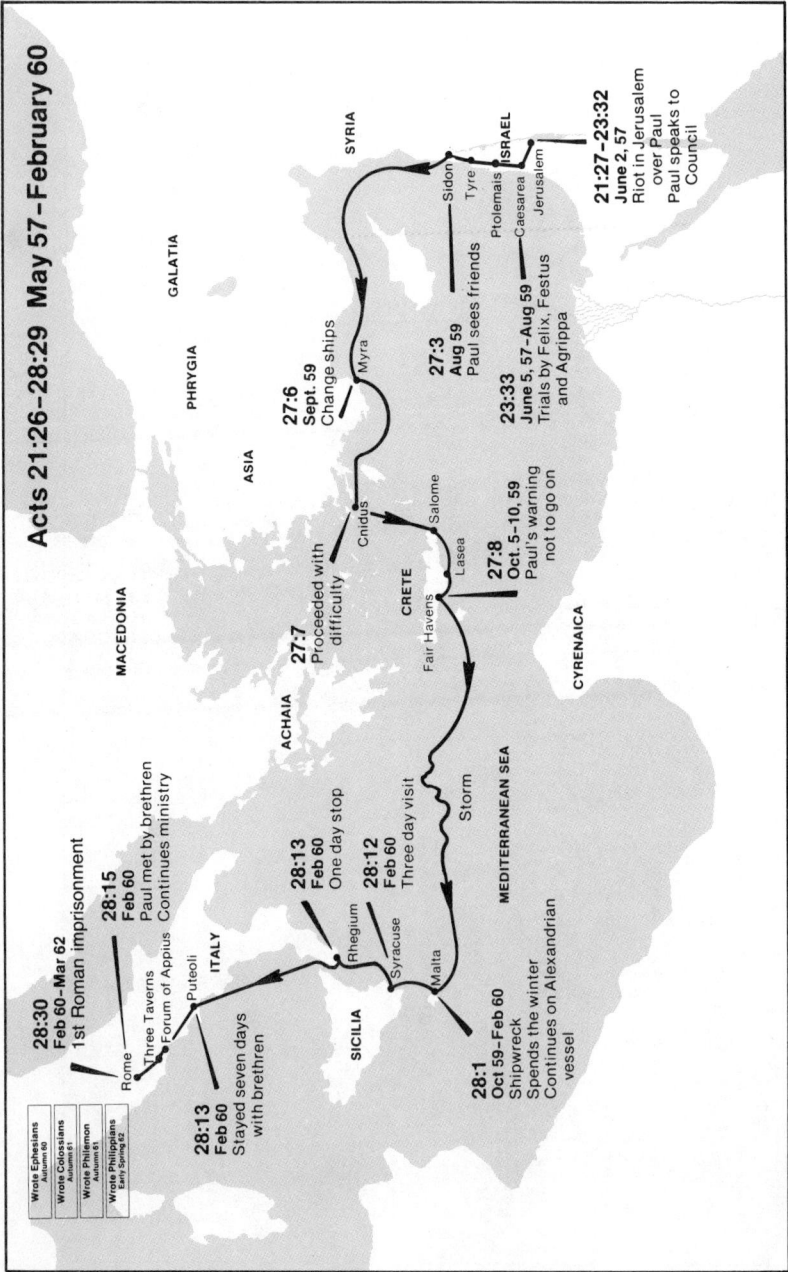

SYRIA

GALATIA

PHRYGIA

ASIA

MACEDONIA

ACHAIA

ITALY

SICILIA

CRETE

CYRENAICA

MEDITERRANEAN SEA

Sidon
Tyre
Ptolemais
Caesarea
Jerusalem

ISRAEL

21:27–23:32
June 2, 57
Riot in Jerusalem
over Paul
Paul speaks to
Council

27:3
Aug 59
Paul sees friends

23:33
June 5, 57–Aug 59
Trials by Felix, Festus
and Agrippa

27:6
Sept. 59
Change ships

Myra

Cnidus

Salome

Lasea

Fair Havens

27:7
Proceeded with
difficulty

27:8
Oct. 5–10, 59
Paul's warning
not to go on

Storm

28:13
Feb 60
One day stop

28:12
Feb 60
Three day visit

Rhegium

Syracuse

Malta

28:1
Oct 59–Feb 60
Shipwreck
Spends the winter
Continues on Alexandrian
vessel

28:30
Feb 60–Mar 62
1st Roman imprisonment

28:15
Feb 60
Paul met by brethren
Continues ministry

Three Taverns
Forum of Appius
Puteoli
Rome

28:13
Feb 60
Stayed seven days
with brethren

Wrote Ephesians
Autumn 60

Wrote Colossians
Autumn 61

Wrote Philemon
Autumn 61

Wrote Philippians
Early Spring 62

60

Introduction
to the
Pauline Epistles

The Pauline epistles are of inestimable value because Paul, under the inspiration of the Holy Spirit, was able to address specific problems and issues of his time with perspectives that are universal and timeless. In these 13 epistles, even the most mundane matters stimulated lofty thoughts in the mind of the apostle which he was able to express with astounding versatility. Paul constantly adapted his style to the changing situations he encountered; he could be logical, personal, rhetorical, lyrical, formal, practical, or emotional. These pithy epistles condense an enormous number of ideas into a small space, so that every reading can yield new insights.

The use of the epistle as a medium of divine revelation was unheard of until the time of Paul and his contemporaries. This very personal form of communication was appropriate to the new message that believers have been made adopted children in the household of God by His grace. The epistles of Paul and others are intimately related to the needs and contingencies of real life, and they issue out of the affliction, joy, sorrow, and compassion of these godly writers. The epistles have an abundance of doctrine, but it is designed for practical application, not theoretical speculation.

Because of their form and personal character, Paul's writings are properly called letters. They generally follow the standard form of letters in Paul's day: the sender's name and office, the name of the recipient, a greeting or wish for prosperity, the main body of the letter, a farewell with closing greetings and good wishes, and the signature. This shell was filled with the richness of revelation, and a transformation took place that makes it appropriate to call these writings epistles as well as letters. Their literary quality and length distinguished them from ordinary letters. Even Philemon (335 words) is considerably longer than the usual letters of Paul's day which easily fit on one sheet of papyrus. Paul's epistles required a number of these sheets to be joined and rolled into scrolls.

Paul followed the usual procedure of using a scribe or *amanuensis* for the final form of his letters, but he wrote the concluding lines and signature with his own hand to guarantee authenticity (see Rom. 16:22; 1 Cor. 16:21; Gal. 6:11; Col. 4:18; 2 Thess. 3:17; Philemon was evidently an exception; Philem. 19). It is clear from letters like Romans and Ephesians that Paul had carefully thought out the details of his argument in advance, but the process of dictation allowed a freedom and freshness of speech. Since the limited imperial postal service was only for official business, Paul relied on helpers to carry his letters, but they also conveyed supplementary messages (Eph. 6:21,22; Phil. 2:25-28; Col. 4:7,8).

The New Testament contains nine Pauline letters to churches and four to individuals. It is evident, however, that Paul wrote letters that are now lost (see 1 Cor. 5:9; 2 Cor. 10:9,10; Col. 4:16; 2 Thess. 3:17). Paul's 13 canonical epistles are arranged so that the first nine (to churches) and the last four (to individuals) are in order of decreasing length. The probable chronological order is: Galatians, 1 Thessalonians, 2 Thessalonians, 1 Corinthians, 2 Corinthians, Romans, Colossians, Philemon, Ephesians, Philippians, 1 Timothy, Titus, and 2 Timothy.

Saul was born a Roman citizen in Tarsus of Cilicia, a center of learning. He may have received a Greek education (cf. Acts 17:28; Titus 1:12) before his family moved to Jerusalem. He learned the trade of tent-making (Acts 18:3), but as a full-blooded Jew of the tribe of Benjamin he received the privilege of being educated under Rabbi Gamaliel (Acts 22:3). His keen mind and religious zeal advanced him in Judaism beyond his contemporaries (Gal. 1:14), and as a young Pharisee, Saul was present at the stoning of Stephen (Acts 7:48; 8:1). He energetically persecuted Christians in Judea and decided to carry his campaign northeast to Damascus when his encounter with the resurrected Christ completely changed his life. He spent three years in Arabia and Damascus (Gal. 1:17,18) before being introduced by Barnabas to the apostles in Jerusalem. After 15 days, a plot against him forced his departure (Acts 9:26-30; Gal. 1:18-21), and he spent about 10 years in Cilicia and Syria (primarily Tarsus and Antioch).

Barnabas and Paul brought a contribution from Antioch to Jerusalem for the famine relief of the brethren in Judea (Acts 11:25-30). After their return to Antioch, Barnabas, Paul, and Mark embarked on the first missionary journey (Acts 13-14). Mark left early, but Barnabas and Paul ministered in Cyprus, Pamphylia, and Galatia. After the journey, they went to Jerusalem to settle the issue of the Gentiles and the Mosaic law (Acts 15), and then returned to Antioch. Paul took Silas on his second missionary journey (Acts 15:36-18:22) which concentrated on Macedonia and Greece. Paul's third missionary journey, again originating in Antioch, focused on Asia with Ephesus as his headquarters (Acts 18:23-21:16). Paul went to Jerusalem for the last time with a collection for the poor but he was soon accused of violating the temple and a riot broke out. The Romans brought him to Caesarea where the governor Felix kept him imprisoned for two years (Acts 24:27). Paul defended himself before Felix, his replacement Festus, and Agrippa before his arduous journey to Rome (Acts 24-28:16). There he was imprisoned for two years, and although the book of Acts stops at this point, evidence from Paul's letters to Timothy and Titus and from the early church fathers indicates that he was released from prison. He apparently had an opportunity to visit Spain, Crete, Asia, Macedonia, and Greece before his second Roman imprisonment and execution under Nero in 67-68.

Paul's Christian life was characterized by unflagging dedication to the cause of Christ in the face of suffering. He had a clear sense of divine calling, a strong love for his converts, an unshakable conviction and authority, and a constant spirit of dependence upon Christ in all that he did.

Romans: This most systematic of all the epistles traces the story of the gospel from condemnation to justification to sanctification to glorification. It explains God's program for Jews and Gentiles and concludes with practical exhortations for the outworking of righteousness among believers.

1 Corinthians: This epistle of correction and reproof firmly handles the problems of factions, immorality, lawsuits, and abuse of the Lord's Supper that were destroying the testimony of the Corinthians. Paul also responds to questions raised by the Corinthians on marriage, meat offered to idols, public worship, and the resurrection.

2 Corinthians: Paul wrote this very personal letter to defend his apostolic character, call, and credentials in view of a recent rebellion against him that was led by certain false apostles. Paul was comforted by the repentance of the majority but concerned about the unrepentant minority.

Galatians: This polemic epistle refutes the error of legalism that had suddenly ensnared the churches of Galatia. Paul uses a biographical, theological, and moral argument to demonstrate the superiority of grace over law and magnify the life of liberty over legalism and license.

Ephesians: The first three chapters of Ephesians are one of the most sublime and profound texts in the Bible, because they extol the believer's position in Christ. The remaining three chapters exhort believers to maintain a spiritual walk that is based upon their spiritual wealth.

Philippians: In this joyous letter of affection and gratitude for the Philippians, Paul speaks of the latest developments in his imprisonment and urges his readers to a lifestyle of unity, humility, and godliness. He also warns them about the error of legalism.

Colossians: This may be the most Christocentric epistle in the New Testament, because in it, Paul demonstrates the preeminence of Christ in creation, redemption, and the relationships of life. The Christian is complete in Christ and has no need of other systems of speculation or religious observances.

1 Thessalonians: The first three chapters give a summary of Paul's ministry with the Thessalonians. He commends them for their faith and reminds them of his motives and concerns on their behalf. Chapters 4-5 exhort them to purity of life and teach them about the coming of the Lord.

2 Thessalonians: The Thessalonians were arriving at incorrect conclusions about the day of the Lord and they were becoming anxious about their persecution. Paul explains what must precede this awesome event and exhorts them to remain diligent.

1 Timothy: This letter is Paul's leadership manual for his entrusted servant who was put in charge of the work in Ephesus. In it, Paul counsels Timothy on the problems of false teachers, public prayer, the role of women, the requirements for elders and deacons, and miscellaneous duties.

2 Timothy: Paul's last letter is a combat manual which is designed to build up and encourage Timothy to boldness and steadfastness in view of the hardships of the spiritual warfare. Paul knew his earthly course was over, and in his last recorded testimony he urges Timothy on.

Titus: Titus was left by Paul in Crete to oversee the work there and appoint elders. This conduct manual lists the requirements for elders and instructs Titus in his duties relative to the various groups in the churches.

Philemon: Onesimus, Philemon's runaway slave, had become a believer under Paul's ministry and now he was being sent back to his master with this letter. In it, Paul appeals to Philemon to forgive Onesimus and to regard him no longer as a slave but as a brother in Christ.

Romans

"For I am not ashamed of the gospel, for it is the power of God for salvation to everyone who believes, to the Jew first and also to the Greek. For in it the righteousness of God is revealed from faith to faith; as it is written, 'But the righteous man shall live by faith.' "   Romans 1:16,17 (Also see 3:21-24.)

Focus	Problem of Righteousness 1 — 3:20	Provision of Righteousness 3:21 — 5	Power of Righteousness 6 — 8	Program of Righteousness 9 — 11	Practice of Righteousness 12 — 16		
Divisions	Salutation, Occasion, and Theme 1:1-17	CONDEMNATION: Man's Need of Righteousness 1:18 — 3:20	JUSTIFICATION: God's Provision of Righteousness 3:21 — 5	SANCTIFICATION: The Principle of Righteousness 6 — 8:17	GLORIFICATION: The Hope of Righteousness 8:18-39	VINDICATION: God's Plan of Righteousness 9 — 11	APPLICATION: The Outworking of Righteousness 12 — 15:13	Paul's Plans, Greetings, and Benediction 15:14 — 16
Topics		Sin	Salvation	Separation		Sovereignty	Service	
	Prologue	Principles				Puzzle	Praxis	Postlude
	Basis of the Gospel					Behavior of the Gospel		
	Doctrinal (Truth)					Practical (Transformation)		
Location	Probably Written in Corinth							
Time	A.D. 57							

67

Talk Thru—Paul's *magnum opus* was placed first among his 13 epistles in the New Testament canon. The poet Coleridge regarded Romans as "the most profound book in existence," and the commentator Godet called it "the cathedral of the Christian faith." Because of its majestic declaration of the divine plan of salvation, Luther wrote: "This Epistle is really the chief part of the New Testament and the very purest Gospel. . . . It can never be read or pondered too much, and the more it is dealt with the more precious it becomes, and the better it tastes." The four gospels present the words and works of the Lord Jesus, but Romans, "the gospel according to Paul," delves more into the significance of His life. Using a question-and-answer format in Romans, Paul creates the most systematic presentation of doctrine in the Bible. But the theology of Romans is balanced by practical exhortation, because Paul sees the believer's position as the basis for his practice. The theme of righteousness which runs through the book is reflected in the following outline: Problem of Righteousness (1:1-3:20); Provision of Righteousness (3:21-5:21); Power of Righteousness (6-8); Program of Righteousness (9-11); and Practice of Righteousness (12-16).

Problem of Righteousness (1:1-3:20): The prologue (1:1-17) consists of a salutation (1:1-7), a statement of Paul's desire to minister in Rome (1:8-15), and the theme of the book (1:16,17). This two-verse theme is the basic text of Romans because it combines the three crucial concepts of salvation, righteousness, and faith. *Salvation:* a believer is saved *from* the penalty of sin (past), the power of sin (present), and the presence of sin (future), and he is saved *to* a new position, a new life, and an entrance into God's heavenly presence. *Righteousness:* this speaks of perfect conformity to an unchanging standard; the sinner who trusts in Christ receives the righteousness of Christ in his position before God. *Faith:* as the instrumentality for salvation and a gracious gift of God, faith includes an acknowledgment of need and a trust in Christ alone for salvation.

In 1:18-3:20, Paul builds an airtight case for the condemnation of all people under the holy God. Paul's perceptive diagnosis of the human condition shows that Gentiles and Jews seek to justify themselves by using relative standards, not realizing that God's required standard is nothing short of perfection. Paul realizes that the bad news (condemnation) must be understood before the good news (justification) can be appreciated. The Gentiles are without excuse because they have suppressed the knowledge of God they received from nature and their conscience (1:18-32; their seven-step regression is traced in 1:21-31). The Jews are also under the condemnation of God, and Paul overcomes every objection they could raise to this conclusion (2:1-3:8). God judges according to truth (2:2-5), works (2:6-10), and impartiality (2:11-16), and both the moral and religious Jews fail to meet His standard. The divine verdict (3:9-20) is universal: *"all* have sinned and fall short of the glory of God" (3:23).

Provision of Righteousness (3:21-5:21): This section on justification develops the theme of God's provision for man's need. The first 11 verses are the core of the book (3:21-31), revealing that in Christ, God is both Judge and Savior. Three crucial words are found in these verses: (1) *Justification:* this judicial term means that the believer in Christ is "declared righteous" by the holy God. The Lord is not unjust when He justifies sinners because He bases this pronouncement upon the death of Christ on their behalf. (2) *Redemption:* through His death, Christ paid the ransom price of sin by purchasing believers out of slavery to sin and setting them free from the penalty of sin. (3) *Propitiation:* the blood of Christ has satisfied the demands of the righteous God who cannot overlook sin. God in Christ does not give the believer his due, because His holy wrath has been appeased by the sacrifice of His sinless Son. Justification is by grace (the source of salvation, 3:21-24), by blood (the basis of salvation, 3:25,26), and by faith (the condition of salvation, 3:27-31).

Chapter 4 illustrates the principle of justification by faith apart from works in the life of Abraham. Justification issues in reconciliation between God and man (5:1-11). *Reconciliation* speaks of the change in a person's state of alienation from and hostility toward God because of the substitutionary work of Jesus Christ on his behalf. It is brought about by the love of God which is causeless (5:6), measureless (5:7,8), and ceaseless (5:9-11). In 5:12-21 Paul contrasts the two Adams and the opposite results of their two acts. The disobedience of the first Adam made him the head of all who are under sin, but the obedience of the second Adam (Christ) made Him the head of the race of redeemed humanity. The sin of the first Adam was *imputed* to us (placed on our account), leading to alienation. But the righteousness of the second Adam is imputed to all who trust in Him, leading to reconciliation.

Power of Righteousness (6-8): Chapter 6 describes the believer's relationship to sin: in his position he is dead to the principle of sin (6:1-14) and the practice of sin (6:15-23). The reality of identification with Christ is the basis for the sanctified Christian life. The believer must *know* his position in Christ, *reckon* it as true, and *present* himself to God as dead to sin but alive to God in Christ Jesus. Paul views devotion as a response to spiritual truth, not a condition of it. After describing the Christian's emancipation from the law (chapter 7), Paul looks at the work of the Holy Spirit who indwells and empowers every believer (8:1-17). The next major topic after condemnation, justification, and sanctification is glorification (8:18-39). All Christians can anticipate a time when they will be perfectly conformed to Jesus Christ not only in their position (present), but also in their practice (the future resurrection).

Program of Righteousness (9-11): It appears that God has rejected His people Israel, but it is really Israel that has rejected her Messiah. Paul deals with the problem of Israel in the plan of God in three ways: (1) God is the sovereign Lord who is responsible to no one for His work of election and rejection (chapter 9). He elected Israel in the past but because of disbelief, the nation has been set aside in the present. (2) Although God is sovereign, humans are responsible for the consequences of their decisions (chapter 10), and this is true of their decision to accept or reject Jesus. (3) Israelites, the "natural branches" of God's olive tree, were cut off and Gentiles were added in (chapter 11). But God's rejection of Israel is only *partial* (there is a spiritual "remnant" that has trusted in Christ) and *temporary* (they will be grafted back in; 11:23-27). Paul appropriately quotes frequently from the Old Testament in this section, and he emphasizes that God will be faithful to His covenant promises.

Practice of Righteousness (12-16): Paul recognizes that behavior must be built upon belief, and this is why the practical exhortations of this epistle appear after his teaching on the believer's position in Christ. The salvation described in the first 11 chapters should transform a Christian's life in relation to God (12:1,2), society (12:3-21), the state (13:1-14), and other believers (14:1-15:13). A changed life is not a condition for salvation, but it should be the natural outcome of saving faith. The epistle closes with Paul's statement of his plans (15:14-33), a long series of personal greetings (16:1-16), and an admonition followed by a doxology (16:17-27).

Title—Although some manuscripts omit "in Rome" in 1:7,15, the title *Pros Romaious*, "To the Romans," has been associated with the epistle almost from the beginning.

Author—All critical schools agree on the Pauline authorship (1:1) of this foundational book. The vocabulary, style, logic, and theological development are consistent with Paul's other epistles. Paul dictated this letter to an amanuensis named Tertius (16:22) who was allowed to add his own greeting.

The problem is not the authorship but the unity of the epistle. Some Latin (but no Greek) manuscripts omit 15:1-16:24, and the closing doxology (16:25-27) is placed at the end of chapter 14 in some manuscripts. These variations have led some to conclude that the last two chapters were not originally part of the epistle, or that Paul issued it in two editions. But most scholars recognize that chapter 15 logically fits in with the rest of the epistle. There is more debate over chapter 16, because Paul greets 26 people by name in a church he had never visited. Some hold that this was a separate letter, perhaps written to Ephesus, that was appended to this epistle. Such a letter would be grotesque (nothing but greetings) especially in the ancient world, and it is simpler to understand the list of greetings as Paul's effort as a stranger to the Roman church to list his mutual friends. Paul met these people in the cities of his missionary journeys. Significantly, the only other Pauline epistle that lists individual greetings was addressed to the believers at Colossae, another church Paul had never visited. It may be that some copies of Romans dropped this portion because it did not seem relevant.

Date and Setting—Paul did not found the church at Rome, and the tradition that Peter was its founder is contrary to the evidence. It is possible that it began when some of the Jews and proselytes who came to Christ on the day of Pentecost (cf. Acts 2:10) returned to Rome, but it is more likely that Christians from churches established by Paul in Asia, Macedonia, and Greece settled in Rome and led others to Christ. According to this epistle, Gentiles were predominant in the church at Rome (1:13; 11:13; 11:28-31; 15:15,16), but there were also Jewish believers (2:17-3:8; 3:21-4:1; 7:1-14; 14:1-15:12).

Rome was founded in 753 B.C., and by the time of Paul it was the greatest city in the world with over one million inhabitants (one inscription says over four million). It was full of magnificent buildings, but the majority of people were slaves—opulence and squalor coexisted in the Imperial City. The church in Rome was well-known (1:8), and it had been established for several years by the time of this letter (see 14:14; 15:23). The believers there were probably numerous (they evidently met in several places; 16:1-16), and the historian Tacitus referred to the Christians who were persecuted under Nero in A.D. 64 as "an immense multitude." The gospel filled the gap left by the practically defunct polytheism of Roman religion.

Paul wrote Romans in A.D. 57, near the end of his third missionary journey (Acts 18:23-21:14; cf. Rom. 15:19). It was evidently written during his three-month stay in Greece (Acts 20:3-6), more specifically, in Corinth. Paul was staying with Gaius of Corinth (16:23; cf. 1 Cor. 1:14), and he also mentioned "Erastus, the city treasurer" (16:23; a first-century inscription in Corinth mentions him: "Erastus, the commissioner of public works, laid this pavement at his own expense"). Paul's collection from the churches of Macedonia and Achaia for the needy Christians in Jerusalem was complete (15:26), and he was ready to deliver it (15:25). Instead of sailing directly to Jerusalem, Paul avoided a plot by the Jews by first going north to Philippi. He evidently gave this letter to Phoebe from the church at Cenchrea near Corinth, and she carried it to Rome (16:1,2).

Theme and Purpose—The theme of Romans is found in 1:16,17: God offers the gift of His righteousness to everyone who comes to Christ by faith. Paul wrote Romans to reveal God's sovereign plan of salvation (1-8), to show how Jews and Gentiles fit into that plan (9-11), and to exhort them to live righteous and harmonious lives (12-16). In his sweeping presentation of God's plan of salvation, Paul moves from condemnation to glorification, and from positional truth to practical truth. Key words like *righteousness, faith, law, all,* and *sin* each appear at least 60 times in this epistle.

Paul did not write Romans to address specific problems in the church but to prepare the brethren for his long-awaited visit to that strategic church (15:22-24). He had laid the foundation for the gospel in the eastern provinces through his three missionary journeys, and now he desires to begin a significant work in the western provinces. Rome, the most influential city in the Empire, would be the logical base of operations for Paul's future missionary endeavors, just as Antioch was during his first three journeys. Paul had tried to visit Rome a number of times in the past, but each time he had been hindered (1:13; 15:22). By writing this letter, Paul hoped to build up the believers there in their knowledge and faith and to encourage this mixed church of Jews and Gentiles to work together as one body. Paul also asked them for their prayer support because of the dangerous opposition that awaited him in Jerusalem.

Contribution to the Bible—Romans was not the first of Paul's epistles, but it was appropriately placed at the beginning of the Pauline corpus not only because it was Paul's longest work, but because it provides the doctrinal foundation upon which the other epistles are built. It is the most systematic and detailed exposition of theological truth in the Scriptures. Romans concentrates on the doctrines of hamartiology (sin) and soteriology (salvation): just as all men (Jews and Gentiles) are sinners, so God has graciously extended His offer of salvation to all who will place their faith in Christ.

Romans is the most formal of Paul's writings—it is more of a treatise than a letter. Paul was a stranger to most of the Roman believers (hence the long introduction), and he did not seek to refute any specific errors in their church. This is primarily a preventative, not a corrective epistle, and Paul made skillful use of a debate format to refute the kinds of objections he had encountered during two decades of reflecting upon and defending the gospel. The result is one of the most forceful, logical, and eloquent works ever penned. It is safe to say Romans has influenced the subsequent history of the church more than any other epistle.

Christ in Romans—Paul presents Jesus Christ as the second Adam whose righteousness and substitutionary death have provided justification for all who place their faith in Him. He offers His righteousness as a gracious gift to sinful men, having borne God's condemnation and wrath for their sinfulness. His death and resurrection are the basis for the believer's redemption, justification, reconciliation, salvation, and glorification.

1 Corinthians

"Whether, then, you eat or drink or whatever you do, do all to the glory of God."

1 Corinthians 10:31

"But let all things be done properly and in an orderly manner."

1 Corinthians 14:40

Focus	Reproofs to the Church					Replies to the Church				
	1 6					7 16				
D i v i s i o n s	Salutation and Thanksgiving	Problem of Factions	Problem of Specific Immorality	Problem of Lawsuits	Problem of General Immorality	Perspectives on Marriage	Perspectives on Food Offered to Idols	Perspectives on Public Worship	Perspectives on the Resurrection	Concluding Matters
	1:1-9	1:10 4	5	6:1-8	6:9-20	7	8 11:1	11:2 14	15	16
T o p i c s	Four Problems					Four Perspectives				
	Divisions		Discipline			Discussion		Disorders		Disbelief
	Corporate					Private		Public		
	Condemnation					Counsel				
Location	Written in Ephesus									
Time	A.D. 56									

75

Talk Thru—Through the missionary efforts of Paul and others, the church got into Corinth, but Paul found it very difficult to keep Corinth out of the church. The pagan lifestyle of Corinth exerted a profound influence upon the Christians in that corrupt city—problems of every kind plagued them. In this disciplinary letter, Paul is forced to exercise his apostolic authority as he firmly deals with problems of divisiveness, immorality, lawsuits, selfishness, abuses of the Lord's Supper and spiritual gifts, and denial of the resurrection. This epistle is quite orderly in its approach as it sequentially addresses a group of problems that have come to Paul's attention. Paul also gives a series of perspectives on various questions and issues raised by the Corinthians in a letter. He uses the introductory phrase "Now concerning" or "Now . . ." to delineate these topics (7:1,25; 8:1; 11:2; 12:1; 15:1; 16:1). Chapters 1-6 concern Paul's reproofs to the church, and chapters 7-16 list Paul's replies to the church.

Reproofs to the Church (1-6): Personality cults centering around Paul, Apollos, and Peter have led to divisions and false pride among the Corinthians (1). It is not their wisdom or cleverness that has brought them to Christ, because divine wisdom is contrary to human wisdom. The truth of the gospel is spiritually apprehended (2), and the factions that exist among the saints at Corinth are an indication of their spiritual immaturity (3). They should pride themselves in Christ, not in human leaders who are merely His servants (4).

The next problem Paul addresses is that of incest between a member of the church and his stepmother (5). The Corinthians exercised no church discipline in this matter, and Paul orders them to remove the offender from their fellowship until he repents. Another source of poor testimony is the legal action of believer against believer in heathen courts (6:1-8). They must learn to arbitrate their differences within the Christian community. Paul concludes this section with a warning against immorality in general (6:9-20).

Replies to the Church (7-16): In these chapters the apostle Paul gives authoritative answers to thorny questions raised by the Corinthians. His first counsel concerns the issues of marriage, celibacy, divorce, and remarriage (7). The next three chapters are related to the problem of meat offered to idols (8-11:1). Paul illustrates the twin principles of Christian liberty and the law of love from his own life, and concludes that believers must sometimes limit their liberty for the sake of weaker brothers (cf. Rom. 14). The apostle then turns to matters related to public worship, including improper observance of the Lord's Supper and selfish use of spiritual gifts, especially tongues (11:2-14:40). Gifts are to be exercised in love for the edification of the whole body. The Corinthians also had problems with the resurrection, which Paul seeks to correct in chapter 15. His historical and theological defense of the resurrection includes teaching on the nature of the resurrection body. The Corinthians were probably struggling over this issue because the idea of a resurrected body was disdainful in Greek thought. The epistle closes with Paul's instruction for the collection he will make for the saints in Jerusalem (16:1-4), followed by miscellaneous exhortations and greetings (16:5-24).

Title—The oldest recorded title of this epistle is *Pros Korinthious A,* in effect, the "First to the Corinthians." The *A* was no doubt a later addition to distinguish this book from 2 Corinthians.

Author—Pauline authorship of 1 Corinthians is almost universally accepted. Recorded attestation stretches back to A.D. 95 when Clement of Rome wrote to the Corinthian church and cited this epistle in regard to their continuing problem of factions among themselves.

Date and Setting—Corinth was a key city in ancient Greece until it was destroyed by the Romans in 146 B.C. Julius Caesar rebuilt it as a Roman colony in 46 B.C. and it grew and prospered, becoming the capital of the province of Achaia. Its official language was Latin, but the common language remained Greek. In Paul's day Corinth was the metropolis of the Peloponnesus because it was strategically located on a narrow isthmus between the Aegean Sea and the Adriatic Sea that connects the Peloponnesus with northern Greece. Because of its two seaports it became a commercial center, and many small ships were rolled or dragged across the Corinthian isthmus to avoid the dangerous 200-mile voyage around southern Greece. Nero and others attempted to build a canal at the narrowest point, but this was not achieved until 1893.

The city was filled with shrines and temples, but the most prominent was the temple of Aphrodite on top of a 1,800-foot prominence called the Acrocorinthus. Worshipers of the "goddess of love" made free use of the 1,000 *Hieroduli* (consecrated prostitutes). This cosmopolitan center thrived on commerce, entertainment, vice, and corruption—pleasure-seekers came there to spend money on a moral holiday. Corinth became so notorious for its immorality that the term *Korinthiazomai* ("to act like a Corinthian") became a synonym for debauchery and prostitution.

In Paul's day the population of Corinth was about 700,000, about two-thirds consisting of slaves. The diverse population produced no philosophers, but Greek philosophy influenced any speculative thought that was there. In spite of these obstacles to the gospel, Paul was able to establish a church in Corinth on his second missionary journey (3:6,10; 4:15; Acts 18:1-17). Persecution in Macedonia drove him south to Athens, and from there he proceeded to Corinth. He made tents with Aquila and Priscilla and reasoned with the Jews in the synagogue. Silas and Timothy joined him (they evidently brought a gift from Philippi; 2 Cor. 11:8,9; Phil. 4:15) and Paul began to devote all his time to the gospel. Paul wrote 1 and 2 Thessalonians, moved his ministry from the synagogue to the house of Titius Justus because of opposition, and converted Crispus, the leader of the synagogue. Paul taught the Word of God in Corinth for 18 months in A.D. 51-52. After Paul's departure, Apollos came from Ephesus to minister in the Corinthian church (3:6; Acts 18:24-28).

When Paul was teaching and preaching in Ephesus during his third missionary journey, he was disturbed by reports from the household of Chloe concerning quarrels in the church at Corinth (1:11). The church sent a delegation of three men (16:17) who apparently brought a letter that requested Paul's judgment on certain issues (7:1). Paul wrote this epistle as his response to the problems and questions of the Corinthians (he had already written a previous letter; 5:9). It may be that the men who came from Corinth brought this letter back with them. Paul was planning to leave Ephesus (16:5-8), indicating that 1 Corinthians was written in A.D. 56.

Theme and Purpose—The basic theme of this epistle is

the application of Christian principles on an individual and social level. The cross of Christ is a message that is designed to transform the lives of believers and make them different, as people and as a corporate body, from the surrounding world. But the Corinthians were destroying their Christian testimony because of immorality and disunity. Paul wrote this letter as his corrective response to the news of problems and disorders among the Corinthians. It was designed to refute improper attitudes and conduct and to promote a spirit of unity among the brethren in their relationships and worship. Paul's concern as their spiritual father (4:14,15) was tempered with love, and he wanted to avoid visiting them "with a rod" (4:21).

Contribution to the Bible—This epistle is extremely practical in its thrust, and it focuses on basic social, moral, and spiritual issues. Unlike Romans, 1 Corinthians is not rhetorically elegant; it is plain, earnest, and unvarnished. The unusual simplicity and directness of this letter is appropriate to the practical content. The sentences are uncomplicated, and Paul forcefully amplifies his thoughts with abundant literary devices (narrative, sarcasm, appeal, etc.). Although it is informal, 1 Corinthians makes several important contributions to New Testament doctrine. This is particularly true of the doctrines of the church as an organism, the role of spiritual gifts, and the resurrection.

No other epistle gives a better look at the problems and conditions in an apostolic church. Even though planted and nurtured by Paul himself, the church at Corinth bristled with social, ethical, spiritual, and doctrinal problems. This was a difficult letter for Paul to write, but his profound wisdom and insight dominate its pages and reveal the apostle's patient love and self-control.

The wide variety of subjects discussed in this long epistle (only Romans is longer) is easy to follow because of its logical and orderly development.

Christ in 1 Corinthians—This book proclaims the relevance of Christ Jesus to every area of the believer's life. He "became to us wisdom from God, and righteousness and sanctification, and redemption" (1:30), and these are the themes Paul addresses in this book.

2 Corinthians

"For we do not preach ourselves but Christ Jesus as Lord, and ourselves as your bond-servants for Jesus' sake."
2 Corinthians 4:5 (Also see 5:10,20,21; 10:5.)

Focus	Paul's Conduct and Character (1–7)					Paul's Collection (8–9)			Paul's Credentials (10–13)			
Divisions	Salutation and Thanksgiving	Paul's Alteration of His Plans	Paul's Attitudes and Actions in Ministry	Paul's Admonition to the Corinthians	Paul's Assurance over the Effects of His Letter	Paul's Appeal to the Church to Give	Paul's Approval of His Messengers	Paul's Affirmation of Liberality	Paul's Apostolic Authority	Paul's Apostolic Credentials	Paul's Approaching Visit to Corinth	Exhortation, Greetings, Benediction
	1:1-11	1:12–2:11	2:12–6:10	6:11-7:1	7:2-16	8:1-15	8:16–9:5	9:6-15	10	11–12:13	12:14–13:10	13:11-14
Topics	Explanation					Exhortation			Vindication			
	Testimonial					Practical			Apologetic			
	Account					Appeal			Answer			
	Addressed to the Repentant Majority								Addressed to the Rebellious Minority			
Location	Written in Macedonia (Possibly Philippi)											
Time	A.D. 56											

Talk Thru—Second Corinthians describes the anatomy of an apostle. The Corinthian church had been swayed by false teachers who stirred the people against Paul, especially in response to 1 Corinthians, Paul's disciplinary letter. They claimed that Paul was fickle (1:17,18,23), proud and boastful (3:1; 5:12), fleshly (10:2), unimpressive in appearance and speech (10:10; 11:6), unstable in thought (5:13; 11:16-19), not qualified as one of the original apostles (11:5, 12:11,12), and dishonest (12:16-19). Paul sent Titus to Corinth to deal with these difficulties and made his own journey to Troas and Macedonia. There he was met by Titus who informed him that most of the brethren repented of their error (7:5-16). Much relieved, Paul wrote this letter to express his thanksgiving for the repentant majority (1-9) and to appeal to the rebellious minority to accept his apostolic authority (10-13). Throughout this letter Paul defends his apostolic conduct, character, and call. The three major sections are: Paul's Conduct and Character (1-7), Paul's Collection (8-9), and Paul's Credentials (10-13).

Paul's Conduct and Character (1-7): After his salutation and thanksgiving for God's comfort in his afflictions and perils (1:1-11), Paul explains why he delayed his planned visit to Corinth. It was not a matter of vacillation—the apostle wanted them to have enough time to repent (1:12-2:4). Paul graciously asks them to restore the repentant offender to fellowship (2:5-11). At this point, Paul embarks on an extended defense of his ministry in terms of his message, circumstances, motives, and conduct (2:12-6:10). He then admonishes the believers to separate themselves from defilement (6:11-7:1), and expresses his comfort at Titus' news of their change of heart (7:2-16).

Paul's Collection (8-9): This is the longest discussion of the principles and practice of giving in the New Testament. The example of the Macedonians' liberal giving for the needy brethren in Jerusalem (8:1-6) is followed by an appeal to the Corinthians to keep their promise by doing the same (8:7-15). In this connection, Paul commends the messengers he sent to Corinth to make arrangements for their "previously promised bountiful gift" (8:16-9:5). Their generosity will be more than amply rewarded by God (9:6-15).

Paul's Credentials (10-13): Paul concludes this epistle with a defense of his apostolic authority and credentials that is directed to the still rebellious minority in the Corinthian church.

His meekness in their presence in no way diminishes his authority as an apostle (10). To demonstrate his apostolic credentials, Paul is forced to boast about his knowledge, integrity, accomplishments, sufferings, visions, and miracles (11:1-12:13). He reveals his plans to visit them for the third time and urges them to repent so that he will not have to use severity when he comes (12:14-13:10). The letter ends with an exhortation, greetings, and a benediction (13:11-14).

Title—To distinguish this epistle from 1 Corinthians, it was given the title *Pros Korinthious B*, the "Second to the Corinthians." The *A* and *B* were probably later additions to *Pros Korinthious*.

Author—External and internal evidence amply support the Pauline authorship of this letter. As with Romans, the problem of 2 Corinthians is its unity, not its authorship. Many critics theorize that chapters 10-13 were not a part of this letter in its original form because their tone contrasts with that of chapters 1-9. It is held that the sudden change from a spirit of joy and comfort to a spirit of concern and self-defense points to a "seam" between two different letters. A multitude of hypotheses have been advanced to explain the problem, but the most popular is that 10-13 is part of a lost letter referred to in 2:4. There are several problems with these attempts to dissect 2 Corinthians. Chapters 10-13 do not fit Paul's description of the "lost" letter of 2:4 because they are firm but not "sorrowful" and because they do not refer to the offender about whom that letter was written (2:5-11). Also, this earlier material would have been appended at the beginning of 2 Corinthians, not at the end. There is simply no external (manuscripts, church fathers, tradition) or internal basis for challenging the unity of this epistle. The difference in tone between 1-9 and 10-13 is easily explained by the change of address from the repentant majority to the rebellious minority.

Date and Setting—Part of the background of 2 Corinthians can be found in 1 Corinthians, Date and Setting. Paul was in Ephesus when he wrote 1 Corinthians and expected Timothy to visit Corinth and return to him (1 Cor. 16:10,11). Timothy evidently brought Paul a report of the opposition that had developed against him in Corinth, and Paul made a brief and painful visit to the Corinthians (this visit is not mentioned in Acts but can be inferred from 2 Cor. 2:1; 12:14; 13:1,2). Upon returning to Ephesus, Paul regretfully wrote his "sorrowful" letter to urge the church to discipline the leader of the opposition (2:1-11; 7:8). Titus carried this letter and Paul, anxious to learn the results, went to Troas and then to Macedonia to meet Titus on his return trip (2:12,13; 7:5-16). Paul was greatly relieved by Titus' report that the majority of the Corinthians had repented of their rebelliousness against Paul's apostolic authority. However, a minority opposition still persisted, evidently led by a group of Judaizers (10-13). There in Macedonia Paul wrote 2 Corinthians and sent it with Titus and another brother (8:16-24). This took place late in A.D. 56, and the Macedonian city from which it was written may have been Philippi. Paul then made his third trip to Corinth (12:14; 13:1,2; Acts 20:1-3), where he wrote the book of Romans.

There is an alternative view that the "sorrowful" letter of 2:4 and 7:8 is in fact 1 Corinthians and not a lost letter. This would require the offender of 2 Corinthians 2:5-11; 7:12 to be identified with the offender of 1 Corinthians 5.

Theme and Purpose—The major theme of 2 Corinthians is Paul's defense of his apostolic credentials and authority. This is especially evident in the portion directed to the still rebellious minority (10-13), but the theme of vindication is also clear in chapters 1-9. Certain "false apostles" mounted an effective campaign against Paul in the church at Corinth, and Paul had to take a number of steps to overcome the opposition. This epistle expresses the apostle's joy over the triumph of the true gospel in Corinth (1-7), and it acknowledges the "godly sorrow" and repentance of the bulk of the believers there. It also urges the Corinthians to fulfill their promise of making a liberal contribution for the poor among the Christians in Judea (8-9). This collection would not only assist the poor, but it would also demonstrate the concern of Gentile Christians in Macedonia and Achaia for Jewish Christians in Judea, thus displaying the unity of Jews and Gentiles in the body of Christ.

The opposition addressed in 10-13 apparently consisted of Jews (Palestinean or Hellenistic; 11:22) who claimed to be apostles (11:5,13; 12:11) but who preached a false gospel (11:4) and were enslaving in their leadership (11:20). Chapters 10-13 were written to expose these "deceitful workers" and defend Paul's God-given authority and ministry as an apostle of Jesus Christ.

Contribution to the Bible—This epistle is full of autobiographical material and many regard it as the most personal book in the New Testament. The mind of Paul is prominent in Romans, but 2 Corinthians reveals the apostle's heart. His character, motives, priorities, desires, and emotions are exposed more clearly in this epistle than in any other. The personal anecdotes offer a glimpse into aspects of Paul's personal life that would otherwise be unknown. These include persecution and hardships not recorded in Acts (11:23-27), extra details of his escape from Damascus (11:32,33), his vision and revelation of Paradise (12:1-7), and his thorn in the flesh (12:7-10).

The language of this epistle is characterized by unusual constructions, broken sentences, mixed metaphors, and sudden shifts in feeling and tone. Paul's emotional stress can also be seen in the many digressions; 2 Corinthians is perhaps the most unsystematic of all his writings. Nevertheless, this book makes important doctrinal contributions to the Bible. In it, Paul contrasts the old and the new covenants (3), explains the supernatural warfare over the reception of the gospel (4:1-7), gives a proper perspective on suffering for Christ (4:8-18), contributes new insights on the resurrection and judgment of Christians (5:1-13), describes the ministry of reconciliation and the double imputation of Christ (5:14-21), affirms the importance of separation from the ways of the world (6:14-7:1), offers the most thorough biblical perspective on Christian giving (8-9), and exposes the strategies of Satan (2:10,11; 4:4; 11:3,13-15; 12:7).

Christ in 2 Corinthians—Christ is presented as the believer's: comfort (1:5), triumph (2:14), Lord (4:5), light (4:6), judge (5:10), reconciliation (5:19), substitute (5:21), gift (9:15), owner (10:7), and power (12:9).

Galatians

"It was for freedom that Christ set us free; therefore keep standing firm and do not be subject again to a yoke of slavery."
Galatians 5:1 (Also see 2:20,21; 3:3,13,14; 5:22,23.)

Focus	Biographical Argument					Theological Argument		Moral Argument		
	1				2	3	4	5		6
Divisions	Definition of the Gospel	Distortion of the Gospel	Divine Revelation of the Gospel	Debut of Paul's Gospel	Debate over the Gospel	Demonstration of the Gospel	Demand of the Gospel	Diagnosis of the Gospel	Discharge of the Gospel	Distinction of the Gospel
	1:1-5	1:6-10	1:11-24	2:1-10	2:11-21	3:1 4:7	4:8-31	5:1-12	5:13 6:10	6:11-18
Topics	Validity of the Gospel: Apostleship					Vindication of the Gospel: Appeal		Victory of the Gospel: Application		
	Personal Explanation					Doctrinal Exposition		Practical Exhortation		
	Justification by Faith Defended					Justification by Faith Demonstrated		Justification by Faith Developed		
	Liberty to Legalism		Legalism to Liberty			Legalism Versus Liberty		Life of Liberty		
Location	South Galatian Theory: Probably Written in Syrian Antioch North Galatian Theory: Probably Written in Ephesus or Macedonia									
Time	South Galatian Theory: A.D. 49 North Galatian Theory: A.D. 53-56									

Talk Thru—The epistle to the Galatians has been called "the Magna Carta of Christian liberty." It is Paul's manifesto of justification by faith and the liberty it produces. Paul directed this great charter of Christian freedom to a people who were willing to give up the priceless liberty they possessed in Christ. The oppressive theology of certain Jewish legalizers was influencing the believers in Galatia to trade their freedom in Christ for bondage to the law. Paul wrote this forceful epistle to refute the false gospel of works and to demonstrate the superiority of justification by faith. This carefully written polemic approaches the problem from three directions: Biographical Argument (1-2), Theological Argument (3-4), and Moral Argument (5-6).

Biographical Argument (1-2): Paul affirms his divinely given apostleship and defines the gospel (1:1-5) that has been distorted by false teachers among the Galatians (1:6-10). Paul launches into his biographical argument for the true gospel of justification by faith by showing that he received his message not from men but directly from God (1:11-24). When he submitted his teaching of Christian liberty to the apostles in Jerusalem, they all acknowleged the validity and authority of his message (2:1-10). Paul even had to correct Peter on the matter of freedom from the law (2:11-21).

Theological Argument (3-4): In this section Paul uses eight lines of reasoning to develop his theological defense of justification by faith: (1) The Galatians began by faith, and their growth in Christ must continue to be by faith (3:1-5). (2) Abraham was justified by faith, and the same principle applies today (3:6-9). (3) Christ has redeemed all who trust in Him from the curse of the law (3:10-14). (4) The promise made to Abraham was not nullified by the law (3:15-18). (5) The law was given to drive men to faith, not to save them (3:19-22). (6) Believers in Christ are adopted sons of God and no longer in bondage to the law (3:23-4:7). (7) The Galatians must recognize their inconsistency and turn back to their original freedom in Christ (4:8-20). (8) Abraham's two sons allegorically reveal the superiority of the Abrahamic promise to the Mosaic law (4:21-31).

Moral Argument (5-6): The Judaizers seek to place the Gentile believers in Galatia under bondage to their perverted gospel of justification by law, but Paul warns them that law and grace are two contrary principles (5:1-12). So far, Paul has been contrasting the liberty of faith with the legalism of law, but at this point he warns the Galatians of the opposite extreme of license or *antinomianism* (5:13-6:10). The Christian is not only set free from the bondage of law, but he is also free of the bondage of sin because of the power of the indwelling Spirit. Liberty is not an excuse to indulge in the deeds of the flesh; it is the privilege of bearing the fruit of the Spirit by walking in dependence upon Him. This letter closes with a contrast between the Judaizers who are motivated by pride and a desire to avoid persecution, and Paul who has suffered for the true gospel but boasts only in Christ (6:11-18).

Title—The book is called *Pros Galatas,* "To the Galatians," and it is the only letter of Paul that is specifically addressed to a number of churches ("to the churches of Galatia," 1:2). The name *Galatians* was given to this Celtic people because they originally lived in Gaul before their migration to Asia Minor.

Author—The Pauline authorship and the unity of this epistle are virtually unchallenged.

Date and Setting—The term Galatia was used in an ethnographic sense and a political sense. The original ethnographic sense refers to the central part of Asia Minor where these Celtic tribes eventually settled after their conflicts with the Romans and Macedonians. Later in 189 B.C. Galatia came under Roman domination, and in 25 B.C. Augustus turned it into a Roman province. The political or provincial Galatia included southern territory that was not originally part of Galatia (for example, the cities of Pisidian Antioch, Iconium, Lystra, and Derbe).

The *North Galatian theory* holds that Paul was speaking of Galatia in its earlier and more restricted sense. According to this theory, the "churches of Galatia" were north of the cities Paul visited on his first missionary journey. Paul visited (ethnographic) Galatia for the first time on his second missionary journey, evidently on his way to Troas (Acts 16:6). On his third missionary journey, Paul revisited the Galatian churches he had established (Acts 18:23) and wrote this epistle either in Ephesus (53-56) or Macedonia (56). This theory is supported by the church fathers, but this may be due to the exclusive use of the ethnographic sense of Galatia by the second century. Advocates of this view also point to Luke's apparent use of Galatia in the northern sense (Acts 16:6; 18:23). Similarities between Galatians and Romans (written in 57) also help this late-date theory for Galatians. But it is hurt by the fact that Acts does not say that Paul evangelized North Galatia. In fact, he would have had to take a radical detour to the northeast on his second missionary journey to do so, whereas no such detour would have been necessary if he went to South Galatia.

According to the _South Galatian theory_, Paul was referring to Galatia in its wider political sense as a province of Rome. This means that the churches he had in mind in this epistle were in the cities he evangelized on his first missionary journey with Barnabas (Acts 13:13-14:23). This was just prior to the Jerusalem Council (Acts 15), so the Jerusalem visit in Galatians 2:1-10 must have been the Acts 11:27-30 famine relief visit. Galatians was probably written in Syrian Antioch in A.D. 49 just before Paul went to the Council in Jerusalem. This theory is supported in several ways: (1) Paul consistently referred to geography in the political sense in his epistles. (2) If Galatians was written after the Jerusalem Council as the North Galatian theory holds, it is probable that Paul would have referred to that authoritative decree to bolster his argument in this epistle, but it is not mentioned. (3) It is unlikely that Peter would have acted as he did in Galatians 2:11-21 after the Jerusalem Council. (4) This theory fits against the background in Acts 13-14, but the North Galatian theory has no corresponding background. (5) The South Galatian cities that Paul visited were more strategic from an evangelistic point of view than those in the North because of their location, population, and commerce. (6) Barnabas (mentioned three times in chapter 2) would have been more familiar to the South Galatian churches than to the North Galatian churches because he did not accompany Paul on his second missionary journey when the churches in North Galatia were supposedly established.

Neither theory can be proven conclusively, but the weight of evidence seems to favor the newer South Galatian viewpoint. Fortunately, this is just a matter of background, not interpretation. In either case, Paul wrote this epistle in response to a report that the Galatian churches had suddenly succumbed to the false teaching of certain Judaizers who professed Jesus but sought to place Gentile converts under the requirements of the Mosaic law (1:7; 4:17,21; 5:2-12; 6:12,13).

Theme and Purpose—Justification by faith apart from works of the law is the theme of this urgent and corrective book. The three major sections reveal three purposes for which Galatians was written: Chapters 1-2 were written to defend Paul's apostolic authority, because this establishes his gospel message. Chapters 3-4 were written to give a theological defense of the principle of justification by faith to refute the false teaching of justification by law. Paul used the law itself to build his case. Chapters 5-6 were written to show that liberty from the law does not mean lawlessness, as Paul's opponents evidently claimed.

Contribution to the Bible—Although Galatians and Romans have several themes in common, the polemic tone of Galatians stands in contrast to the irenic tone of Romans. Galatians is written in the sharp language of conflict, its severe words reflecting the urgency of the crisis that had so quickly come upon the believers in that region. Avoiding even his customary thanksgiving, Paul immediately launches into his rebuke. The logical development of Galatians is uninterrupted by digressions as Paul carefully develops his crucial theme. But there is a wide variety of feelings and approaches in this epistle. The severity is broken by tender appeals, and Paul uses personal experience, Old Testament exegesis, logic, warning, rebuke, and even an allegory to develop his argument. This epistle has had a profound impact upon the history of the church.

Christ in Galatians—Christ has freed the believer from bondage to the law (legalism) and to sin (license) and has placed him in a position of liberty. The cross is the basis for the believer's deliverance from the curse of sin, law, and self (1:4; 2:20; 3:13; 4:5; 5:24; 6:14).

Ephesians

''I, therefore, the prisoner of the Lord, entreat you to walk in a manner worthy of the calling with which you have been called.''

Ephesians 4:1 (Also see 2:10.)

Focus	Calling of the Body							Conduct of the Body					
	1						3	4					6
D i v i s i o n s	Prologue	Praise for Redemption	Prayer for Spiritual Perception	Power of God in Redemption	People of God in One Body	Proclamation of the Mystery	Prayer for Spiritual Power	Working of the Body	Walk of Integrity	Walk of Holiness	Wives, Husbands, Children, Workers	Warfare against Wickedness	Parting Words
	1:1-2	1:3-14	1:15-23	2:1-10	2:11-22	3:1-13	3:14-21	4:1-16	4:17-32	5:1-21	5:22-6:19	6:10-20	6:21-24
T o p i c s	Privileges of the Believer							Responsibilities of the Believer					
	Spiritual Wealth							Spiritual Walk					
	Positional Truth: Belief							Practical Truth: Behavior					
	Doctrine: No Imperatives							Exhortation:35 Imperatives					
Loca-tion	Written During Paul's First Roman Imprisonment												
Time	A.D. 60-61												

Talk Thru—All who have trusted in Christ possess the priceless bounty of "every spiritual blessing in the heavenly places in Christ" (1:3). Unfortunately, most believers live as though they are spiritual paupers because they are either unaware of or fail to appropriate the divine resources that are at their disposal. Paul wrote this epistle to make Christians more aware of their position in Christ and to motivate them to draw upon their spiritual position in their earthly practice: "walk in a manner worthy of the calling with which you have been called" (4:1; see 2:10). The first half of Ephesians outlines the believer's heavenly possessions: adoption, redemption, inheritance, power, life, grace, citizenship, and the love of Christ. There are no imperatives in chapters 1-3 because these are all divine gifts. But chapters 4-6 have 35 imperatives because the last half of Ephesians speaks of the believer's responsibility to conduct himself according to his calling. Thus, Ephesians begins in heaven but ends in the home, and in all the relationships of daily life. The two divisions are: Calling of the Body (1-3) and Conduct of the Body (4-6).

Calling of the Body (1-3): After a two-verse prologue, Paul extols the triune God for the riches of redemption in one long Greek sentence (1:3-14). This hymn to God's grace praises the Father for choosing us (1:3-6), the Son for redeeming us (1:7-12), and the Spirit for sealing us (1:13,14). The saving work of each divine Person is "to the praise of His glory" (1:6,12,14). Before continuing on, Paul offers the first of two very significant prayers (1:15-23; cf. 3:14-21). Here he asks that the readers would receive spiritual illumination so that they would come to perceive what is in fact true of them. Next, Paul describes the power of God's grace by contrasting their former deadness with their present spiritual life in Christ, a salvation attained not by human works but by divine grace (2:1-10). This redemption includes Jews but extends also to Gentiles who were previously "strangers to the covenants of promise" (2:12). In Christ, the two for the first time have become members of one body (2:11-22). The truth that Gentiles would become "fellow heirs and fellow members of the body" (3:6) was previously a mystery that has only now been revealed (3:1-13). Paul's second prayer (3:14-21) expresses his desire that the readers would be strengthened with the power of the Spirit and would apprehend the love of Christ.

Conduct of the Body (4-6): The pivotal verse of Ephesians is 4:1, because it draws a sharp line between the positional and the practical divisions of this book. There is a cause-effect relationship between chapters 1-3 and 4-6 because the spiritual walk of a Christian must be rooted in his spiritual wealth. As Paul emphasized in Romans, behavior does not determine blessing; blessing should determine behavior.

Because of the unity of all believers in the body of Christ, growth and maturity come from "the proper working of each individual part" (4:1-16). This involves the exercise of spiritual gifts in love. Paul exhorts the readers to "lay aside the old self" and "put on the new self" that will be manifested by a walk of integrity before other men (4:17-32). They are also to maintain a walk of holiness as children of light (5:1-21). Every relationship (wives, husbands, children, parents, slaves, masters) must be transformed by their new life in Christ (5:22-6:9). Paul's colorful description of the spiritual warfare and the armor of God (6:10-20) is followed by a word about Tychicus and a benediction (6:21-24).

Title—The traditional title of this epistle is *Pros Ephesious,* "To the Ephesians." Many ancient manuscripts, however, omit *en Epheso*, "at Ephesus," in 1:1. This has led a number of scholars to challenge the traditional view that it was directed specifically to the Ephesians. The encyclical theory claims that it was a circular letter sent by Paul to the churches of Asia. It is argued that Ephesians is really a Christian treatise that was designed for general use—it has no controversy and deals with no problems in a specific church. This is also supported by the formal tone (no terms of endearment) and distant phraseology ("having heard" of their faith, 1:15; if they "have heard" of his message, 3:2). These things seem inconsistent with the relationship Paul must have had with the Ephesians after a ministry of almost three years among them. On the other hand, the absence of personal greetings is not a support for the encyclical theory because Paul would have done this to avoid favoritism. The only letters that greet specific people are Romans and Colossians, and these were addressed to churches Paul had not visited. Some scholars accept an ancient tradition that Ephesians is in fact Paul's letter to the Laodiceans (Col. 4:16), but there is no way to be sure. If Ephesians was a circular letter, it eventually became associated with Ephesus, the chief of the Asian churches. Another plausible option is that this epistle *was* directly addressed to the Ephesians, but written in a way that would make it relevant to all the churches of Asia.

Author—All external evidence strongly supports the Pauline authorship of Ephesians, but critics in recent years have turned to internal grounds to challenge this unanimous ancient tradition. It has been argued that the vocabulary and style are different from other Pauline epistles, but this overlooks Paul's flexibility under different circumstances (compare Romans and 2 Corinthians). The theology of Ephesians in some ways reflects a later development, but this must be attributed to Paul's own growth and meditation on the church as the body of Christ. It is not necessary to theorize that Ephesians was written by a pupil or admirer of Paul like Timothy, Luke, Tychicus, or Onesimus.

Date and Setting—At the end of his second missionary journey, Paul visited Ephesus where he left Priscilla and Aquila (Acts 18:18-21). This strategic city was the commercial center of Asia Minor, but heavy silting required a special canal to be maintained so that ships could reach the harbor. Ephesus was a religious center as well, especially famous for its magnificent temple of Diana (Roman name) or Artemis (Greek name), one of the seven wonders of the ancient world (cf. Acts 19:35). The practice of magic and the local economy were closely related to this temple. When Paul came to Ephesus on his third missionary journey, he remained there for close to three years (Acts 19; 20:31), and the Word of God spread throughout the province of Asia. Paul's effective ministry began to seriously hurt the traffic in magic and images, leading to an uproar in the huge Ephesian theater. Paul left for Macedonia after this but met with the Ephesian elders on his way to Jerusalem (Acts 20:17-38).

Paul wrote the "Prison Epistles" (Ephesians, Philippians, Colossians, and Philemon) during his first Roman imprisonment in A.D. 60-62. These epistles all refer to his imprisonment (Eph. 3:1; 4:1; 6:20; Phil. 1:7,13,14; Col. 4:3,10,18; Philem. 9,10,13,23), and fit well against the background in Acts 28:16-31. This is especially true of Paul's references to the "praetorian guard" (Phil. 1:13) and "Caesar's household" (Phil. 4:22). Some commentators believe that the imprisonment in one or more of these epistles refers to Paul's Caesarean imprisonment or to a hypothetical Ephesian imprisonment, but the weight of evidence is still in favor of the traditional view that they were written in Rome. Ephesians, Colossians, and Philemon were evidently written about the same time (compare Eph. 6:21,22 with Col. 4:7-9) in A.D. 60-61. Philippians was written in A.D. 62, not long before Paul's release.

Theme and Purpose—The theme of Ephesians is the believer's responsibility to walk in accordance with his heavenly calling in Christ Jesus (4:1). Ephesians was not written to correct specific errors in a local church, but to prevent problems in the church as a whole by encouraging the body of Christ to mature in Him. It was also written to make believers more aware of their position in Christ because this is the basis for their practice on every level of life.

Contribution to the Bible—Unlike Galatians, which is a very personal and controversial letter, Ephesians is formal and impersonal in its style and noncontroversial in its subject matter. Paul communicates only two facts about himself in this epistle: his imprisonment and his reason for sending Tychicus. And unlike the rest of his epistles, the benediction is in the third person (6:23,24). Ephesians abounds with sublime thought and rich vocabulary, especially in chapters 1-3, where theology and worship are intertwined. Many regard it as the most profound book in the New Testament.

Christ in Ephesians—Paul's important phrase "in Christ" (or its equivalent) appears about 35 times, more than in any other New Testament book. The believer is in Christ (1:1), in the heavenly places in Christ (1:3), chosen in Him (1:4), adopted through Christ (1:5), in the Beloved (1:6), redeemed in Him (1:7), given an inheritance in Him (1:11), given hope in Him (1:12), sealed in Him (1:13), made alive together with Christ (2:5), raised and seated with Him (2:6), created in Christ (2:10), brought near by His blood (2:13), growing in Christ (2:21), partaker of the promise in Christ (3:6), and given access through faith in Him (3:12).

Philippians

"Make my joy complete by being of the same mind, maintaining the same love, united in spirit, intent on one purpose."
Philippians 2:2

"Rejoice in the Lord always; again I will say, rejoice!"
Philippians 4:4 (Also see 1:21; 2:5-11; 3:20; 4:8.)

Focus	Personal Affairs 1:1 — 1:26		Practical Appeals 1:27 — 2:30		Promised Attainment 3:1 — 4:1	Proper Attitudes 4:2 — 4:23		
D i v i s i o n s	Salutation	Rejoicing in Harmony	Rejoicing in Hardship	Rejoicing in Humility	Rejoicing in Helpers	Rejoicing in Heaven	Rejoicing in Holiness	Rejoicing in Help	Greetings and Benediction
	1:1-2	1:3-11	1:12 — 1:26	1:27 — 2:18	2:19 — 2:30	3:1 — 4:1	4:2-9	4:10 — 4:20	4:21-23
T o p i c s	Partakers of Christ		People of Christ		Pursuit of Christ	Power of Christ		
	Experience		Examples		Exposition	Exhortation		
	Circumstances		Call to Unity and Humility		Confutation of Legalism	Counsel and Contentment		
	Situation and Suffering		Submission and Service		Safeguard and Salvation	Sanctification and Sharing		
Location	Written Near the End of Paul's First Roman Imprisonment							
Time	A.D. 62							

Talk Thru—Philippians is the epistle of joy and encouragement in the midst of adverse circumstances. In it, Paul freely expresses his fond affection for the Philippians in view of their consistent testimony and support, and lovingly urges them to center their actions and thoughts on the person, pursuit, and power of Christ. Paul also seeks to correct the problem of disunity and rivalry (2:2-4) and to prevent the problem of legalism and antinomianism (3:1-19). Philippians focuses on: Personal Affairs (1:1-26); Practical Appeals (1:27-2:30); Promised Attainment (3:1-4:1); and Proper Attitudes (4:2-23).

Personal Affairs (1:1-26): Paul's usual salutation (1:1,2) is followed by his thanksgiving, warm regard, and prayer on behalf of the Philippians (1:3-11). For years, they have participated in the apostle's ministry, and he prays for their continued growth in the real knowledge of Christ. Paul shares the circumstances of his imprisonment and rejoices in the spread of the gospel in spite of and because of his situation (1:12-26). As he considers the outcome of his approaching trial, he expresses his willingness to "depart and be with Christ" or continue on in ministry.

Practical Appeals (1:27-2:30): Paul encourages the Philippians to remain steadfast in the face of opposition and coming persecution (1:27-30). This will require a spirit of unity and mutual concern borne out of an attitude of humility (2:1-4), and the greatest example of humility is the incarnation and crucifixion of Christ (2:5-11). The *kenosis* or emptying of Christ does not mean that He divested Himself of His deity, but that He withheld His preincarnate glory and voluntarily restricted His use of certain attributes (e.g., omnipresence, omniscience). Paul asks the Philippians to apply this attitude to their lives (2:12-18) and gives two more examples of sacrificial ministry (Timothy and Epaphroditus, 2:19-30).

Promised Attainment (3:1-4:1): It almost appears that Paul is about to close his letter ("Finally, my brethren," 3:1) when he decides to launch into a warning about the continuing problem of legalism (3:1-16). Paul refutes this teaching with important autobiographical details about his previous attainments in Judaism. Compared to the goal of knowing Christ, these pursuits are rubbish. True righteousness is achieved by faith, not by law, and Paul scornfully refers to these Judaizers as "dogs" (their term for Gentiles) and "evil workers" (their attempt to achieve salvation by works). Paul seems to be refuting the opposite extreme of antinomianism in 3:17-4:1, but some believe this may still refer to the legalists. Paul yearns for the promised attainment of the resurrected body.

Proper Attitudes (4:2-23): In a series of exhortations, Paul urges the Philippians to a lifestyle of unity, prayerful dependence, and holiness (4:2-9). He rejoices over their gift, but explains that the power of Christ enables him to live above his circumstances (4:10-20). This joyous letter from prison closes with greetings and a benediction (4:21-23).

Title—This epistle is called *Pros Philippesious,* "To the Philippians." The church at Philippi was the first church Paul founded in Macedonia.

Author—The external and internal evidence for the Pauline authorship of Philippians is very strong, and there are few doubts concerning its authenticity. Its unity, however, has been attacked because of the sudden transition in content and tone at 3:1. This abrupt change has led some critics to surmise that an editor inserted a portion of another letter at this point. Apart from the lack of external evidence (manuscripts and tradition) and disagreement over where this interpolation ends, this theory is hurt because it is unnecessary. As an informal letter, Philippians has a number of quick transitions.

Date and Setting—In 356 B.C., King Philip of Macedonia (the father of Alexander the Great) took and expanded this town and renamed it Philippi. The Romans captured it in 168 B.C., and in 42 B.C. the defeat of the forces of Brutus and Cassius by those of Anthony and Octavian (later Augustus) took place outside of the city. Octavian turned it into a Roman colony (cf. Acts 16:12) and it became a military outpost. The citizens of this colony were regarded as citizens of Rome and given a number of special privileges. Because Philippi was a military city and not a commercial center, there were not enough Jews for a synagogue when Paul came (Acts 16:13).

Paul's "Macedonian Call" in Troas during his second missionary journey led to his ministry in Philippi with the conversion of Lydia and others. Paul and Silas were beaten and imprisoned, but this resulted in the conversion of the Philippian jailer. The magistrates were placed in a dangerous position by beating Roman citizens without a trial (Acts 16:37-40), and this embarrassing event may have prevented future reprisals against the new Christians in Philippi. Paul visited the Philippians again on his third missionary journey (Acts 20:1,6). When they heard of his Roman imprisonment, the Philippian church sent Epaphroditus with financial help (4:18; they had helped Paul in this way on at least two other occasions according to 4:16). Epaphroditus almost died of an illness and remained with Paul long enough for the Philippians to receive word of his malady. Upon his recovery, Paul sent him back to Philippi with this letter (2:25-30).

Silas, Timothy, Luke, and Paul first came to Philippi in A.D. 51, 11 years before Paul wrote this letter. Philippians 1:13 and 4:22 suggest that it was written from Rome, although some commentators argue for Caesarea or Ephesus. Paul's life was at stake, and he was evidently expecting the verdict of the Imperial Court before long (2:20-26).

Theme and Purpose—This letter was written to convey Paul's love and gratitude for the believers at Philippi and to exhort them to a lifestyle of unity, holiness, and joy. Paul evidently enjoyed a very warm relationship with the Philippian church, perhaps his favorite. They were more sensitive and responsive to his financial needs than any other church (2 Cor. 8:11; Phil. 4:15-18) and appeared to have no major problems in their midst. Philippians was not written because of any crisis, but to express Paul's affection for them, his gratitude for their gift, his encouragement concerning their Christian growth, his admonitions against false teaching, and his thoughts about his circumstances. Paul gave the Philippians the latest news of his imprisonment and growing ministry in the propagation of the gospel (1:12-20), and prepared them for the coming of Timothy and possibly himself (2:19-24). He warned them of the twin dangers of legalism and antinomianism (3), but this was more of a preventative than a corrective measure. On the other hand, Paul recognized a growing problem of disunity in the Philippian church and sought to correct it before it became severe.

Contribution to the Bible—This warm and informal letter verbalizes Paul's love for a group of people to an unparalleled degree. The spontaneous words of affection to the "beloved" Philippians are not diluted by the problems of doctrine, discipline, or disorder that persistently marred Paul's relationship with some churches. Because of its informality, Philippians rapidly shifts from topic to topic without regard to a strict outline, just as one would expect from a personal letter. It also reveals Paul's true motivation and devotion to the cause of the gospel (see especially chapter 3). One of the predominant words in this epistle is *joy* or *rejoice*, appearing 16 times in its four chapters. By the power of God, Paul was enabled to live above his difficult circumstances with joy, and he sought the same for his Philippian readers. Other significant words are *attitude* or *think* (used 10 times) and *gospel* (used nine times). Although there is a small amount of doctrinal teaching, Philippians is centered around the person and power of Christ, and 2:5-11 is perhaps the most crucial Christological passage in the Pauline epistles. It was written to illustrate practical humility as a means of unity among believers, but it is in fact one of the most sublime texts in Scripture. Condensed in these seven verses are profound insights concerning the preexistence, incarnation, humiliation, and exaltation of Jesus Christ.

Christ in Philippians—The great *kenosis* passage is one of several portraits of Christ in this epistle. In chapter 1, Paul sees Christ as his life ("For me to live is Christ," 1:21). In chapter 2, Christ is the model of true humility ("Have this attitude in yourselves which was also in Christ Jesus," 2:5). Chapter 3 presents Him as the One "who will transform the body of our humble state into conformity with the body of His glory," 3:21. In chapter 4, He is the source of Paul's power over circumstances ("I can do all things through Him who strengthens me," 4:13).

Colossians

"For in Him all the fulness of Deity dwells in bodily form, and in Him you have been made complete, and He is the head over all rule and authority."

Colossians 2:9,10 (Also see 1:28; 3:1,2,17.)

Focus	Supremacy of Christ				Submission to Christ			
	1			2	3			4
D i v i s i o n s	Commencing Salutation	Concern for the Colossians' Knowledge and Walk	Christ Preeminent in All Things	Christianity Contrasted with False Systems	Changed Lives	Changed Relationships	Communicating to Outsiders	Comments and Greetings
	1:1-2	1:3 1:14	1:15 1:23	1:24 2:23	3:1 3:17	3:18 4:1	4:2-6	4:7 4:18
T o p i c s	Colossians in Christ	Character of Christ	Completeness in Christ		Conduct through Christ			Concluding Matters
	Prayer for the Colossians	Person of Christ	Power of Christ		Program of Christ			Personal Concerns
	Basis: Doctrinal				Behavior: Practical			
	"that you may be filled with . . . spiritual wisdom and understanding" (1:9)				"so that you may walk in a manner worthy of the Lord" (1:10)			
Location	Written During Paul's First Roman Imprisonment							
Time	A.D. 60-61							

Talk Thru—Colossians is perhaps the most Christocentric book in the Bible. In it Paul stresses the preeminence of the person of Christ and the completeness of the salvation He provides in order to combat a growing heresy that was threatening the church at Colossae. This heresy devaluated Christ by elevating speculation, ritualism, mysticism, and asceticism. But Christ, the Lord of creation and Head of the body, is completely sufficient for every spiritual and practical need of the believer. The last half of this epistle explores the application of these principles to daily life, because doctrinal truth (chapters 1-2) must bear fruit in practical conduct (chapters 3-4). The two major topics are: Supremacy of Christ (1-2) and Submission to Christ (3-4).

Supremacy of Christ (1-2): Paul's salutation (1:1,2) is followed by an unusually extended thanksgiving (1:3-8) and prayer (1:9-14) on behalf of the believers at Colossae. Paul expresses his concern that the Colossians come to a deeper understanding of the person and power of Christ. Even here Paul begins to develop his major theme of the preeminence of Christ, but the most potent statement of this theme is in 1:15-23. He is supreme both in creation (1:15-18) and in redemption (1:19-23), and this majestic passage builds a positive case for Christ as the most effective refutation of the heresy that will be exposed in chapter 2. Paul describes his own ministry of proclaiming the mystery of "Christ in you, the hope of glory" to the Gentiles (1:24-29) and assures the readers that although he has not personally met them, he strongly desires that they become deeply rooted in Christ alone (2:1-7). This is especially important in view of false teachers (see Date and Setting) who would defraud them through false philosophy (2:8-10), legalistic rituals (2:11-17), improper worship (2:18,19), and useless asceticism (2:20-23). In each case, Paul contrasts the error with the corresponding truth about Christ.

Submission to Christ (3-4): The believer's union with Christ in His death, resurrection, and exaltation is the foundation upon which his earthly life must be built (3:1-4). Because of his death with Christ, the Christian must regard himself as dead to the old sins and put them aside (3:5-11); because of his resurrection with Christ, the believer must regard himself as alive to Him in righteousness and put on the new qualities which are prompted by Christian love (3:12-17). Turning from the inward life (3:1-17) to the outward life (3:18-4:6), Paul outlines the transformation that faith in Christ should make in relationships inside and outside the home. This pithy epistle concludes with a statement concerning its bearers (Tychicus and Onesimus), greetings and instructions, and a farewell note (4:7-18).

Title—This epistle became known as *Pros Kolossaeis*, "To the Colossians," because of 1:2. Paul also wanted it to be read in the neighboring church at Laodicea (4:16).

Author—The external testimony to the Pauline authorship of Colossians is ancient and consistent, and the internal evidence is very good as well. It not only claims to be Pauline (1:1,23; 4:18), but the personal details and close parallels with Ephesians and Philemon make the case even stronger. Nevertheless, the authenticity of this letter has been challenged on the internal grounds of vocabulary and thought. In its four chapters, Colossians uses 55 Greek words that do not appear in Paul's other epistles. But Paul commanded a wide vocabulary, and the circumstances and subject of this epistle, especially the references to the Colossian heresy, account for these additional words. The high Christology of Colossians has been compared to John's later concept of Christ as the Logos (cf. 1:15-23 and John 1:1-18), with the conclusion that these concepts were too late for Paul's time. But there is no reason to assume that Paul was unaware of Christ's work as Creator, especially in view of Philippians 2:5-11. It is also wrong to assume that the heresy refuted in Colossians 2 refers to the fully developed form of Gnosticism that did not appear until the second century. The parallels only indicate that Paul was dealing with a nascent form of Gnosticism.

Date and Setting—Colossae was a minor city about 100 miles east of Ephesus in the region of the seven Asian churches of Revelation 1-3. Located in the fertile Lycus Valley by a mountain pass on the road from Ephesus to the East, Colossae was once a populous center of commerce and famous for its glossy black wool. But by the time of Paul, it had been eclipsed by its neighboring cities Laodicea and Hierapolis (cf. 4:13) and was on the decline. Apart from this letter, Colossae exerted almost no influence on early church history. It is evident from 1:4-8 and 2:1 that Paul had never visited the church at Colossae which was founded by Epaphras. On his third missionary journey, Paul devoted almost three years to an Asian ministry centered in Ephesus (cf. Acts 19:10; 20:31), and Epaphras probably came to Christ during this time. He carried the gospel to the cities of the Lycus Valley and years later came to visit Paul in his imprisonment (4:12,13; Philem. 23).

Colossians, Philemon, and Ephesians were evidently written at about the same time and under the same circumstances, judging from the overlap in their themes and personal names (cf. Col. 4:9-17 and Philem. 2,10,23,24). Although Caesarea and Ephesus have been suggested, the bulk of the evidence indicates that Paul wrote all four Prison Epistles during his first Roman imprisonment (see Ephesians and Philippians, Date and Setting). If so, Paul wrote it in A.D. 60-61 and sent it with Tychicus and the converted slave Onesimus to Colossae (4:7-9; cf. Eph. 6:21, Philem. 10-12).

Epaphroditus' visit and report about the conditions in Colossae prompted this letter. Although the Colossians had not yet succumbed (2:1-5), an encroaching heresy was threatening the predominantly Gentile (1:21,27; 2:13) Colossian church. The nature of this heresy can only be deduced from Paul's incidental references to it in his refutation in 2:8-23. It was apparently a syncretistic religious system that amalgamated elements from Greek speculation (2:4,8-10), Jewish legalism (2:11-17), and Oriental mysticism (2:18-23). It involved a low view of the body (2:20-23) and probably nature as a whole. Circumcision, dietary regulations, and ritual observances were included in this system which utilized asceticism, worship of angels as intermediaries, and mystical experiences as an approach to the spiritual realm. Any attempt to fit Christ into a system like this would undermine His person and redemptive work.

Theme and Purpose—The resounding theme in Colossians is the preeminence and sufficiency of Christ in all things. The believer is complete in Him alone and lacks nothing because "in Him all the fulness of Deity dwells in bodily form" (2:9); He has "all the treasures of wisdom and knowledge" (2:3). There is no need for speculation, mystical visions, or ritualistic regulations as though faith in Christ were insufficient. Paul's predominant purpose, then, was to refute a threatening heresy that was devaluating Christ by a positive presentation of His true attributes and accomplishments. A proper view of Christ is the antidote for heresy. Paul also wrote this epistle to encourage the Colossians to "continue in the faith firmly established and steadfast" (1:23) so that they will grow and bear fruit in the knowledge of Christ (1:10). A firm adherence to the true gospel will give them stability and resistance to opposing influences. Another purpose in the mind of the apostle is reflected in 3:1-4:6. Paul wanted the Colossians to understand the implications of the preeminence of Christ not only for doctrine, but also for practice. The supremacy of Christ is one side of the coin—submission to Christ is the other. The believer's position in Him (3:1-4) provides the basis and power for a transformed life in every area.

Contribution to the Bible—Colossians is characterized by its high Christology: as the exalted Creator and Redeemer, He is central to all belief and behavior. Paul uses rich language and even redefines the terms used by the heretical movement by filling them with orthodox meaning (e.g., *pleroma*, "fulness," and *gnosis*, "knowledge"). Even though the style is not as piercing or rigorous as that in Galatians or Romans, the intense concepts betray an underlying controversy. There are no Old Testament references in this epistle.

The twin epistles Ephesians and Colossians can be compared and contrasted in several ways:

EPHESIANS	COLOSSIANS
Written in prison, carried by Tychicus	Written in prison, carried by Tychicus
Stresses wisdom, knowledge, fullness, mystery	Stresses wisdom, knowledge, fullness, mystery
Similar passages: (1)1:7, (2)1:10, (3)1:15-17, (4)1:18, (5)1:19,20, (6)1:21-23	Similar passages: (1)1:4, (2)1:20, (3)1:3,4, (4)1:27, (5)2:12, (6)1:16-19
Emphasizes the church as the body of Christ	Emphasizes Christ as the Head of the body
General, universal	Specific, local
First half—position; second half—practice	First half—position; second half—practice
Irenic, calm	Polemic, concern
Reflective, quiet	Spiritual conflict

Christ in Colossians—This singularly Christological book is centered on the cosmic Christ—"the head over all rule and authority" (2:10), the Lord of creation (1:16,17), and the Author of reconciliation (1:20-22; 2:13-15). He is: the basis for the believer's hope (1:5,23,27), the source of the believer's power for a new life (1:11,29), the believer's Redeemer and Reconciler (1:14,20-22; 2:11-15), the embodiment of full deity (1:15,19; 2:9), the Creator and Sustainer of all things (1:16,17), the Head of the church (1:18), the resurrected God-man (1:18; 3:1), and the all-sufficient Savior (1:28; 2:3,10; 3:1-4).

1 Thessalonians

"For who is our hope or joy or crown of exultation? Is it not even you, in the presence of our Lord Jesus at His coming?"
1 Thessalonians 2:19 (Also see 3:13; 4:14; 5:23.)

Focus	Personal Experiences				Practical Exhortations				
	1			3	4				5
D i v i s i o n s	Declaration of the Thessalonians' Faith	Defense of Paul's Conduct	Desire of Paul to Learn of the Thessalonians' Progress	Deepening of the Thessalonians' Faith	Directions for the Thessalonians' Growth	Doctrine Concerning the Dead in Christ	Description of the Day of the Lord	Dealing with Integrity	Development and Directions
	1:1 1:10	2:1 2:16	2:17 3:10	3:11-13	4:1 4:12	4:13 4:18	5:1 5:11	5:12 5:22	5:23-28
T o p i c s	Commendation	Character	Concern		Commandments	Consolation		Conduct	
	Retrospective				Prospective				
	Salvation of the Thessalonians				Sanctification of the Thessalonians				
	Implantation				Irrigation				
Location	Written in Corinth								
Time	A.D. 51								

Talk Thru—After Paul's forced separation from the Thessalonians, he grew increasingly concerned about the progress of their faith. His great relief upon hearing Timothy's positive report prompted him to write this warm epistle of commendation, exhortation, and consolation. They are commended for remaining steadfast under afflictions, exhorted to "excel still more" in their Christian walk, and consoled concerning their loved ones who have died in Christ. The theme of the coming of the Lord recurs throughout this epistle, and 4:13-5:11 is one of the fullest New Testament developments of this crucial truth. The two major sections of 1 Thessalonians are: Personal Experiences (1-3) and Practical Exhortations (4-5).

Personal Experiences (1-3): Paul's typical salutation in the first verse combines the customary Greek ("grace") and Hebrew ("peace") greetings of his day and enriches them with Christian content. The opening chapter is a declaration of thanksgiving for the Thessalonians' metamorphosis from heathenism to the Christian hope. The triad of faith, love, and hope (1:3) properly characterizes the new lives of these believers. In 2:1-16, Paul reviews his brief ministry in Thessalonica and defends his conduct and motives, apparently to answer enemies who were trying to impugn his character and message. His devotion to the Thessalonian believers was evident from his affection (like a mother, 2:7) and admonition (like a father, 2:11). Prevented from returning to Thessalonica, Paul became troubled because of uncertainty over their spiritual condition. He sent Timothy to minister to them and was greatly relieved when Timothy reported the stability of their faith and love (2:17-3:10). Paul therefore closes this historical section with a prayer that their faith may continue to deepen (3:11-13).

Practical Exhortations (4-5): The apostle deftly moves into a series of exhortations and instructions by encouraging the Thessalonians to keep on progressing. He reminds them of his previous teaching on sexual and social matters (4:1-12), especially because these Gentile believers lacked the moral upbringing in the Mosaic law provided in the Jewish community. Now rooted in the Word of God (2:13), the readers must resist the constant pressures of pagan society.

Paul had taught them about the return of Christ, and they

became distressed over the death of some in their number. In 4:13-18, Paul comforted them with the assurance that all who die in Christ will be resurrected at His *parousia* ("presence, coming, advent"). The apostle continues his discourse on eschatology by describing the coming day of the Lord (5:1-11). In view of this day, believers are to be "alert and sober" as "sons of light" who are destined for salvation, not wrath. Paul requests the readers to deal with integrity toward one another and to remain on a growing spiritual edge (5:12-22). The epistle closes with a wish for their sanctification, three requests, and a benediction (5:23-28).

Title—Because this is the first of Paul's two canonical letters to the church at Thessalonica, it received the title *Pros Thessalonikeis A*, the "First to the Thessalonians."

Author—First Thessalonians went unchallenged as a Pauline epistle until the 19th century, when radical critics claimed that its dearth of doctrinal content made its authenticity suspect. But this is a weak objection on two counts: (1) the proportion of doctrinal teaching in Paul's epistles varies widely, and (2) 4:13-5:11 is a foundational passage for New Testament eschatology. Paul had quickly grounded the Thessalonians in Christian doctrine, and the only problematic issue when this epistle was written concerned the matter of Christ's return. The external and internal evidence points clearly to Paul.

Date and Setting—In Paul's time, Thessalonica was a prominent seaport and the capital of the Roman province of Macedonia. This prosperous city was located on the Via Egnatia, the main road from Rome to the East, within sight of Mount Olympus, purported home of the Greek pantheon. Cassander expanded and strengthened this site around 315 B.C. and renamed it after his wife, the half-sister of Alexander the Great. The Romans conquered Macedonia in 168 B.C. and organized it into a single province 22 years later with Thessalonica as the capital city. It became a "free city" under Augustus with its own authority to appoint a governing board of magistrates who were called "politarchs." Its strategic location assured it of commercial success, and it boasted a population of perhaps 200,000 in the first century. It still survives under the shortened name Salonika.

Thessalonica had a sizeable Jewish population, and the ethical monotheism of Judaism attracted many Gentiles who had become disenchanted with Greek paganism. These "God-fearers" quickly responded to Paul's reasoning in the synagogue when he ministered there on his second missionary journey (Acts 17:1-10). The Jews became jealous at Paul's success and organized a mob to oppose the Christian missionaries. Not finding Paul and Silas, they dragged Jason (their host) before the politarchs and accused him of harboring traitors of Rome. The brethren evidently had to pledge the departure of Paul and Silas who left that night for Berea. After a time, the Thessalonian Jews raised an uproar in Berea, so that Paul departed for Athens, leaving orders for Silas and Timothy to join him there (Acts 17:11-16). Luke's account in Acts may give the impression that Paul was in Thessalonica for less than a month ("three Sabbaths," 17:2), but other evidence suggests a longer stay: (1) Paul received two separate offerings from Philippi, 100 miles away, while he was in Thessalonica (Phil. 4:15,16). (2) According to 1:9 and 2:14-16, most of the Thessalonian converts were Gentiles who came out of idolatry. This would imply an extensive ministry directly to the Gentiles after Paul's initial work with the Jews and Gentile God-fearers. (3) Paul worked "night and day" (2:9; 2 Thess. 3:7-9) during his time there. He may have begun to work immediately, but his time spent in tent-making would require a longer stay to accomplish the extensive ministry of evangelism and teaching that took place in that city. After Silas and Timothy met Paul in Athens (3:1,2), he sent Timothy to Thessalonica (Silas also went back to Macedonia, probably Philippi), and his assistants later rejoined him in Corinth (Acts 18:5; cf. 1 Thess. 1:1 where Silas is called Silvanus). There he wrote this epistle in A.D. 51 as his response to Timothy's good report.

Theme and Purpose—The basic theme of this epistle is the salvation and sanctification of the Thessalonians. The contents reveal five basic purposes for which 1 Thessalonians was written: (1) Paul wanted to express his thanksgiving for their faith and love now that he heard of their steadfastness in the face of persecution. (2) Paul defended himself against slanderous attacks that evidently originated from the Jewish opposition. He reminds the Thessalonians of his conduct and motives while among them, in refutation of those who claimed that he was a religious charlatan and mercenary. (3) The Thessalonians needed encouragement and exhortation to resist the temptations of moral impurity and slothful behavior. (4) Paul sought to dispel their ignorance about the relationship of the dead in Christ to His *parousia*. He comforted them with the revelation that Christians who are alive when Christ comes to meet them will have no advantage over those who have already died, since both groups will "meet the Lord in the air." (5) Paul instructed the Thessalonians concerning their spiritual leaders, conduct, and worship (5:12-22).

Contribution to the Bible—This book contains one of the most helpful and illuminating biblical passages on the return of the Redeemer (4:13-5:11). In fact, all five chapters refer to this great event: 1:10; 2:19; 3:13; 4:13-18; 5:1-11,23. First Thessalonians alludes to several other doctrines, but Paul did not feel a need to develop them. He evidently taught them well during his short stay, and wanted to make this more of a personal than a doctrinal letter. Like 2 Corinthians, it reveals Paul's tenderness, affection, and great concern for the spiritual welfare of his converts. The purity of his motives, compassion, and dedication—in short, his innermost feelings—are manifest in these pages.

Christ in 1 Thessalonians—Christ is seen as the believer's hope of salvation both now and at His coming. When He returns, He will deliver (1:10; 5:4-11), reward (2:19), perfect (3:13), resurrect (4:13-18), and sanctify (5:23) all who trust in Him.

2 Thessalonians

"But we should always give thanks to God for you, brethren beloved by the Lord, because God has chosen you from the beginning for salvation through sanctification by the Spirit and faith in the truth."

2 Thessalonians 2:13 (Also see 2:1,2; 3:3.)

Focus	Discouraged Believers 1			Disturbed Believers 2			Disobedient Believers 3		
Divisions	Commencing Salutation	Consolation and Encouragement in Persecution	Concern for Their Progress	Confusion over the Day of the Lord	Coming of the Man of Lawlessness	Calling and Comfort of Believers	Confidence in Their Progress	Commands to the Indolent	Concluding Benediction
	1:1-2	1:3 1:10	1:11-12	2:1-2	2:3 2:12	2:13-17	3:1 3:5	3:6 3:15	3:16-18
Topics	Encouragement to the Persecuted			Explanation to the Perplexed			Exhortation to the Unproductive		
	Appreciation			Agitation			Admonition		
	Commendation and Comfort			Confusion and Correction			Confidence and Commands		
	Intervention and Intercession			Instructions and Identification			Injunctions and Idleness		
Location	Written in Corinth								
Time	A.D. 51								

Talk Thru—This epistle is the theological sequel to 1 Thessalonians which developed the theme of the coming day of the Lord (1 Thess. 5:1-11). But not long after the Thessalonians received that letter, they fell prey to false teaching or outright deception, thinking the day of the Lord had already begun. Paul wrote this brief letter to correct this error and to encourage these believers in their faith which was being tested under the fires of persecution. He also reproved those who had decided to cease working because the coming of Christ was nigh. Second Thessalonians deals with discouraged believers (1), disturbed believers (2), and disobedient believers (3).

Discouraged Believers (1): After his two-verse salutation, Paul gives thanks for the growing faith and love of the Thessalonians and assures them of their ultimate deliverance from those who are persecuting them (1:3-10). They are encouraged to patiently endure their afflictions, knowing that the Lord Jesus will judge their persecutors when He is "revealed from heaven with His mighty angels in flaming fire" (1:7). Before Paul moves to the next topic, he concludes this section with a prayer for the spiritual welfare of his readers (1:11,12).

Disturbed Believers (2): Because of the severity of their afflictions, the Thessalonians became susceptible to false teaching (and possibly a fraudulent letter in the name of Paul) which claimed that they were already in the day of the Lord (2:1,2). This was particularly disturbing because Paul's previous letter gave them the comforting hope that they were not destined for the wrath of that day (1 Thess. 5:9). Paul therefore assures them that the day of the Lord is yet future and cannot come until certain precedents occur (2:3-12). A great spiritual rebellion must take place, climaxed by the revealing of the satanically-empowered man of lawlessness (2:3, 4, 8, 9). It has been suggested that Paul was thinking of Caligula's (unfulfilled) order in A.D. 40 that his image be worshipped in the Jerusalem temple. Another guess is that this is a reference to the so-called "Nero *redivivus*" myth that this deceased emperor would return again from the East (this would require post-Pauline authorship). But a comparison of this passage with Daniel 9:27; 12:11; Matthew 24:15; 1 John 2:18; Revelation 11:7; 13:1-10 shows that the man of lawlessness is the antichrist who will be fully manifested when the restrainer is removed

(2:6-9). The Thessalonians knew the identity of this restrainer, but we cannot be sure of what Paul had in mind. The two prominent views are the restraining work of the Holy Spirit and that of human government. In any case, the concurrently developing mysteries of lawlessness and of Christ will continue in conflict until the climax of Christ's victorious appearance. Again Paul concludes with a word of encouragement and a benedictory prayer before moving to his final topic (2:13-17).

Disobedient Believers (3): Paul requests the Thessalonian church to pray on his behalf and expresses his confidence in their progress as a whole (3:1-5). Having thus commended, corrected, and comforted his readers, the tactful apostle closes his letter with a sharp word of command to those who were using the truth of Christ's return as an excuse for indolence (3:6-15; cf. 1 Thess. 4:11,12). The doctrine of the Lord's return requires a balance between waiting and working. It is a perspective that should encourage holiness, not idleness. This final section, like the first two, closes on a benedictory note (3:16-18).

Title—As the second letter in Paul's Thessalonian correspondence, this was entitled *Pros Thessalonikeis B,* the "Second to the Thessalonians."

Author—The external attestation to the authenticity of 2 Thessalonians as a Pauline epistle is even stronger than that for 1 Thessalonians. Internally, the vocabulary, style, and doctrinal content support the claims in 1:1 and 3:17 that it was authored by Paul. But like other Pauline epistles, 2 Thessalonians began to come under critical attack in the 19th century. One area of criticism has been its relationship to 1 Thessalonians. The obvious resemblances between the two epistles (compare 1 Thess. 1:2,3; 3:11-13; 4:1 with 2 Thess. 1:3; 2:16,17; 3:1) have led some to believe that the second was a skillful later imitation of the first. But a closer analysis shows that the parallels do not extend to more than a third of their contents; a similar situation exists between Ephesians and Colossians. Also, the Thessalonian letters were written within a short time of one another and to the same recipients, so it is to be expected that the issues would be related.

On the other hand, critics have pointed to differences between these epistles as an evidence against Pauline authorship of the second. Much is made of the warm and affectionate tone of 1 Thessalonians in contrast to the presumably cold and distant tone of 2 Thessalonians. While there is a difference in tone, 2 Thessalonians remains a comforting and supportive letter with only one rebuke to some in the church (3:6-15). Paul's initial relief caused him to write like a nursing mother in 1 Thessalonians, while doctrinal and practical difficulties led him to write like a father in 2 Thessalonians (cf. 1 Thess. 2:7,11).

Others have claimed that the Old Testament allusions in 2:1-12 suggest a Jewish audience in contrast to the Gentile audience of 1 Thessalonians, but it can be argued that the readers were familiar with these things because of Paul's teachings (2:5), not because they were Jewish. Another argument is that the eschatological teaching of the two epistles is contradictory. The first emphasizes the nearness of the Lord's return, while the second teaches that certain obvious events must occur before His return. This can be solved by noting that 1 Thessalonians 4:13-18 and 2 Thessalonians 2:1-12 are dealing with two different aspects of the second coming.

Date and Setting—See 1 Thessalonians, Date and Setting, for the background to the Thessalonian correspondence. This letter was probably written a few months after 1 Thessalonians while Paul was still in Corinth with Silas and Timothy (1:1; cf. Acts 18:5). The bearer of the first epistle may have brought Paul an update on the new developments that prompted him to write this letter. They were still undergoing persecution, and the false teaching about the day of the Lord led some of them to over-react by giving up their jobs. The problem of idleness in 1 Thessalonians 4:11,12 had become more serious (3:6-15). By this time, Paul was beginning to see the opposition he would have to face as a result of his ministry in Corinth (3:2; see Acts 18:5-10).

Some scholars have argued that the order of these two epistles should be reversed, but this goes against manuscript evidence, tradition, Paul's mention of a previous letter in 2 Thessalonians 2:15, and the logical development from 1 to 2 Thessalonians in doctrine and disorder.

Theme and Purpose—The theme of this epistle is Paul's comfort and correction of the Thessalonians in view of their problems of religious persecution, doctrinal misunderstanding, and practical abuse. Paul's three major purposes correspond to the three chapters: (1) The apostle wanted to applaud their continuing growth in faith and love and encourage them to endure their persecution in the knowledge that God will vindicate His name and glorify all who have trusted in Christ. (2) The second chapter was written to correct the fallacious teaching that the day of the Lord was already upon them. This teaching, coupled with the afflictions they were suffering, was causing great disturbances among the Thessalonian believers who were wondering when their "gathering together to Him" (2:1; cf. 1 Thess. 4:13-18) would take place. Paul made it clear that the day of the Lord had not overtaken them (cf. 1 Thess. 5:4). (3) The doctrinal error of chapter 2 was causing a practical error that Paul sought to overcome in chapter 3. Some of the believers abandoned their work and began to live off others, apparently assuming that the end was at hand. Paul commanded them to follow his example by supporting themselves and instructed the rest of the church to discipline them if they failed to do so.

Contribution to the Bible—This is the shortest of Paul's nine letters to churches, but it provides crucial information concerning the end times and clarifies issues that would otherwise be very obscure. Even so, there has been a wide difference of opinion regarding the nature of the man of lawlessness and the restrainer. The two Thessalonian epistles, along with the Olivet Discourse (Matt. 24-25) and the book of Revelation, form the three major prophetic texts of the New Testament. Their early date places them among the first New Testament books to be written and reveals that apostolic doctrine had already become a settled body of truth. Paul refers to his teaching among the Thessalonians as "the traditions" which they had received (2:15; 3:6). These two epistles refer to almost every central doctrine of the Christian faith even though they are not doctrinal treatises like Romans or Ephesians.

In spite of its brevity, Paul offers four prayers on behalf of the readers of this letter (1:11,12; 2:16,17; 3:5; 3:16). It closes with a greeting in his own handwriting as a mark of authentication against the possibility of fraud (3:17; cf. 2:2).

Christ in 2 Thessalonians—The return of Christ is mentioned more times (318) in the New Testament than any other doctrine, and this is certainly the major concept in chapters 1 and 2 of this epistle. The return of the Lord Jesus is a reassuring and joyful hope for believers, but His revelation from heaven holds awesome and terrifying implications for those who have not trusted in Him (1:6-10; 2:8-12).

1 Timothy

"But in case I am delayed, I write so that you may know how one ought to conduct himself in the household of God, which is the church of the living God, the pillar and support of the truth."

1 Timothy 3:15 (Also see 1:18; 6:13,14.)

Focus	Reminders				Regulations		Responsibilities				
	1:1			1:20	2:1	3:13	3:14				6:21
D i v i s i o n s	Prologue	Problem of False Doctrine	Paul's Reflections on God's Grace	Pursuing the True Faith	Public Prayer and the Role of Women	Prerequisites for Overseers and Deacons	Purpose of the Letter	Preserving Pure Doctrine	Pastoral Responsibilities	Personal Principles	Parting Appeal
	1:1-2	1:3-11	1:12-17	1:18-20	2:1 2:15	3:1 3:13	3:14-15	3:16 4:16	5:1 6:2	6:3 6:19	6:20-21
T o p i c s	Warning				Wor-ship	Wise Leaders	Work		Wid-ows	Wealth	
	Doctrine				Directions		Defense		Duty		
	Charge				Church		Counsel and Conduct				
	Timothy				The Assembly		Timothy				
Location	Written in Macedonia (Perhaps Philippi)										
Time	After Paul's Release from Roman Imprisonment, A.D. 62-63										

123

Talk Thru—Paul's last three recorded letters, written near the end of his full and fruitful life, were addressed to his authorized representatives Timothy and Titus. These were the only letters Paul wrote exclusively to individuals (Philemon was addressed primarily to its namesake, but also to others), and they were designed to exhort and encourage Timothy and Titus in their ministry of solidifying the churches in Ephesus and Crete. In the 18th century, these epistles came to be known as the "Pastoral Epistles" even though they do not use any terms like shepherd, pastor, flock, or sheep. Still, this term is fairly appropriate for 1 Timothy and Titus because they focus on the oversight of church life. It is less appropriate for 2 Timothy because it is more of a personal than a church-oriented letter. The Pastoral Epistles abound with principles for leadership and righteous living.

In his first letter to Timothy, Paul sought to guide his younger and less experienced assistant in his heavy responsibility as the overseer of the work at Ephesus and other Asian cities. He wrote this leadership manual to challenge Timothy to fulfill his task of combating false teaching with sound doctrine, developing qualified leadership, teaching God's Word, and encouraging Christian conduct. Because of the personal and conversational character of this letter, it is loosely structured. The three basic movements are: Reminders (1:1-20), Regulations (2:1-3:13), and Responsibilities (3:14-6:21).

Reminders (1:1-20): After his opening salutation (1:1,2), Paul warns Timothy about the growing problem of false doctrines, particularly relating to the misuse of the Mosaic law (1:3-11). The aging apostle then rehearses his radical conversion to Christ and calling to the ministry (1:12-17). Timothy, too, has a divine calling, and Paul charges him to fulfill it without wavering in doctrine or conduct (1:18-20). Over and over, Paul personally appeals to Timothy to carry out his weighty commission (see 1:18; 4:6,11-16; 5:21; 6:11-16,20).

Regulations (2:1-3:13): Turning his attention to the church at large, Paul addresses the issues of church worship and leadership. Efficacious public prayer should be a part of worship, and Paul associates this with the role of men in the church (2:1-8). He then turns to the role of women (2:9-15) and emphasizes the importance of the inner quality of godliness. In 3:1-7, Paul lists several qualifications for overseers or bishops.

The word for overseer (*episkopos*) is used synonymously with the word for elder (*presbuteros*) in the New Testament, because both orginally referred to the same office (see Acts 20:17,28; Titus 1:5,7). The qualifications for the office of deacon (*diakonos*, "servant") are listed in 3:8-13. The deacons served as assistants to the overseers, particularly in the more mundane aspects of church life.

Responsibilities (3:14-6:21): In a parenthetical remark, Paul relates the purpose for which he wrote this letter to Timothy (3:14,15). In one succinct statement possibly derived from a very early hymn, he summarizes the essential truth about Christ from His incarnation to His glorification (3:16; cf. 6:15,16). This truth is in contrast to the errors that Paul warns Timothy to guard against (4:1-16). The greatest defense against false doctrine is a consistent proclamation of sound doctrine, and this is what Paul urges his younger assistant to do. Next, the apostle outlines Timothy's responsibilities toward various groups in the church, focusing particularly on widows and elders (5:1-6:2). After moving through these detailed ecclesiastical matters, this letter develops principles concerning false teachers and the relationship between wealth and godliness (6:3-19). Paul gives Timothy a series of personal exhortations and closes with a final appeal (6:11-16, 20,21).

Title—The Greek title for this letter is *Pros Timotheon A,* the "First to Timothy." This name means "honoring God" or "honored by God," and it was probably given to him by his mother Eunice.

Author—Since the early 19th century, the Pastoral Epistles have been castigated more than any other Pauline epistles on the issue of authenticity. The similarity of these epistles requires that they be treated as a unit in terms of authorship because they stand or fall together.

The external evidence solidly supports the conservative position that Paul authored the letters to Timothy and Titus. Post-apostolic church fathers like Polycarp and Clement of Rome allude to them, and they are identified as Pauline by Irenaeus, Tertullian, Clement of Alexandria, and the Muratorian Canon. Only Romans and 1 Corinthians have better attestation among the Pauline epistles. Marcion the heretic failed to include the Pastoral Epistles in his New Testament because they did not fit his erroneous system of theology (Marcion also omitted Matthew, Mark, and John).

The critical attack is leveled wholly on the basis of internal evidence, and even though these letters claim to be written by Paul (1 Tim. 1:1; 2 Tim. 1:1; Titus 1:1), critics assert that they are "pious forgeries" that appeared in the second century. There are several problems with this: (1) Pseudonymous writing was unacceptable to Paul (see 2 Thess. 2:2; 3:17) and to the early church, which was very sensitive to the problem of forgeries. (2) The adjective "pious" should deceive no one—a forgery was as deliberately deceptive then as it is now. This means a basic problem of dishonesty that flies in the face of the high morality of these epistles. (3) The many personal facts and names that appear in the Pastorals would be avoided by a forger who would take refuge in vagueness. Nor would a forger use expressions like those in 1 Timothy 1:13,15 if he was an admirer of Paul. The doctrinal teaching and autobiographical details (cf. 1 Tim. 1:12-17; 2:7; 2 Tim. 1:8-12; 4:9-22; Titus 1:5; 3:12,13) fit very well with "Paul, the aged" (Philem. 9). (4) What purpose or advantage would these epistles serve as later forgeries? There are too many personal elements, and the doctrinal refutations do not refer to second-century Gnosticism (see below). (5) None of the post-apostolic writings or apocryphal books can compare with these three epistles.

Because of these problems, some scholars have opted for a "mediating position" that a Paulinist used genuine Pauline fragments when he wrote these epistles around A.D. 100. But this position does not overcome the moral problem of fraud, and it raises additional difficulties. Determining which parts are genuine is simply subjective guesswork, and even if such fragments did survive, they would have been useless if not recognized by the church as genuinely Pauline. But if they were so recognized, they could not be inserted into forged epistles without detection.

Critics use four basic arguments to deny Pauline authorship of the Pastorals: (1) The geographical, historical, and personal (e.g., names like Onesiphorus, Eubulus, Pudens, Zenas) details in these letters do not fit Luke's account of Paul's life in Acts. But there is no basis for assuming that Paul's story ends in Acts 28. In his letter to the Philippians, Paul was optimistic about his release from Roman imprisonment (Phil. 1:25,26; 2:24), and at that time (62), Christianity had not yet become an illicit religion. The unanimous tradition in the early church affirms this release. (2) The omission of certain Pauline doctrines in the Pastorals and the inclusion of post-Pauline doctrinal developments argue against their authenticity. But it was unnecessary for Paul to include most of his doctrinal teaching since these letters were addressed to his well-taught and trusted associates. And the Pastorals do not refer to the full-orbed Gnostic teachings that challenged the church in the second century. They deal instead with a mixed heresy that included Judaistic features (1 Tim. 1:3-11; Titus 1:10,14-16; 3:9). (3) Critics claim that the church government in the Pastorals reflects second-century conditions when the office of the monarchical bishop emerged. But these epistles refer only to two offices, because the words for bishop and elder were used of the same position (Titus 1:5,7; cf. Acts 20:17,28). From the time of his first missionary journey, it was Paul's practice to appoint elders (Acts 14:23; Phil. 1:1), and the ecclesiastical situation in the Pastorals fits the first century. (4) The differences in vocabulary and style between the Pastorals and the uncontested Pauline epistles point to a different author. There are definite differences, but they are not of a determinative nature. Most of Paul's unique words and phrases can be found in the Septuagint, and this additional vocabulary can be accounted for by the new topics and later conditions of these three letters. Likewise, the calm and sedate style of quiet instruction is explained by the two addressees—Timothy and Titus were responsive and dependable laborers who would not challenge Paul's authoritative instructions. Paul's style varied widely among all his epistles, and the Pastorals can be included within that range. Thus, while there *are* problems, the traditional position is worthy of modern acceptance.

Date and Setting—Pauline authorship of the Pastoral Epistles requires Paul's release from his Acts 28 Roman imprisonment, the continuation of his missionary endeavors, and his imprisonment for a second time in Rome. Unfortunately, the order of events can only be reconstructed from hints, because there is no consecutive history like Acts that chronicles the last years of the apostle. The following reconstruction, therefore, is

only tentative: As he anticipated in Philippians (1:19,25,26; 2:24), Paul was released from his first Roman imprisonment. It is possible that his Jewish accusers decided not to appear at his trial before Caesar. In fulfillment of his promise to the Philippians (Phil. 2:19-23), he sent Timothy to Philippi to relate the good news. Paul himself went to Ephesus (in spite of his earlier expectations in Acts 20:38) and to other Asian churches like Colossae (see Philem. 22). When Timothy rejoined him in Ephesus, Paul instructed his assistant to "remain on at Ephesus" (1 Tim. 1:3) while he journeyed to Macedonia. When he saw that he might be delayed in Macedonia, Paul wrote 1 Timothy, perhaps from Philippi (1 Tim. 3:14,15). After he saw Timothy in Ephesus, the apostle journeyed on to the island of Crete where he left Titus after a period of ministry to continue the work (Titus 1:5). In Corinth, Paul decided to write a letter to Titus because Zenas and Apollos were making a journey that would take them by way of Crete (Titus 3:13). He instructed Titus to join him in Nicopolis after the arrival of his replacement (Artemas or Tychicus) in Crete (Titus 3:12). If he went to Spain as he planned in Romans 15:24,28, Paul probably departed with Titus for that western province after his winter in Nicopolis. Early church tradition holds that Paul did go to Spain. Before the end of the first century, Clement of Rome said that Paul "reached the limits of the West" (1 Clement 5:7). Since he was writing from Rome, he evidently had Spain in mind. Paul may have been in Spain from A.D. 64 to 66. He returned to Greece and Asia (Corinth, Miletus, Troas; 2 Tim. 4:13,20), and may have been arrested in Troas where he left his valuable books and parchments (2 Tim. 4:13-15). Now that Christianity had become an illegal religion in the empire (the burning of Rome took place in 64), Paul's enemies were able to successfully accuse him. He was imprisoned in A.D. 67 and wrote 2 Timothy from his Roman cell after his first defense before the Imperial Court (2 Tim. 1:8,17; 2:9; 4:16,17). He was delivered from condemnation, but he held no hope of release and expected to be executed (2 Tim. 4:6-8,18). He urged Timothy to come before the end (2 Tim. 4:9,21), and according to tradition, the apostle was beheaded west of Rome on the Ostian Way.

Paul wrote 1 Timothy from Macedonia in A.D. 62-63 while Timothy was serving as his representative in Ephesus and perhaps other churches in the province of Asia. Timothy's office was not that of a pastor or elder; he was to appoint elders, combat false doctrine, and supervise church life as an apostolic legate.

Theme and Purpose—The theme of this epistle is Timothy's organization and oversight of the Asian churches as a faithful minister of God. Paul wrote this letter as a leadership manual so that Timothy would have effective guidance in his responsibilities during Paul's absence in Macedonia (3:14,15). Paul wanted to encourage and exhort his younger assistant to become an example to others, exercise his spiritual gifts, and "Fight the good fight of faith" (6:12; cf. 1:18; 4:12-16; 6:20). Timothy's personal and public life must be beyond reproach, and he must know how to deal with matters of false teaching, organization, discipline, proclamation of the Scriptures, poverty and wealth, and the role of various groups. Negatively, he was to refute error (1:7-11; 6:3-5); positively, he was to teach the truth (4:13-16; 6:2,17,18).

Contribution to the Bible—This is a personal letter, but it is rich in principles that are relevant to every Christian worker and Christian church. Because it was written to Timothy, this epistle asumes rather than develops doctrine. Its primary concern is with the practical outworking of Christian truth on an individual and corporate level. First Timothy, along with Titus, provides the most explicit directions for church leadership and organization in the Bible.

The phrase, "It is a trustworthy statement" (1 Tim. 1:15; 3:1; 4:9; 2 Tim. 2:11; Titus 3:8) is peculiar to the Pastoral Epistles. Paul used it in his later years to refer to Christian sayings and confessions.

Christ in 1 Timothy—Christ is the "one mediator between God and man" (2:5), "who was revealed in the flesh, was vindicated in the Spirit, beheld by angels, proclaimed among the nations, believed on in the world, taken up in glory" (3:16). He is the source of spiritual strength, faith, and love (1:12,14). He "came into the world to save sinners" (1:15) and "gave Himself as a ransom for all" (2:6) as "the Savior of all men, especially of believers" (4:10).

2 Timothy

"Suffer hardship with me, as a good soldier of Christ Jesus."
2 Timothy 2:3

"Be diligent to present yourself approved to God as a workman who does not need to be ashamed, handling accurately the word of truth."

2 Timothy 2:15 (Also see 4:2.)

Focus	Power of the Gospel 1		Perseverance of the Gospel Minister 2		Protection of the Gospel Message 3		Proclamation of the Gospel 4		
D i v i s i o n s	Paul's Introduction and Thanksgiving	Paul's Instructions for Timothy to Stand Firm	Timothy's Personal Responsibilities	Timothy's Public Responsibilities	The Dangers of Apostasy	The Defense Against Apostasy	Closing Exhortation to Timothy	Comments and Requests	Concluding Greetings and Benediction
	1:1 1:5	1:6 1:18	2:1 2:13	2:14 2:26	3:1 3:9	3:10 3:17	4:1 4:8	4:9 4:18	4:19-22
T o p i c s	Reminder		Require-ments		Resistance		Requests		
	Courage		Character		Caution		Commitment		
	Divine Call		Duty		Defense		Declaration		
	Retro-spective		Perspective		Prospective				
Loca-tion	Written During Paul's Second Roman Imprisonment								
Time	A.D. 67								

131

Talk Thru—Paul knew as he wrote this final epistle that his days on earth were quickly drawing to a close. About to relinquish his heavy burdens, the godly apostle sought to challenge and strengthen his somewhat timid but faithful associate Timothy in his difficult ministry in Ephesus. In spite of Paul's bleak circumstances, this is a letter of encouragement that urges Timothy on to steadfastness in the fulfillment of his divinely-appointed task. Paul calls Timothy a "good soldier of Christ Jesus" (2:3), and it is clear from the sharp imperatives that this letter is really a combat manual for use in the spiritual warfare: "kindle afresh," "do not be ashamed," "join with me in suffering," "retain the standard," "guard . . . the treasure," "be strong," "suffer hardship," "be diligent," "flee . . . pursue . . . refuse," "I solemnly charge you," "preach . . . be ready . . . reprove, rebuke, exhort," "be sober . . . endure hardship," "be on guard." Central to everything in 2 Timothy is the sure foundation of the Word of God. Paul focuses on the power of the gospel (1), the perseverance of the gospel minister (2), the protection of the gospel message (3), and the proclamation of the gospel (4).

Power of the Gospel (1): After his salutation to his "beloved son" (1:1,2), Paul expresses his thanksgiving for Timothy's "sincere faith" (1:3-5). He then encourages Timothy to stand firm in the power of the gospel and to overcome his fear in the face of opposition (1:6-18). At personal risk, Onesiphorus boldly sought out Paul in Rome, but most of the Asian Christians failed to stand behind Paul at the time of his arrest. Timothy must remain faithful and not fear possible persecution.

Perseverance of the Gospel Minister (2): Paul exhorts his spiritual son to reproduce in the lives of others what he has received in Christ (four generations are mentioned in 2:2). He is responsible to work hard and discipline himself like a soldier, an athlete, and a farmer, following the example of Paul's perseverance (2:1-13). In his dealings with others, Timothy must not get entangled in false speculations, foolish quarrels, or youthful lusts which would hamper his effectiveness. As he pursues "righteousness, faith, love and peace" he must know how to graciously overcome error (2:14-26).

Protection of the Gospel Message (3): Paul anticipates a time of growing apostasy and wickedness when men and women will be increasingly susceptible to empty religiosity and false teaching (3:1-9). Arrogance and godlessness will breed further deception and persecution, but Timothy must not waiver in using the Scriptures to combat doctrinal error and moral evil (3:10-17). The Scriptures are inspired or "God-breathed," and with them Timothy is equipped to carry out the ministry to which he was called.

Proclamation of the Gospel (4): Paul's final exhortation to Timothy (4:1-8) is a classic summary of the task of the man of God to proclaim the gospel in spite of opposing circumstances. This very personal letter closes with an update of Paul's situation in Rome along with certain requests (4:9-22). Paul longed to see Timothy before the end, and he also needed certain articles, especially "the parchments" (probably portions of the Old Testament Scriptures).

Title

—Paul's last epistle received the title *Pros Timotheon B,* the "Second to Timothy." The *B* was probably added when Paul's epistles were collected together to distinguish it from the first letter to Timothy.

Author

—Since the Pastoral Epistles have to be treated as a unit on the matter of authorship, see 1 Timothy, Author for the authorship of 2 Timothy.

Date and Setting

—For a tentative reconstruction of the events following Paul's first Roman imprisonment, see 1 Timothy, Date and Setting. The cruel and unbalanced Nero, emperor of Rome from A.D. 54 to 68, was responsible for the beginning of the Roman persecution of Christians. Half of Rome was destroyed in July A.D. 64 by a fire, and mounting suspicion that Nero was responsible for the conflagration caused him to use the unpopular Christians as his scapegoat. Christianity thus became a *religio illicita,* and persecution of those who professed Christ became severe. By the time of Paul's return from Spain to Asia in A.D. 66, his enemies were able to use the official Roman position against Christianity to their advantage. Fearing for their own lives, the Asian believers failed to support Paul after his arrest (1:15) and no one supported him at his first defense before the Imperial Court (4:16). Abandoned by almost everyone (4:10,11), the apostle found himself in very different circumstances from those of his first Roman imprisonment in Acts 28:16-31. At that time he was merely under house arrest, people could freely visit him, and he had the hope of release. Now he was in a cold Roman cell (4:13), regarded "as a criminal" (2:9), and without hope of acquittal in spite of the success of his initial defense (4:6-8,17,18). Under these conditions, Paul wrote this epistle in the fall of A.D. 67, hoping that Timothy would be able to visit him before the approaching winter (4:21). Timothy was evidently in Ephesus at the time of this letter (cf. 1:18 and 4:19), and on his way to Rome he would go through Troas (4:13) and Macedonia. Priscilla and Aquilla (4:19) probably returned from Rome (Rom. 16:3) to Ephesus after the burning of Rome and the beginning of the persecution. Tychicus may have been the bearer of this letter (4:12).

Timothy's name is found more often in the salutations of the Pauline epistles than any other (2 Cor., Phil., Col., 1 and 2 Thess., 1 and 2 Tim., Philem.). His father was a Greek (Acts 16:1), but his Jewish mother Eunice and grandmother Lois raised him in the knowledge of the Hebrew Scriptures (2 Tim. 1:5; 3:15). Timothy evidently became a convert of Paul (1 Cor. 4:17; 1 Tim. 1:2; 2 Tim. 1:2) when the apostle was in Lystra on his first missionary journey (Acts 14:8-20). When he visited Lystra on his second missionary journey, Paul decided to take Timothy along with him and circumcised him because of the Jews (Acts 16:1-3). Timothy was ordained to the ministry (1 Tim. 4:14; 2 Tim. 1:6) and served as a devoted companion and assistant to Paul in Troas, Berea, Thessalonica, and Corinth (Acts 16-18; 1 Thess. 3:1,2. During the third missionary journey, Timothy labored with Paul and ministered for him as his representative in Ephesus, Macedonia, and Corinth. He was with Paul during his first Roman imprisonment and evidently went to Philippi (2:19-23) after Paul's release. Paul left him in Ephesus to supervise the work there (1 Tim. 1:3) and years later summoned him to Rome (2 Tim. 4:9,21). According to Hebrews 13:23, Timothy was imprisoned and released, but the passage does not say where. Timothy was sickly (1 Tim. 5:23), timid (2 Tim. 1:7), and youthful (1 Tim. 4:12), but he was a gifted teacher who was trustworthy and diligent.

Theme and Purpose—In this letter, Paul commissions Timothy to faithfully carry on the work that the condemned apostle must now relinquish. This combat manual exhorts Timothy to put the spiritual equipment of the Word of God to constant use to overcome growing obstacles to the spread of the gospel. Timothy was in great need of encouragement because of the hardships that he was facing, and Paul used this letter to instruct him on how to handle persecution from without and dissension and deception from within. As a spiritual father, Paul urged his son Timothy to overcome his natural timidity and boldly proclaim the gospel even if it meant that he would suffer for doing so. Paul also wrote this letter to summon Timothy and Mark to visit him in Rome as soon as possible and to bring his papyrus and parchment scrolls along with his cloak. In case they did not reach him in time, this letter would serve as Paul's closing testimony to the believer's victory in Christ in the face of death.

Contribution to the Bible—Second Timothy is, in effect, Paul's last will and testament, and in it Paul reviews the past, analyzes the present, and anticipates his future deliverance to God's heavenly kingdom. This book has provided comfort, encouragement, and motivation to distressed Christian workers over the centuries. It emphasizes the centrality of the Scriptures and contains the clearest biblical statement of their inspiration (3:16,17; also see 2:15; 4:2).

This little epistle is full of personal references to Paul, Timothy, and over 20 other people, a number of whom are mentioned nowhere else in Scripture. It also contains two important prophecies about coming conditions of apostasy, empty profession, and spiritual deception (3:1-9; 4:3,4).

Christ in 2 Timothy—Christ Jesus appeared on earth, "abolished death, and brought life and immortality to light through the gospel" (1:10). He rose from the dead (2:8) and provides salvation and "eternal glory" (2:10) for believers who "died with Him" and will "also live with Him" (2:11). All who have loved His appearing will receive the crown of righteousness (4:8) and reign with Him (2:12; 4:18).

Titus

"But as for you, speak the things which are fitting for sound doctrine."   Titus 2:1

"This is a trustworthy statement; and concerning these things I want you to speak confidently, so that those who have believed God may be careful to engage in good deeds. These things are good and profitable for men."   Titus 3:8 (Also see 3:5,14.)

Focus	Protection of Sound Doctrine 1			Preaching of Sound Doctrine 2		Practice of Sound Doctrine 3		
Divisions	Derivation of Doctrine	Designation of Elders	Description of False Teachers	Duty of Titus	Definition of Doctrine	Demonstration of Applied Doctrine	Denunciation of Dissenters	Diverse Remarks
	1:1 1:4	1:5 1:9	1:10 1:16	2:1 2:10	2:11 2:15	3:1 3:8	3:9-11	3:12-15
Topics	Opening	Organization	Offenders	Operation		Obedience		
	Governing Conduct			Group Conduct		General Conduct		
	Battle			Behavior		Belief		
	Elders and Error			Examples		Effort		
Location	Perhaps Written in Corinth							
Time	After Paul's Release from Roman Imprisonment, A.D. 63							

Talk Thru—Like 1 Timothy, Titus was written by Paul after his release from Roman imprisonment to an associate who was given the task of organizing and supervising a large work as an apostolic representative. Paul left Titus on the island of Crete to "set in order what remains, and appoint elders in every city" (1:5). Not long after Paul's departure from Crete he wrote this letter to encourage and assist Titus in his task. It stresses sound doctrine and warns against those who distort the truth, but it is also a conduct manual because of its emphasis upon good deeds and the conduct of various groups within the churches. This epistle falls into three major sections: Protection of Sound Doctrine (1), Preaching of Sound Doctrine (2), and Practice of Sound Doctrine (3).

Protection of Sound Doctrine (1): The salutation to Titus is really a compact doctrinal statement which lifts up the Word of God as the source of truth and the revelation of eternal life (1:1-4). Paul reminds Titus of his responsibility to organize the churches of Crete by appointing elders (also called overseers; cf. 1:5,7) and rehearses the qualifications these spiritual leaders must meet (1:5-9). This is especially important in view of the disturbances which are being caused by false teachers who are upsetting a number of the believers with their Jewish myths and commandments (1:10-16). The natural tendency toward moral laxity among the Cretans coupled with this kind of deception was a dangerous force that had to be overcome by godly leadership and sound doctrine.

Preaching of Sound Doctrine (2): Titus is given the charge to "speak the things which are fitting for sound doctrine" (2:1), and Paul delineates Titus' role with regard to various groups in the church, including older men, older women, young women, young men, and bondslaves (2:2-10). The knowledge of Christ must affect a transformation in each of these groups so that their testimony will "adorn the doctrine of God" (2:10). The second doctrinal statement of Titus (2:11-14) gives the basis for the appeals Paul has just made for righteous living. God in His grace redeemed believers from slavery to sin and gives them a "blessed hope" that will be realized at the coming of Christ. Paul urges Titus to authoritatively proclaim these truths (2:15).

Practice of Sound Doctrine (3): Paul now moves from conduct in groups (2:1-10) to conduct in general (3:1-11). The behavior of believers as citizens and toward all men must be qualitatively different because of their regeneration and renewal by the Holy Spirit. The third doctrinal statement in this book (3:4-7) emphasizes the kindness, love, and mercy of God who "saved us, not on the basis of deeds which we have done in righteousness" (3:5). Nevertheless, the need for "good deeds" as a result of salvation is stressed six times in the three chapters of Titus (1:16; 2:7,14; 3:1,8,14). Paul exhorts Titus to deal firmly with dissenters who would cause factions and controversies (3:9-11) and closes his letter with three instructions, a greeting, and a benediction (3:12-15).

Title—This third Pastoral Epistle is simply titled *Pros Titon*, "To Titus." This was also the name of the Roman general who destroyed Jerusalem in A.D. 70 and succeeded his father Vespasian as emperor.

Author—Since the Pastoral Epistles have to be treated as a unit on the matter of authorship, see 1 Timothy, Author for the authorship of Titus.

Date and Setting—For a tentative reconstruction of the events following Paul's first Roman imprisonment, see 1 Timothy, Date and Setting. The Mediterranean island of Crete is 156 miles long and up to 30 miles wide, and its first-century inhabitants were notorious for untruthfulness and immorality (cf. 1:12,13). "To act the Cretan" became an idiom meaning "to play the liar." A number of Jews from Crete were present in Jerusalem at the time of Peter's sermon on the day of Pentecost (Acts 2:11), and some of them may have believed in Christ and introduced the gospel to their countrymen. Certainly Paul would not have had opportunity to do evangelistic work during his brief sojourn on Crete while he was en route to Rome (Acts 27:7-13). But the apostle spread the gospel in the cities of Crete after his release from Roman imprisonment and left Titus there to finish organizing the churches (1:5). Because of the problem of immorality among the Cretans, it was important for Titus to stress the need of righteousness in Christian living. False teachers, especially "those of the circumcision" (1:10), were also misleading the believers and causing divisions. Paul wrote this letter around A.D. 63, perhaps from Corinth, taking advantage of the journey of Zenas and Apollos

(3:13) whose destination would take them by way of Crete. Paul was planning to spend the winter in Nicopolis (western Greece), and urged Titus in this letter to join him there upon his replacement by Artemas or Tychicus (13:12). Paul may have been planning to leave Nicopolis for Spain in the spring, and he wanted his useful companion Titus to come along.

Titus is not mentioned in Acts, but the 13 references to him in the Pauline epistles make it clear that he was one of Paul's closest and most trusted companions. This convert of Paul ("my true child in a common faith," Titus 1:4) was probably from Syrian Antioch if he was one of the disciples of Acts 11:26. Paul brought this uncircumcised Greek believer to Jerusalem (Gal. 2:3) where he became a test case on the matter of Gentiles and liberty from the law. Years later when Paul set out from Antioch on his third missionary journey (Acts 18:22), Titus must have accompanied him because he was sent by the apostle to Corinth on three occasions during that time (2 Cor. 2:12,13; 7:5-7,13-15; 8:6, 16-24). He is not mentioned again until the epistle that bears his name when he was left on Crete to carry on the work. He was with Paul during his second Roman imprisonment but left to go to Dalmatia (2 Tim. 4:10), possibly on an evangelistic mission. Paul spoke of this reliable and gifted associate as his "brother" (2 Cor. 2:13), his "partner and fellow worker" (2 Cor. 8:23), and his "child" (Titus 1:4). He lauded Titus' character and conduct in 2 Corinthians 7:13-15 and 8:16,17.

Theme and Purpose

Theme and Purpose—This brief letter focuses on Titus' role and responsibility in the organization and supervision of the churches in Crete. It was written to strengthen and exhort Titus to firmly exercise his authority as an apostolic representative in a situation where churches needed to be put in order, false teachers and dissenters needed to be refuted, and immoral behavior needed to be replaced by good deeds. Paul used this letter to remind Titus of some of the details related to his task, including the qualifications for elders and the behavior expected of various groups in the churches. Paul included three doctrinal sections in this letter to stress that proper belief (orthodoxy) gives the basis for proper behavior (orthopraxy). Because of the opposition Titus would face (1:11,13; 2:15; 3:9-11), this letter was also written to provide official apostolic warrant for Titus' authority. Paul also used this letter to give Titus certain personal instructions (3:12,13).

Contribution to the Bible—Titus and 1 Timothy are similar in date, circumstances, and purposes. Both give instructions on qualifications for leadership, how to deal with false teaching, and the need for sound doctrine and behavior. Both contain encouragement and exhortation to Paul's representatives, but Titus is briefer, more official, and less personal than 1 Timothy. The situation at Ephesus required a stronger emphasis on sound doctrine, while that at Crete required more concentration on conduct. Even so, Titus offers three excellent summaries of Christian theology (1:14; 2:11-14; 3:4-7), and the last two are among the most sublime New Testament portraits of the grace of God.

Christ in Titus—The deity and redemptive work of Christ are beautifully stated in 2:13,14: "looking for the blessed hope and the appearing of the glory of our great God and Savior, Christ Jesus; who gave Himself for us, that He might redeem us from every lawless deed and purify for Himself a people for His own possession, zealous for good deeds."

Philemon

"I appeal to you for my child, whom I have begotten in my imprisonment, Onesimus, who formerly was useless to you, but now is useful both to you and to me."

Philemon 10,11

Focus	Greet-ings	Grati-tude	Grace			General		
	1 3	4 7	8 21			22 25		
D I V I S I O N S	Salutation	Paul's Thanksgiving for Philemon	Paul's Appeal for Onesimus	Paul's Promise to Philemon	Personal Request	Greetings from Co-laborers	Benediction
	1 3	4 7	8 17	18 21	22	23 24	25
T o p i c s	Pre-face	Praise	Plea	Pledge	Personal		
	Com-mence-ment	Commen-dation	Counsel	Confi-dence	Conclusion		
	Family	Fellowship of Faith	Favor of Forgiveness		Friends and Farewell		
	Recip-ients	Relation-ship	Request		Remarks		
Loca-tion	Written During Paul's First Roman Imprisonment							
Time	A.D. 60-61							

Talk Thru—This briefest of Paul's epistles (only 334 words in the Greek text) is a model of courtesy, discretion, and loving concern for the forgiveness of one who would otherwise face the sentence of death. In it, Paul beseeches his "beloved brother and fellow worker" Philemon to forgive his runaway slave Onesimus and receive him as a new brother in Christ. This tactful and highly personal letter can be divided into four components: Greetings (1-3), Gratitude (4-7), Grace (8-21), and General (22-25).

Greetings (1-3): Writing this letter as a "prisoner of Christ Jesus," Paul addressed it personally to Philemon, a Christian leader in Colossae (1). But the apostle also addressed it to Apphia and Archippus (evidently Philemon's wife and son) as well as the church that met in Philemon's house (2). Thus, Philemon's decision regarding Onesimus would have public import as it was viewed by his family and Christian friends.

Gratitude (4-7): The main body of this compact letter begins with a word of thanksgiving for Philemon's faithfulness and love. This honest commendation of Philemon prior to the request is an excellent example of Paul's tactfulness and wisdom.

Grace (8-21): Basing his appeal on Philemon's character, Paul refuses to command Philemon to pardon and receive Onesimus. Instead, "Paul, the aged" (9; he may have been 50 to 60 at this time) seeks to persuade his friend of his Christian responsibility to forgive even as he was forgiven by Christ. Paul does not even mention Onesimus until verse 10, and when he does, he immediately refers to the dramatic change that occurred in Onesimus' life. Onesimus means "useful, profitable," and Paul uses a play on words to illustrate his point: he "formerly was useless (*achreston*) to you, but now is useful (*euchreston*) both to you and to me" (11). Onesimus became Paul's spiritual child and a warm bond developed between them, making it difficult for Paul to send him back to Philemon, as he knew he must. Paul therefore urges Philemon not to punish Onesimus, but to receive him, "no longer as a slave" but as "a beloved brother" (16). Paul places Onesimus' debt on his account, but then reminds Philemon of his greater spiritual debt as one of his converts (18,19).

This was a real test of Philemon's Christian love, but Paul was confident in the outcome: "I know that you will do even more than what I say" (21). This may imply the emancipation of Onesimus or permission for him to engage in ministry.

General (22-25): Paul closes this effective epistle with a hopeful request (22), greetings from his companions (23,24), and a benediction (25). The fact that it was preserved indicates Philemon's favorable response to Paul's pleas.

Title
—Since this letter was addressed to Philemon in verse 1, it became known as *Pros Philemona*, "To Philemon." Like 1 and 2 Timothy and Titus, it was addressed to an individual, but unlike the Pastoral Epistles, Philemon was also addressed to a family and a church (vs. 2).

Author
—The authenticity of Philemon was not called into question until the fourth century when certain theologians concluded that its lack of doctrinal content made it unworthy of the apostle Paul. But men like Jerome and Chrysostom soon vindicated this epistle and it was not challenged again until the 19th century. Some radical critics who denied the authenticity of Colossians also turned against the Pauline authorship of Philemon because of the close connection between the two epistles (e.g., the same people are associated with Paul in both letters: compare Col. 4:9,10,12,14 with Philem. 10,23,24). The general consensus of scholarship, however, recognizes Philemon as Pauline. There could have been no doctrinal motive for its forgery, and it is supported externally by consistent tradition and internally by no less than three references to Paul (vss. 1,9,19).

Date and Setting
—Reconstructing the background of this letter, it appears that a slave named Onesimus robbed or in some other way wronged his master Philemon and escaped. He made his way from Colossae to Rome, where he found relative safety among the masses in the Imperial City. Somehow Onesimus came into contact with Paul—it is possible that he even sought out the apostle for help (Onesimus no doubt heard Philemon speak of Paul). Paul led him to Christ (vs. 10), and although Onesimus became a real asset to Paul, both knew that as a Christian, Onesimus had a responsibility to return to Philemon. That day came when Paul wrote his epistle to the Colossians. Tychicus was the bearer of that letter, and Paul

decided to send Onesimus along with Tychicus to Colossae (Col. 4:7-9; Philem. 12), knowing that it would be safer in view of slave-catchers to send Onesimus with a companion.

Philemon is one of the four Prison Epistles (see Ephesians, Philippians, and especially Colossians, Date and Setting for background). It was written in A.D. 60-61 and dispatched at the same time as Colossians during Paul's first Roman imprisonment (see vss. 1,9,10,13,23). Philemon 22 reflects Paul's confident hope of release: "prepare me a lodging; for I hope that through your prayers I shall be given to you."

Philemon was a resident of Colossae (Col. 4:9,17; Philem. 1,2) and a convert of Paul (vs. 19), perhaps through an encounter with Paul when he was in Ephesus during the third missionary journey. Philemon's house was large enough to serve as a meeting place for a church (vs. 2). He was benevolent to other believers (vss. 5-7), and his son Archippus evidently held a position of leadership in the church (Col. 4:17; Philem. 2). Philemon may have had other slaves in addition to Onesimus, and he was not alone as a slave owner among the Colossian believers (Col. 4:1). Thus this letter and his response would provide guidelines for other master-slave relationships.

✓ According to Roman law, runaway slaves like Onesimus could be severely punished or condemned to a violent death. It is doubtful that Onesimus would have returned to Philemon even with this letter if he was not a Christian.

Theme and Purpose—Philemon develops the transition from bondage to brotherhood that is brought about by Christian love and forgiveness. Just as Philemon was shown mercy through the grace of Christ, so he must graciously forgive his repentant runaway who has returned as a brother in Christ. Paul wrote this letter as his personal appeal that Philemon receive Onesimus even as he would receive Paul. This letter was also addressed to other Christians in Philemon's circle, because Paul wanted it to have an impact on the Colossian church as a whole.

Contribution to the Bible—In this very personal and persuasive letter, Paul skillfully handled a delicate matter with supreme tactfulness and genuine warmth. As in his other epistles, he was able to apply the highest principles to the most

mundane affairs. Christian love and courtesy dominate Philemon, and though it is not written with elegance and formality, its content is marked by loftiness and dignity. Unlike his other epistles, Paul wrote Philemon entirely in his own hand (vs. 19), apparently to emphasize the urgency and personal nature of the request. Paul does not minimize Onesimus' offense, but acting as his advocate and intercessor, he puts himself in Onesimus' place.

Philemon was not written to impart doctrine but to apply it in such a way that the life-changing effects of Christianity would have an impact on social conditions. The power of the gospel overcomes sociological barriers ("neither slave nor free man," Gal. 3:28; cf. Col. 3:11), and Paul is a vivid illustration of this truth: this once self-righteous Pharisee now refers to a Gentile slave as "my child, whom I have begotten" (vs. 10). Philemon is not a direct attack on the institution of slavery, but its Christian principles would ultimately lead to the renunciation of slavery.

Christ in Philemon—The forgiveness that the believer finds in Christ is beautifully portrayed by analogy in Philemon. Onesimus was guilty of a great offense (11,18), but Paul's love motivated him to intercede on his behalf (10-17). Paul laid aside his rights (8) and became Onesimus' substitute by assuming his debt (18,19). By Philemon's gracious act, Onesimus is restored and placed in a new relationship (15,16). In this analogy, we are Onesimus, and Paul's advocacy before Philemon is parallel to Christ's work of mediation before the Father. Onesimus was condemned by law but saved by grace.

Walk Thru the Pauline Epistles

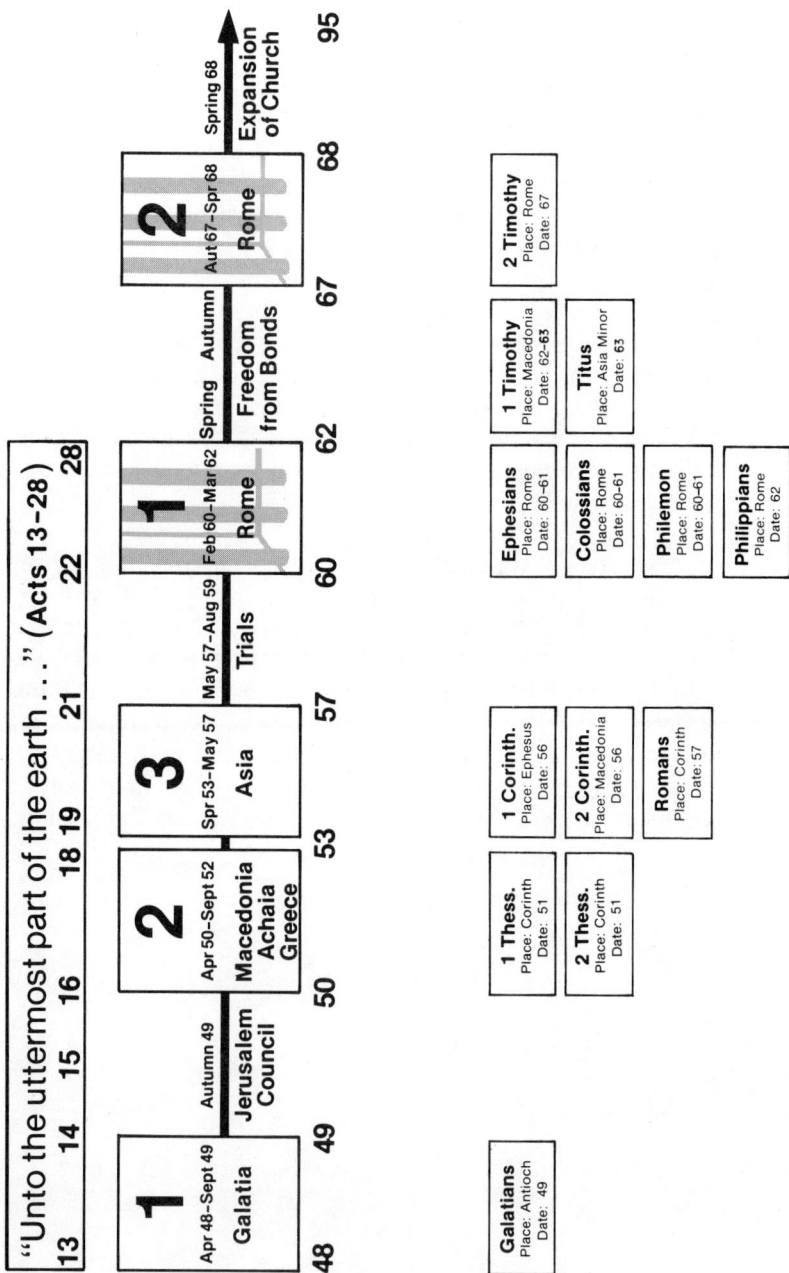

"Unto the uttermost part of the earth . . ." (Acts 13–28)

| 13 | 14 | 15 | 16 | 18 | 19 | 21 | 22 | 28 |

1
Apr 48–Sept 49
Galatia

Autumn 49
Jerusalem Council

2
Apr 50–Sept 52
Macedonia
Achaia
Greece

3
Spr 53–May 57
Asia

May 57–Aug 59
Trials

1
Feb 60–Mar 62
Rome

Spring — Autumn
Freedom from Bonds

2
Aut 67–Spr 68
Rome

Spring 68
Expansion of Church

| 48 | 49 | 50 | 53 | 57 | 60 | 62 | 67 | 68 | 95 |

Galatians
Place: Antioch
Date: 49

1 Thess.
Place: Corinth
Date: 51

2 Thess.
Place: Corinth
Date: 51

1 Corinth.
Place: Ephesus
Date: 56

2 Corinth.
Place: Macedonia
Date: 56

Romans
Place: Corinth
Date: 57

Ephesians
Place: Rome
Date: 60–61

Colossians
Place: Rome
Date: 60–61

Philemon
Place: Rome
Date: 60–61

Philippians
Place: Rome
Date: 62

1 Timothy
Place: Macedonia
Date: 62–63

Titus
Place: Asia Minor
Date: 63

2 Timothy
Place: Rome
Date: 67

148

Summary of the Pauline Epistles

Book	No. of Chapters	Author	Key Word	Place Written	Date Written	Recipients
Romans	16	Paul	Paid in Full	Corinth	57	Beloved of God in Rome
1 Corinthians	16	Paul	Spanking the Saints	Ephesus	56	Church of God at Corinth, those sanctified in Christ Jesus
2 Corinthians	13	Paul	Anatomy of an Apostle	Macedonia	56	Church of God at Corinth and all saints throughout Achaia
Galatians	6	Paul	Unshackled	Antioch	49	Churches of Galatia
Ephesians	6	Paul	Body-Building	Rome	60-61	Saints of Ephesus
Philippians	4	Paul	How to be Happy Though Humble	Rome	62	Saints in Christ Jesus in Philippi
Colossians	4	Paul	Commander-in-Chief	Rome	60-61	Saints and faithful brothers in Christ at Colossae
1 Thessalonians	5	Paul	Stay on Target	Corinth	51	Church of the Thessalonians
2 Thessalonians	3	Paul	Working Waiters	Corinth	51	Church of the Thessalonians
1 Timothy	6	Paul	Leadership Manual	Macedonia	62-63	Timothy, my true child in the faith
2 Timothy	4	Paul	Combat Manual	Rome	67	Timothy, my beloved son
Titus	3	Paul	Conduct Manual	Corinth	63	Titus, my true child in a common faith
Philemon	1	Paul	Bondage to Brotherhood	Rome	60-61	Philemon, our beloved brother

Introduction to the Non-Pauline Epistles and Revelation

The Non-Pauline Epistles—These eight epistles exert an influence out of proportion to their length (less than 10% of the New Testament). They supplement the 13 Pauline epistles by offering different perspectives on the richness of Christian truth. Each of the five authors—James, Peter, John, Jude, and the author of Hebrews—has a distinctive contribution to make from his own point of view. Like the four complementary approaches to the life of Christ in the gospels, these writers provide a sweeping portrait of the Christian life in which the total is greater than the sum of the parts. Great as Paul's epistles are, the New Testament revelation after Acts would be severely limited by one apostolic perspective if the writings of these five men were not included.

With the exception of James, these letters were written near the end of Paul's life or after his time. As Paul anticipated in Acts 20:29,30; 1 Timothy 4:1-3; and 2 Timothy 4:3,4, the problem of heretical teachings would reach alarming proportions in the church. It is significant that most of the non-Pauline epistles deal rather firmly with these dangerous doctrines. The churches of this time were threatened not only by external opposition and persecution, but also by internal attacks from false prophets.

The term "general epistle" appears in the King James Version titles of James, 1 and 2 Peter, 1 John, and Jude, but it was not used in the oldest manuscripts. These epistles were not addressed to specific churches or individuals, and they came to be known as the general or "catholic" (universal) epistles. The epistles of 2 and 3 John are also included in this group even though they are addressed to specific people. Because of this problem, and because Hebrews is not regarded as a general epistle, it would be safer to designate Hebrews, James, 1 and 2 Peter, 1, 2, and 3 John, and Jude as the non-Pauline epistles (assuming that Paul did not write Hebrews; see Hebrews, Author). The Pauline epistles are titled by their addressees, but the non-Pauline epistles (except Hebrews) are titled by their authors.

These epistles were usually placed before the Pauline epistles in Greek manuscripts, but early catalogs of the canonical New Testament books generally listed them in the order used today. This seems preferable because of their date, length, and content. It also reflects the delay most of them endured in being admitted into the canon of authoritative books. All but the first epistles of Peter and John were disputed for a period of time for various reasons before being officially recognized as canonical. This illustrates the great care taken by the early church in critically distinguishing between authoritative and later apocryphal books.

Hebrews: This beautifully styled epistle was written to demonstrate the superiority of Christ over all that preceded Him. The readers were evidently in danger of slipping back into Judaism because of growing opposition to them as Christians. They needed to mature and become stable in their faith. The author presents the superiority of Christ's person, priesthood, and power.

James: James wrote this incisive and practical catalog of the characteristics of true faith to exhort his Hebrew-Christian readers to examine the reality of their own faith. If it does not produce a qualitative change in character or control (1-3), its genuineness must be questioned. James also rebukes those who succumb to the pursuit of worldly pleasure and wealth rather than God, and encourages a patient endurance in light of the coming of the Lord.

1 Peter: The recipients of this letter were being maligned for their faith in Christ and needed Peter's words of comfort and counsel. He begins by giving them a fresh perspective on the riches of their salvation and their need for holy lives. He then encourages them to develop an attitude of submission in view of their suffering. Undeserved suffering for the name of Christ must be met by an attitude of humble dependence on God.

2 Peter: Unlike 1 Peter, which dealt with external opposition, 2 Peter copes with the problem of internal opposition, in the dangerous form of false teachers who would entice believers into their errors of belief and conduct. Peter counters this peril with an appeal for growth in the true knowledge of Christ as the best way to overcome the seduction of heresy.

1 John: John's first epistle explores the dimensions of fellowship between redeemed people and God. He is a God of light, and believers must walk in integrity before Him; He is a God of love, and believers must manifest love for one another; and He is a God of life, and believers can be assured of eternal life in Christ.

2 John: This note was written to commend the readers for remaining steadfast in apostolic truth and to remind them to walk in love in obedience to the Lord's commandment. John also urged them not to show hospitality to any teachers whose doctrine about Christ is unsound.

3 John: John had received a report from the traveling teachers he commissioned, telling of Gaius' warm hospitality on their behalf. The apostle personally thanks Gaius for his walk in the truth and support of these missionaries, in contrast to Diotrephes, who rejected them and told others to do the same.

Jude: In spite of its brevity, this is the most intense exposé of false teachers in the New Testament. Jude reveals their conduct and character and makes liberal use of the Old Testament to predict their judgment. On the positive side, Jude encourages his readers to build themselves up in the truth and contend earnestly for the faith.

Revelation—This most controversial book is the culmination not only of the New Testament but of the Bible as a whole, since it completes the story begun in Genesis. As the only New Testament book that concentrates on prophecy, the Apocalypse has been approached from a number of interpretive directions.

After a dramatic description of his overwhelming vision of

the glorious Christ, John records seven messages to seven Asian churches (1-3). Chapters 4-19 portray unparalleled judgment upon rebellious mankind, the scenes shifting back and forth from heaven to earth. Jesus Christ is not only the Lamb that was slain, but also the Lion who has received all authority to stand in judgment of men and angels. After describing the second advent and the judgments that follow, John records his vision of the new heaven and new earth and surveys the marvels of the new Jerusalem (20-22).

Hebrews

"Therefore leaving the elementary teaching about Christ, let us press on to maturity . . ."
Hebrews 6:1a (Also see 2:1-3,9; 4:12,13,16; 7:25; 10:19-22; 12:2.)

Focus	A Superior Person				A Superior Priesthood				A Superior Power				
	1			4:13	4:14			10:18	10:19				13
Divisions	Supremacy of Christ	Superiority of Christ over Angels	Superiority of Christ over Moses	Superiority of Christ's Rest	Superiority of Christ's Priesthood	Superiority of Christ's Covenant	Superiority of Christ's Sanctuary	Superiority of Christ's Sacrifice	Danger of Discarding Faith	Demonstrations of Faith	Discipline and Endurance	Duty and Dedication	Departing Benediction and Words
	1:1-3	1:4 2:18	3:1-6	3:7 4:13	4:14 7:28	8:1-13	9:1-11	9:12—10:18	10:19-39	11:1-40	12:1-29	13:1-19	13:20-25
Topics	Majesty of Christ				Ministry of Christ				Message on Conduct				
	Better than Angels, Moses, and Joshua				Better Priesthood, Covenant, Sanctuary, and Sacrifice				Basis of a Better Life				
	Doctrine								Discipline				
	Precepts								Practice				
Location	Place of Writing Unknown												
Time	Probably A.D. 64-68												

Talk Thru—Hebrews stands alone among the New Testament epistles in its style and approach, and it is the only New Testament book that remains a real mystery in terms of authorship. This profound work builds a case for the superiority of Christ through a cumulative argument in which Christ is presented as "better" in every respect. In His person He is better than the angels, Moses, and Joshua, and in His performance He provides a better priesthood, covenant, sanctuary, and sacrifice. Evidently, the readers were in danger of reverting back to Judaism because of the suffering they were beginning to experience due to their faith in Christ. But in reverting, they would be retreating from the substance back into the shadow. In addition to his positive presentation of the supremacy of Christ, the writer intersperses five solemn warnings about the peril of turning away from Christ (2:1-4; 3:7-4:13; 5:11-6:20; 10:19-39; 12:25-29). These parenthetical warnings build from neglect (2:1-4) to refusal (12:25-29). After using the Old Testament to demonstrate Christ's superior person (1:1-4:13) and superior priesthood (4:14-10:18), the writer applies these truths in a practical way to show Christ's superior power (10:19-13:25) to transform lives.

A Superior Person (1:1-4:13): Instead of the usual salutation, this epistle immediately launches into the theme of the book—the supremacy of Christ (1:1-3). Christianity is built upon the highest form of divine disclosure: the personal revelation of God through His incarnate Son. Christ is therefore greater than the prophets, and He is also greater than the angels, the mediators of the Mosaic law (1:4-2:18; see Acts 7:53; Heb. 2:2). This is seen in His name, His position, His worship by the angels, and His incarnation. The Son of God partook of flesh and blood and was "made like His brethren in all things" (2:17) in order to bring "many sons to glory" (2:10). Christ is also superior to Moses (3:1-6), for Moses was a servant in the house of God, but Christ is the Son over God's household. Because of these truths, the readers are exhorted to avoid divine judgment due to disbelief (3:7-4:13). It was their disbelief that prevented the generation of the exodus from becoming the generation of the conquest, and the rest that Christ offers is so much greater than that which was provided by Joshua. The readers are therefore urged to enter the eternal rest which is possessed by faith in Christ.

A Superior Priesthood (4:14-10:18): The high priesthood of Christ is superior to the Aaronic priesthood (4:14-7:28). Because of His incarnation, Christ can "sympathize with our weaknesses," having been "tempted in all things as we are, yet without sin" (4:15). Christ was not a Levite, but He qualified for a higher priesthood according to the order of Melchizedek. The superiority of Melchizedek to Levi is seen in the fact that Levi in effect paid tithes through Abraham to Melchizedek (7:9,10), Abraham was blessed by Melchizedek, and "the lesser is blessed by the greater" (7:7). The parenthetical warning in 5:11-6:20 exhorts the readers to "press on to maturity" by moving beyond the basics of salvation and repentance. This difficult passage has been interpreted in many ways, but it cannot properly be used as an attack on the security of the believer, not only because this contradicts the New Testament teaching on regeneration, but because it would lead to the unacceptable position that a person could not be restored after falling away. This passage seems to be saying that one cannot keep going back to the original point of regeneration after coming to Christ; the believer must move beyond the basics of salvation.

By divine oath (7:21), Christ has become a permanent and perfect high priest and "the mediator of a better covenant" (8:6). The new covenant has made the old covenant obsolete (8:6-13). Similarly, our great high priest ministers in "a greater and more perfect tabernacle, not made with hands, that is to say, not of this creation" (9:11; cf. 9:1-10). And unlike the former priests, He offers Himself as a sinless and voluntary sacrifice once for all (9:12-10:18).

A Superior Power (10:19-13:25): The author applies what he has been saying about the superiority of Christ by warning his readers of the danger of discarding their faith in Christ (10:19-39). Like chapter 6, this is a difficult passage because of its stern tone; it is a solemn admonition against the perils of apostasy. The faith that the readers must maintain is defined in 11:1 and illustrated in 11:2-39. The triumphs and accomplishments of faith in the lives of Old Testament believers should encourage the recipients of "something better" (11:40) in Christ to fix their "eyes on Jesus, the author and perfector of faith" (12:2). Just as Jesus endured great hostility, those who believe in Him will sometimes have to endure divine discipline for the sake of holiness (12:1-29). The readers are warned not to turn away from Christ during such times, but to place their hope in Him. The character of their lives must be shaped by their dedication to Christ (13:1-19), and this will be manifested in their love, hospitality, concern, purity, contentment, and obedience. The author concludes this epistle with one of the finest benedictions in Scripture (13:20,21) and some personal words (13:22-25).

Title—Although the King James Version uses the title "The Epistle of Paul the Apostle to the Hebrews," there is no early manuscript evidence to support it. The oldest and most reliable title is simply *Pros Ebraious*, "To Hebrews."

Author—Like Melchizedek, the ancestry of Hebrews is unknown. Uncertainty plagues not only its authorship, but also its location, date, and readership. The question of authorship delayed its recognition in the West as part of the New Testament canon in spite of early support by Clement of Rome. Not until the fourth century was it generally accepted as authoritative in the western church, and the testimony of Jerome and Augustine settled the issue. In the eastern church, there was no problem of canonical acceptance because it was regarded as one of the "14" epistles of Paul. The issue of its canonicity was again raised during the Reformation, but the spiritual depth and quality of Hebrews bears witness to its inspiration regardless of its anonymity.

Hebrews 13:18-24 tells us that this book was not anonymous to the original readers; they evidently knew the author well. But for some reason, early church tradition is divided over the identity of the author. Part of the church attributed it to Paul, others preferred Barnabas, Luke, or Clement, and some opted for anonymity. Thus, external evidence will not help determine the author; internal evidence must be the final court of appeal, but here too, the results are ambiguous. Some aspects of the language, style, and theology of Hebrews are very similar to Paul's epistles, and the author refers to Timothy as well (13:23). But there are also significant differences that have led the majority of biblical scholars to reject Pauline authorship of this book: (1) The Greek style of Hebrews is far more polished and refined than that found in any of Paul's recognized epistles. (2) In view of Paul's consistent claims to be an apostle and an eyewitness of Christ, it is very doubtful that he would have used the phraseology found in 2:3: "After it was at the first spoken through the Lord, it was confirmed to us by those who heard." (3) The lack of Paul's customary salutation which includes his name goes against the firm pattern found in all his other epistles. (4) While Paul used both the Hebrew text and the Septuagint to quote from the Old Testament, the writer of Hebrews apparently did not know Hebrew and quoted exclusively from the Septuagint. (5) Paul's common use of compound titles to refer to the Son of God is not followed in Hebrews which usually refers to Him as Christ, Jesus, and Lord. (6) Hebrews concentrates on Christ's present priestly ministry, but Paul's writings have very little to say about the present work of Christ. Thus, Hebrews appears not to have been written by Paul, though the writer shows a Pauline influence. The authority of Hebrews in no way depends upon its Pauline authorship, especially since it does not claim to have been written by Paul.

Tertullian referred to Barnabas as the author of Hebrews, but it is unlikely that this resident of Jerusalem (Acts 4:36,37) would include himself as one of those who relied on others for eyewitness testimony about Jesus (2:3). Other suggestions include Luke, Clement of Rome, Apollos, Silvanus (Silas), Philip, and even Priscilla. Some of these are real possibilities, but we must agree with the third century theologian Origen who wrote, "Who it was that really wrote the Epistle, God only knows."

Date and Setting—Because of the exclusive use of the Septuagint and the polished Greek style found in Hebrews, some recent scholars have argued that this book was written to a Gentile readership. However, the bulk of the evidence favors the traditional view that the original recipients of this letter were Jewish Christians. Besides the ancient title "To Hebrews," there is also the frequent use of the Old Testament as an unquestioned authority, the assumed knowledge of the sacrificial ritual, and the many contrasts between Christianity and Judaism which are designed to prevent the readers from lapsing back into Judaism.

Many places have been suggested for the locality of the

readers, but the destination cannot be determined with any certainty. In the past, Jerusalem was most frequently suggested, but this view is hindered by four problems: (1) It is unlikely that a book addressed to Palestineans would quote exclusively from the Septuagint rather than the Hebrew Old Testament. (2) Palestinean believers were poor (Rom. 15:26), but these readers were able to financially assist other Christians (6:10). (3) Residents of Jerusalem would not be characterized by the description in 2:3 because some would have been eyewitnesses of the ministry of Christ. (4) "You have not resisted to the point of shedding blood" (12:4) does not fit the situation in Jerusalem. The majority view today is that the recipients of Hebrews probably lived in Rome. The statement "Those from Italy greet you" in 13:24 seems to mean that Italians away from Italy are sending their greetings home.

The recipients of this letter were believers (3:1) who came to faith through the testimony of eyewitnesses of Christ (2:3). They were not novices (5:12), and they had successfully endured hardships because of their stand for the gospel (10:32-34). Unfortunately, they had become "dull of hearing" (5:11) and were in danger of drifting away (2:1; 3:12). This would make them particularly susceptible to the renewed persecutions that were coming upon them (12:4-12), and the author found it necessary to check the downward spiral with "this word of exhortation" (13:22). While there is disagreement over the specific danger involved, the classic position that the readers were on the verge of lapsing back into Judaism to avoid persecution directed at Christians seems to be supported by the whole tenor of the book. Hebrews repeatedly stresses the superiority of Christianity over Judaism, and this would be pointless if the readers were about to return to Gnosticism or heathenism.

The place of writing is unknown, but a reasonable estimate of the date can be made. Hebrews was quoted in A.D. 95 by Clement of Rome, but its failure to mention the ending of the Old Testament sacrificial system with the destruction of Jerusalem in A.D. 70 indicates that it was written prior to that date. Timothy was still alive (13:23), persecution was mounting, and the old Jewish system was about to be removed (12:26,27). All this suggests a date of around A.D. 64-68.

Theme and Purpose—The basic theme of Hebrews is found in the use of the word "better" (1:4; 6:9; 7:7,19,22; 8:6; 9:23; 10:34; 11:16,35,40; 12:24 (the words "perfect" and "heavenly" are also prominent) to describe the superiority of Christ in His person and work. He offers a better revelation, position, priesthood, covenant, sacrifice, and power. The writer develops this theme to prevent the readers from giving up the substance for the shadow by abandoning Christianity and retreating into the old Judaic system. This epistle was also written to exhort them to become mature in Christ and put away their spiritual dullness and degeneration. Thus, it places heavy stress on doctrine, concentrating on Christology and soteriology (salvation).

Contribution to the Bible—Among the New Testament epistles Hebrews is unique in form. It has no introductory salutation like other letters, and there is no evidence that such a salutation was ever removed at some early point. Hebrews instead launches immediately into its theme, and it reads more like a sermonic essay than a letter. The author regarded it as a "word of exhortation" (13:22), and it may have been a modified sermon or series of sermons. Only 13:18-25 sounds like a real epistle. Hebrews is characterized by a very precise and scholarly style, elegantly written and carefully constructed. Its literary quality and vigorous rhetoric are unexcelled in the New Testament. This book abounds with quotations and allusions to the Old Testament which are authoritatively used to demonstrate the superiority and finality of the person and priesthood of Christ. Hebrews makes important doctrinal contributions to the New Testament, especially in its revelation of the present priestly ministry of Christ on behalf of the believer. It develops the doctrine of the atoning work of Christ in relation to the new covenant. It also explores the typological significance of the offerings and feasts in Leviticus; Hebrews is a divine commentary on the prophetic meaning of the ceremonial law. Throughout this epistle, the application of doctrine to practice is stressed in its negative warnings and positive exhortations (see "let us . . ." in 4:1,11,14,16; 6:1; 10:22,23,24; 12:1 two times, 28; 13:13,15).

Christ in Hebrews—Christ is our eternal High Priest according to the order of Melchizedek. He identified with man in His incarnation and offered no less a sacrifice than Himself on our behalf.

Sacrifices Under the Law (10:1-4)	Sacrifice of Christ (10:5-18)
Reminders of sin	Remover of sin
Repeated constantly	Once for all time
Anticipation	Fulfillment
Shadows	Substance
Blood of animals	Blood of Christ
Involuntary	Voluntary

Hebrews presents Christ as the divine-human Prophet, Priest, and King. His deity (1:1-3,8) and humanity (2:9,14,17,18) are asserted with equal force, and over 20 titles are used to describe His attributes and accomplishments (e.g., heir of all things, Apostle and High Priest, mediator, author and perfecter of faith). He is superior to all that went before and offers the supreme sacrifice, priesthood, and covenant.

James

". . . But let everyone be quick to hear, slow to speak and slow to anger."

James 1:19 (Also see 1:22.)

Focus	Character of Faith					Control of Faith		Conflicts of Faith		Consummation of Faith	
	1￼ ￼ ￼ ￼2					3		4￼ ￼5:6		5:7￼ ￼5:20	
D i v i s i o n s	Persevering under Trials	Progress of Temptation	Planting the Word	Personal Favoritism	Performance of Faith	Power of the Tongue	Portrait of Pure Wisdom	Perversity of Pleasures	Pride of the Rich	Patient Endurance	Prayer and Restoration
	1:1-12	1:13-18	1:19-27	2:1-13	2:14-26	3:1￼ 3:12	3:13 3:18	4:1￼ 4:12	4:13￼ 5:6	5:7￼ 5:12	5:13 5:20
T o p i c s	Will		Word	Works		Words	Wisdom	Worldliness	Wealth	Wait	Wholeness
	Endurance		Efficacy			Exposition		Exhortation		Encouragement	
	Resisting		Responding			Restraining		Rebuking		Remaining	
	"...be quick to hear..."					"slow to speak..."		"and slow to anger" (1:19)			
Location	Probably Jerusalem										
Time	Probably A.D. 46-49										

163

Talk Thru—James is an intensely practical manual on the outworking of true faith in everyday life. It explores Christian conduct from several perspectives and shifts abruptly from topic to topic. Faith perseveres under trials, resists temptations, responds to the Word, overcomes prejudice, produces good works, controls the tongue, manifests wisdom, submits to God rather than worldly pleasures, depends on God rather than wealth, and waits patiently for the return of the Lord. Biblical faith moves from assent to actions, from words to works.

James is the Proverbs of the New Testament because it is written in the terse moralistic style of wisdom literature. It is evident that James was profoundly influenced by the Old Testament (especially the wisdom literature like Proverbs) and by the Sermon on the Mount. But James' impassioned preaching against inequity and social injustice also earns him the title of the Amos of the New Testament. Because of the many subjects in this epistle, it is difficult to outline; suggestions have ranged from no connection between the various topics to a unified scheme. The outline used here is: Character of Faith (1-2), Control of Faith (3), Conflicts of Faith (4:1-5:6), and Consummation of Faith (5:7-20).

Character of Faith (1-2): The first two chapters of this epistle develop the qualities of genuine faith in regard to trials and temptations, response to the Scriptures, and practical behavior. After a one-verse salutation to geographically dispersed Hebrew Christians (1:1), James quickly introduces his first subject, outward tests of faith (1:2-12). These trials are designed to produce mature endurance and a sense of dependence upon God as a believer turns to Him and asks for wisdom and enablement. Inward temptations (1:13-18) do not come from the One who bestows "every good thing" (1:17). These solicitations to evil must be checked at an early stage or they can give birth to disastrous consequences.

A righteous response to testing requires that one be "quick to hear, slow to speak and slow to anger" (1:19,20), and this broadly summarizes the remainder of the epistle. Quickness of hearing involves an obedient response to God's Word (1:21-27). True hearing means more than mere listening; the Word must be received and applied. After stating this principle (1:21,22), James develops it with an illustration (1:23-25) and an application (1:26,27). A genuine faith should produce a change in *attitude* from partiality to the rich to a love for the poor as well as the rich (2:1-13). True faith should also result in *actions* as a belief that behaves (2:14-26). In Romans 4, Paul used the example of Abraham to show that justification is by faith, not by works. But James says that Abraham was justified by works (2:21). In spite of the apparent contradiction, Romans 4 and James 2 are really two sides of the same coin. In context, Paul is writing about justification before God while James writes of the evidence of justification before men. While God knows the heart, men need an external manifestation of the heart attitude to know the difference between profession and reality. A faith that produces no change is not saving faith.

Control of Faith (3): Moving from works to words, James shows how a living faith controls the tongue ("slow to speak," 1:19). The tongue is small, but it has the power to accomplish great good or evil. But only the power of God applied by an active faith can tame the tongue (3:1-12). Just as there is a wicked and a righteous use of the tongue, so there is a demonic and a divine manifestation of wisdom (3:13-18). James contrasts seven characteristics of human wisdom with seven qualities of divine wisdom (see Proverbs, Contribution to the Bible).

Conflicts of Faith (4:1-5:6): The strong pulls of worldliness (4:1-12) and wealth (4:13-5:6) create conflicts which are harmful to the growth of faith. The world system is at enmity with God, and the pursuit of its pleasures produces covetousness, envy, fighting, and arrogance (4:1-6). The believer's only alternative is submission to God out of a humble and repentant spirit. This will produce a transformed attitude toward others as well (4:7-12). This spirit of submission and humility should be applied to any attempts to accrue wealth (4:13-17), especially because wealth can lead to pride, injustice, and selfishness (5:1-6).

Consummation of Faith (5:7-20): James encourages his readers to patiently endure the sufferings of the present life in view of the future prospect of the coming of the Lord (5:7-12). They may be oppressed by the rich or by other circumstances, but as the example of Job teaches, believers can be sure that God has a gracious purpose in His dealings with them. James concludes his epistle with some practical words on prayer and restoration (5:13-20). The prayers of righteous men (like elders in local churches) are efficacious for the healing and restoration of believers. When sin is not dealt with, it can be a contributing cause of illness and even death.

Title—The name *Iakobos* (James) in 1:1 is the basis for the early title *Iakobou Epistole*, "Epistle of James." *Iakobos* is the Greek form of the Hebrew name Jacob, a common Jewish name in the first century.

Author—Four men are named James in the New Testament: (1) James, the father of Judas (not Iscariot), is mentioned twice (Luke 6:16; Acts 1:13) as the father of one of the 12, but is otherwise completely unknown. (2) James, the son of Alphaeus (Matt. 10:3; Mark 3:18; Luke 6:15; Acts 1:13), elsewhere called James the Less (Mark 15:40), was one of the 12 disciples. Apart from being listed with the other disciples, this James is completely obscure, and it is doubtful that he is the authoritative figure behind the epistle. Some attempts have been made to identify this James with the Lord's brother (Gal. 1:19), but this view is difficult to reconcile with the gospel accounts. (3) James, the son of Zebedee and brother of John (Matt. 4:21; 10:2; 17:1; Mark 3:17; 10:35; 13:3; Luke 9:54; Acts 1:13), was one of Jesus' intimate disciples, but his martyrdom by A.D. 44 (Acts 12:2) makes it very unlikely that he wrote this epistle. (4) James, the Lord's brother (Matt. 13:55; Mark 6:3; Gal. 1:19), was one of the "pillars" in the church in Jerusalem (Acts 12:17; 15:13-21; 21:18; Gal. 2:9,12). Tradition points to this prominent figure as the author of the epistle, and this best fits the evidence of Scripture. There are several clear parallels between the language of the letter drafted under his leadership in Acts 15:23-29 and the epistle of James (e.g., the unusual word *chairein*, "greetings" is found only in Acts 15:23; 23:26—and James 1:1). The Jewish character of this epistle with its stress upon the law, along with the evident influence by the Sermon on the Mount (e.g., 4:11,12; 5:12), complement what we know about James "the Just" from Scripture and early tradition.

It has been argued that the Greek of this epistle is too sophisticated for a Galilean like James, but this assumes that he never had the opportunity or aptitude to develop proficiency in *Koine* ("common") Greek. As a prominent church leader, it would have been to his advantage to become fluent in the universal language of the Roman Empire.

For various reasons, some assert that James was a step-brother of Jesus by a previous marriage of Joseph, or that the "brothers" of Jesus mentioned in Matthew 13:55 and Mark 6:3 were really His cousins. However, the most natural under-standing of the gospel accounts is that James was the half-brother of Jesus, being the offspring of Joseph and Mary after the birth of Jesus (cf. Matt. 1:24,25). He apparently did not accept the claims of Jesus until the Lord appeared to him after His resurrection (1 Cor. 15:7). He and his brothers were among the believers who awaited the coming of the Holy Spirit on the day of Pentecost (Acts 1:14). It was not long before he became an acknowledged leader of the Jerusalem church (Acts 12:17; Gal. 2:9,12), and he was a central figure in the Jerusalem Council in Acts 15. Even after Paul's third missionary journey, James continued to observe the Mosaic law as a testimony to other Jews (Acts 21:18-25). Early tradition stresses his Jewish piety and his role in bringing others to an understanding of Jesus as the Messiah. He evidently suffered a violent martyr's death not long before the fall of Jerusalem.

The brevity and limited doctrinal emphasis of James kept it from wide circulation, and by the time it became known in the church as a whole, there was uncertainty about the identity of the James in 1:1. Growing recognition that it was written by the Lord's brother led to its acceptance as a canonical book.

Date and Setting—James is addressed "to the twelve tribes who are dispersed abroad" (1:1), and it is apparent from verses like 1:19; 2:1,7 that this refers to Hebrew Christians out-side of Palestine. Their place of meeting is called a "synagogue" in the Greek text of 2:2, and the whole epistle reflects Jewish thought and expressions (e.g., 2:19,21; 4:11,12; 5:4,12). There are no references to slavery or idolatry, and this also fits an originally Jewish readership.

These Jewish believers were beset with problems that were testing their faith, and James was concerned that they were succumbing to impatience, bitterness, materialism, disunity, and spiritual apathy. As a resident of Jerusalem and a leader of the church, James no doubt had frequent contact with Jewish

Christians from a number of Roman provinces. He therefore felt a responsibility to exhort and encourage them in their struggles of faith.

According to Josephus, James was martyred in A.D. 62 (Hegesippus, quoted in Eusebius, fixed it at A.D. 66). Those who accept him as the author of this epistle have proposed a date of writing ranging from A.D. 45 to the end of his life. But there are several reasons for thinking that this may be the earliest book of the New Testament (c. 46-49): (1) There is no mention of Gentile Christians or their relationship to Jewish Christians as would be expected in a later epistle. (2) Apart from references to the person of Christ, there is practically no distinctive Christian theology in James, suggesting an early date when Christianity was viewed in terms of Messianic Judaism. (3) The allusions to the teachings of Christ have such little verbal agreement with the synoptic gospels that they probably preceded them. (4) James uses the word "synagogue" ("assembly," 2:2) in addition to "church" and indicates a very simple organization of elders and teachers (3:1; 5:14) which was patterned after the early synagogue. (5) The expectation of the imminent return of the Lord (5:7-9) is consistent with an early date. (6) James does not mention the issues involved in the Acts 15 Council in Jerusalem (A.D. 49).

Theme and Purpose—Throughout his epistle, James

develops the theme of the characteristics of true faith. He effectively uses these characteristics as a series of tests to help his readers evaluate the reality of their relationship to Christ. The purpose of this work is not doctrinal or apologetic but practical, as James seeks to challenge these believers to examine the quality of their daily lives in terms of attitudes and actions. A genuine faith will produce real changes in a person's conduct and character, and the absence of change is a symptom of a dead faith.

Contribution to the Bible—Martin Luther took a

dim view of James and called it "a right strawy epistle" compared to other New Testament books that bear clearer testimony to the work of Christ and the way of salvation. But James and Paul are supplementary, not contradictory, and this epistle assumes a knowledge of these doctrines on the part of the readers. Because of its very practical nature, James has little formal theology, but it is not devoid of doctrinal statements (see 1:12,13,17,18; 2:1,10-13,19; 3:9; 4:5; 5:7-9).

James writes with a very concise, authoritative, and unvarnished style. Combining the pithy maxims of wisdom literature with the impassioned rhetoric of Amos, James' pointed barbs are borne out of an uncompromising ethical stance. His Greek is of a good quality and he communicates his thoughts effectively by means of vivid imagery (especially from nature), illustrations, and figures of speech. Unlike Paul, James says nothing about his personal circumstances. This is a formal and sometimes severe epistle, authoritatively written and full of imperatives (54 in only 108 verses). Nevertheless, its liberal use of "[my] brethren" (11 times) and "my beloved brethren" (3 times) tempers the harshness with warmth and concern.

James was probably written before or during Paul's first missionary journey at a time when the church was almost exclusively made up of Jewish believers. This explains its strong Jewish perspective with its abundant references to the law and Old Testament imagery (James alludes to 22 Old Testament books).

As the most practical book in the New Testament, James is as relevant today as it was in the first century. Its exhortations concerning trials and temptations, response to the Word, preferential treatment because of social status, control of the tongue, and the lure of worldliness are strongly needed in the contemporary church.

James 3:15-17 describes human and divine wisdom in terms strikingly similar to those found in the book of Proverbs. Human wisdom is *earthly* (Prov. 14:2), *natural* (Prov. 7:18), *demonic* (Prov. 27:20), *jealous* (Prov. 6:34), *selfish* (Prov. 28:25), *disorderly* (Prov. 11:29), and *evil* (Prov. 8:13). By contrast, divine wisdom is *pure* (Prov. 15:26), *peaceable* (Prov. 3:1,2), *gentle* (Prov. 11:2), *reasonable* (Prov. 14:15), *full of mercy and good fruits* (Prov. 11:17; 3:18), *unwavering* (Prov. 21:6), and *without hypocrisy* (Prov. 28:13).

Christ in James—In 1:1 and 2:1 James refers to the "Lord Jesus Christ," and in 5:7,8 he anticipates "the coming of the Lord." Compared to other New Testament writers, James says little about Christ, and yet his speech is virtually saturated with

allusions to the teaching of Christ. The Sermon on the Mount is especially prominent in James' thinking (there are about 15 indirect references; e.g., Jas. 1:2 and Matt. 5:10-12; Jas. 1:4 and Matt. 5:48; Jas. 2:13 and Matt. 6:14,15; Jas. 4:11 and Matt. 7:1,2; Jas. 5:2 and Matt. 6:19). This epistle portrays Christ in the context of early Messianic Judaism.

1 Peter

"For you have been called for this purpose, since Christ also suffered for you, leaving you an example for you to follow in His steps."

1 Peter 2:21 (Also see 1:3; 4:12,13.)

Focus	Salvation			Sub-mission	Suffering		
	1:1 2:10			2:11 3:12	3:13 5:14		
D i v i s i o n s	Salutation	Salvation and Security of Believers	Sanctification of Believers	Submission of Believers	Suffering of Believers	Shepherding and Steadfastness of Believers	Statement of Theme and Greetings
	1:1 1:2 1:3 1:12		1:13 2:10	2:11 3:12	3:13 4:19	5:1 5:11	5:12 5:14
T o p i c s	Hope	Holiness		Harmony	Hardship	Humility	
	Attainment of Believers			Appeal to Believers	Attitude and Actions of Believers		
	"For you have been called for this purpose . . ."			"since Christ also suffered for you . . ."	"leaving you an example for you to follow in His steps" (2:21)		
	Calling	Character		Conduct			
Loca-tion	Probably Rome, Possibly Babylon						
Time	About A.D. 63-64						

Talk Thru—Peter addressed this epistle to "aliens and strangers" in a world that was growing increasingly hostile to Christians. These believers were beginning to suffer because of their stand for Christ, and Peter used this letter to give them counsel and comfort by stressing the reality of their living hope in the Lord. By standing firm in the grace of God (5:12) they would be able to endure their "fiery ordeal" (4:12), knowing that there was a divine purpose behind their pain. This letter logically proceeds through the themes of salvation (1:1-2:10), submission (2:11-3:12), and suffering (3:13-5:14).

Salvation (1:1-2:10): Addressing his letter to believers in several Roman provinces, Peter briefly describes the saving work of the triune Godhead in his salutation (1:1,2). He then extols God for the riches of this salvation by looking in three temporal directions (1:3-12). First, Peter anticipates the future realization of the Christian's manifold inheritance (1:3-5). Second, he looks at the present joy that this living hope produces in spite of various trials (1:6-9). Third, he reflects upon the prophets of the past who predicted the gospel of God's grace in Christ (1:10-12).

The proper response to this salvation is the pursuit of sanctification or holiness (1:13-2:10). This involves a purifying departure *from* conformity with the world *to* godliness in behavior and love. With this in mind, Peter exhorts his readers to "grow in respect to salvation" by applying the "living and abiding word of God" and acting as a holy priesthood of believers.

Submission (2:11-3:12): Peter turns to the believer's relationships in the world and appeals for an attitude of submission as the Christlike way to harmony and true freedom. Submission for the Lord's sake to those in governmental (2:13-17) and social (2:18-20) authority will foster a good testimony to outsiders. Before moving on to submission in marital relationships (3:1-7), Peter again picks up the theme of Christian suffering (mentioned in 1:6,7 and 2:12,18-20) and uses Christ as the supreme model: He suffered sinlessly, silently, and as a substitute for the salvation of others (2:21-25; cf. Isaiah 52:13-53:12). Peter summarizes his appeal for Christlike submission and humility in 3:8-11.

Suffering (3:13-5:14): Anticipating that growing opposition

172

to Christianity will require a number of his readers to defend their faith and conduct, Peter encourages them to be ready to do so in an intelligent and gracious way (3:13-16). Three times he tells them that if they must suffer, it should be for righteousness' sake and not as a result of sinful behavior (3:17; see 2:20; 4:15,16). The end of this chapter (3:18-22) is an extremely difficult passage to interpret, and several options have been offered. Verses 19 and 20 may mean that Christ addressed demonic spirits or the spirits of those who were alive before the flood between His death and resurrection, or it may mean that Christ preached through Noah to his pre-flood contemporaries. Verse 21 teaches that the inner attitude of repentance and identification with the work of Christ saves a person, and this attitude is reflected in water baptism.

As believers in Christ, the readers are no longer to pursue the lusts of the flesh as they did formerly, but rather the will of God (4:1-6). In view of the hardships that they may suffer, Peter exhorts them to be strong in their mutual love and exercise their spiritual gifts in the power of God so that they will be built up (4:7-11). They should not be surprised when they are slandered and reviled for their faith because the sovereign God has a purpose in all things, and the time of judgment will come when His name and all who trust in Him will be vindicated (4:12-19). They must therefore "entrust their souls to a faithful Creator in doing what is right" (4:19).

In a special word to the elders of the churches in these Roman provinces, Peter urges them to be diligent but gentle shepherds over the flocks which have been divinely placed under their care (5:1-4). The readers as a whole are told to clothe themselves with humility toward one another and toward God who will exalt them at the proper time (5:5-7). They are to resist the adversary in the sure knowledge that their calling to God's eternal glory in Christ will be realized (5:8-11). Peter ends his epistle by stating his theme ("the true grace of God") and conveying greetings and a benediction (5:12-14).

Title—This epistle begins with the phrase *Petros apostolos Iesou Christou*, "Peter, an apostle of Jesus Christ." This is the basis of the early title *Petrou A*, the "First of Peter."

Author—The early church universally acknowledged the authenticity and authority of 1 Peter. The internal evidence supports this consistent external testimony in several ways. The apostle Peter's name is given in 1:1, and there are definite similarities between certain phrases in this letter and Peter's sermons in the book of Acts (compare 1 Pet. 1:20 and Acts 2:23; 1 Pet. 4:5 and Acts 10:42). Twice in Acts Peter used the Greek word *xylon*, "wood, tree," to speak of the cross, and this distinctive use is also found in 1 Peter (see Acts 5:30; 10:39; 1 Pet. 2:24). There are a number of allusions in this epistle to events in the life of Christ that had special significance to Peter (e.g., 2:23; 3:18; 4:1; 5:1; cf. 5:5 and John 13:4).

Nevertheless, critics since the 19th century have challenged the authenticity of 1 Peter on several grounds. Some claim that 1:1,2 and 4:12-5:14 were later additions that turned an anonymous address or a baptismal sermon into a Petrine epistle. Others argue that the sufferings experienced by readers of this letter must refer to the persecution of Christians that took place after the time of Peter in the reigns of the emperors Domitian (81-96) or Trajan (98-117). There is no basis for the first argument, and the second argument falsely assumes that Christians were not being reviled for their faith during the life of Peter. Another challenge asserts that the quality of the Greek of this epistle is too high for a Galilean like Peter. But Galileans were bilingual (Aramaic and Greek), and writers like Matthew and James were skillful in their use of Greek. It is also likely that Peter used Silvanus as his scribe (5:12; Paul calls him Silvanus in 2 Cor. 1:19; 1 Thess. 1:1; 2 Thess. 1:1; Luke calls him Silas in Acts 15:40-18:5), and Silvanus may have smoothed out Peter's speech in the process.

Date and Setting—This letter is addressed to "those who reside as aliens," or more literally, "sojourners of the dispersion" (1:1). This, coupled with the injunction to keep their behavior "excellent among the Gentiles" (2:12), gives the initial appearance that the bulk of the readers were Hebrew Christians. A closer look, however, forms the opposite view that most of these believers were Gentiles. They were "called out of darkness" (2:9), and they "once were not a people," but now they are the people of God (2:10). Their former "way of life inherited from [their] forefathers" was characterized by ignorance and futility (1:14,18; cf. Eph. 4:17). Because they no longer engage in debauchery and idolatry, they are maligned by their countrymen (4:3,4). These descriptions do not fit a predominantly Hebrew Christian readership. Though Peter was an apostle to the circumcision (Gal. 2:9), he also ministered to Gentiles (Acts 10:34-48; Gal. 2:12), and a letter like this would not be beyond the scope of his ministry.

This epistle was addressed to Christians throughout Asia Minor, indicating the spread of the gospel in regions not evangelized in Acts (Pontus, Cappadocia, Bithynia; 1:1). It is possible that Peter visited and ministered in some of these areas, but there is no evidence. He wrote this letter in response to the news of growing opposition to the believers in Asia Minor (1:6; 3:13-17; 4:12-19; 5:9,10). Hostility and suspicion were mounting against Christians in the empire, and they were being reviled and abused for their lifestyles and subversive talk about another Kingdom. Christianity had not yet received the official Roman ban, but the stage was being set for the persecution and martyrdom of the near future.

Peter's life was dramatically changed after the resurrection, and he occupied a central role in the early church and in the spread of the gospel to the Samaritans and Gentiles (Acts 2-10). After the Acts 15 Jerusalem Council, little is recorded of Peter's activities. He evidently traveled extensively with his wife (1 Cor. 9:5) and ministered in various Roman provinces. According to tradition, Peter was crucified upside down in Rome before Nero's death in A.D. 68.

This epistle was written from "Babylon" (5:13), but scholars are divided as to whether this refers literally to Babylon in Mesopotamia or symbolically to Rome. There is no tradition that Peter went to Babylon, and in his day it had few inhabitants. On the other hand, tradition consistently indicates that Peter spent the last years of his life in Rome. As a center of idolatry, the term "Babylon" was an appropriate figurative designation for Rome (compare the later use of Babylon in Rev. 17-18). Peter used other figurative expressions in this epistle (e.g., "dispersion" in 1:1 and "she" in 5:13) and it is not surprising that he would do the same with Rome. His mention of Mark (5:13) also fits this view because Mark was in Rome during Paul's first imprisonment (Col. 4:10). This epistle was probably written shortly before the outbreak of persecution under Nero in A.D. 64.

Theme and Purpose—The basic theme of 1 Peter is the proper response to Christian suffering. Knowing that his readers would be facing more persecution than ever before, Peter wrote this letter to give them a divine perspective on these trials so that they would be able to endure them without wavering in their faith. They should not be surprised at their ordeal because the One they follow also suffered and died (2:21; 3:18; 4:1,12-14). Rather, they should count it a privilege to share the sufferings of Christ. Peter therefore exhorts them to be sure that their hardships are not being caused by their own wrongdoings, but for their Christian testimony. They are not the only believers who are suffering (5:9), and they must recognize that God brings these things in the lives of His children not as a punishment but as a stimulus to growth in Christlikeness. Peter wanted to overcome an attitude of bitterness and anxiety and replace it with dependence on and confidence in God.

Another theme is stated in 5:12: "I have written to you briefly, exhorting and testifying that this is the true grace of God." In this epistle, Peter frequently speaks of the believer's position in Christ and future hope, and he does so to remind his readers that they are merely sojourners on this planet—their true destiny is eternal glory at the revelation of Jesus Christ. The grace of God in their *salvation* (1:1-2:10) should give them an attitude of *submission* (2:11-3:12) in the context of *suffering* for the name of Christ (3:13-5:14).

Contribution to the Bible—There are evidences of Pauline influence in the style and content of 1 Peter. Peter knew Paul and his epistles, but the similarities do not imply that Peter was dependent on Paul, since both men shared common apostolic doctrine. Peter wrote this letter with real warmth and sympathy for the plight of his readers, but this does not diminish its forcefulness. The chain of 34 imperatives from 1:13 to 5:9 is highly authoritative, yet borne out of a heart of compassion. In some ways, 1 Peter is the Job of the New Testament because of its theme of undeserved suffering and steadfast submission to the sovereignty of God. This epistle,

like Peter's sermon in Acts 2, reveals a thorough acquaintance with the Old Testament and an effective use of its contents. It is also characterized by a number of allusions to Peter's personal experiences with Christ and to the future prospect of all believers in Christ. Passages like 1:2-12, 18-20; 2:21-25; 3:18-22; 4:12-19 make a significant contribution to the theology of the New Testament.

Christ in 1 Peter

—This epistle presents Christ as the believer's example and hope in times of suffering in a spiritually hostile world. He is the basis for the Christian's "living hope" and inheritance (1:3,4), and the love relationship available with Him by faith is a source of inexpressible joy (1:8). His suffering and death provide redemption for all who trust in Him: "and He Himself bore our sins in His body on the cross, that we might die to sin and live to righteousness; for by His wounds you were healed" (2:24; cf. 1:18,19; 3:18). Christ is the Chief Shepherd and Guardian of believers (2:25; 5:4), and when He appears, those who know Him will be glorified.

2 Peter

"And so we have the prophetic word made more sure, to which you do well to pay attention as to a lamp shining in a dark place, until the day dawns and the morning star arises in your hearts."

2 Peter 1:19 (Also see 1:13; 3:11,18.)

Focus	Progress 1			Peril 2			Parousia 3		
Divisions	Greetings	Growth in Christ	Ground of Belief	Danger and Deeds of False Teachers	Doom of False Teachers	Description of False Teachers	Mockery in the Last Days	Manifestation of the Day of the Lord	Maturity in View of the Day of the Lord
	1:1　1:2	1:3　1:11	1:12　1:21	2:1　2:3a	2:3b　2:9	2:10　2:22	3:1　3:7	3:8　3:13	3:14　3:18
Topics	Development in the Truth			Denunciation of Error			Day of the Lord		
	Confidence			Conflict			Consummation		
	Holiness			Heresy			Hope		
	Walking	Witness-ing		Warning			Waiting		
Location	Probably Rome								
Time	About A.D. 64-66								

Talk Thru—Peter wrote his first epistle to encourage the proper response among his readers to *external* opposition. His second epistle focuses on *internal* opposition caused by false teachers whose "destructive heresies" (2:1) can seduce believers into error and immorality. While 1 Peter speaks of the new *birth* through the living Word, 2 Peter stresses the need for *growth* in the grace and knowledge of Christ. The best antidote for error is a mature understanding of the truth. Peter opens his epistle with an appeal for progress in Christian maturity (1) and follows this with a piercing description of the peril caused by false teachers (2). The third chapter anticipates the awaited *parousia* (coming or advent) of Christ and its implications for unbelievers and believers.

Progress (1): Peter's salutation (1:1,2) is really an introduction to the major theme of chapter 1—the true knowledge of Jesus Christ. The readers are reminded of the "precious and magnificent promises" which are theirs because of their calling to faith in Christ (1:3,4). They have been called away from the corruption of the world to conformity with Christ, and Peter urges them to progress in their growth by forging a chain of eight Christian virtues from faith to love (1:5-7). If a believer does not transform profession into practice, he becomes spiritually useless, perverting the purpose for which he was called (1:8-11).

This letter was written not long before Peter's death (1:14) to remind believers of the riches of their position in Christ and their responsibility to hold fast to the truth (1:12-21). Peter knew that his "exodus" or departure from this earth was imminent, and he left this letter as a written legacy. As an eyewitness of the life of Christ (he illustrates this with a portrait of the transfiguration in 1:16-18), Peter affirms the authority and reliability of the prophetic word. The clearest biblical description of the divine-human process of inspiration is found in 1:21: "men moved by the Holy Spirit spoke from God."

Peril (2): Peter's discussion of true prophecy leads him to an extended denunciation of false prophecy in the churches. These false teachers were especially dangerous because they arose within the church and exploited the confidence of believers (2:1-3a). Nevertheless, God will deliver His own and punish those who seek to destroy their faith. This truth is vividly illustrated in three examples from the book of Genesis (2:3b-9).

Peter's extended description of the characteristics of these false teachers (2:10-22) exposes the futility and corruption of their strategies. Their teachings and lifestyles reek of arrogance and selfishness, but their crafty words are capable of enticing immature believers.

Parousia (3): Again Peter states that this letter is designed to stir up the minds of his readers "by way of reminder" (3:1; cf. 1:13). This very timely chapter is designed to remind them of the certain truth of the imminent parousia (this Greek word, used in 3:4,12, refers to the second coming or advent of Christ) and to refute those mockers who will deny this doctrine in the last days. These scoffers will claim that God does not powerfully intervene in world affairs, but Peter calls attention to three (two past and one future) divinely-induced catastrophic events: creation, the flood, and the dissolution of the present heavens and earth (3:1-7). It may appear that the promise of Christ's return will not be fulfilled, but this is untrue for two reasons: God's perspective on the passing of time is quite unlike that of men, and the apparent delay is due to His patience in waiting for more to come to a knowledge of Christ (3:8,9). Nevertheless, the day of consummation *will* come, and all the matter of this universe will evidently be transformed into energy from which God will fashion a new cosmos (3:10-13).

In light of this coming day of the Lord, Peter exhorts his readers to lives of holiness, steadfastness, and growth (3:14-18). He mentions the letters of "our beloved brother Paul" and significantly places them on a level with the Old Testament Scriptures (3:15,16). After a final warning about the danger of false teachers, the epistle closes with an appeal to growth and a doxology.

Title—The statement of authorship in 1:1 is very clear: "Simon Peter, a bond-servant and apostle of Jesus Christ." To distinguish this epistle from the first by Peter it was given the Greek title *Petrou B*, the "Second of Peter."

Author—There is no other book in the New Testament that poses as many problems of authenticity as 2 Peter. Unlike 1 Peter, this letter has very weak external testimony, and its genuineness is hurt by internal difficulties as well. Because of these obstacles, many scholars reject the Petrine authorship of

181

this epistle, but this does not mean that there is no case for the opposite position.

External Evidence: The external testimony for the Petrine authorship of 2 Peter is weaker than that for any other New Testament book, but by the fourth century it became generally recognized as an authentic work of the apostle Peter. There are no undisputed second-century quotations from 2 Peter, but in the third century it is quoted in the writings of several church fathers, notably Origen and Clement of Alexandria. Third-century writers were generally aware of 2 Peter and respected its contents, but it was still catalogued as a disputed book. The fourth century saw the official acknowledgment of the authority of 2 Peter in spite of some lingering doubts. There are several reasons why 2 Peter was not quickly accepted as a canonical book: (1) Slow circulation kept it from being widely known. (2) Its brevity and contents greatly limited the number of quotations from it in the writings of early church leaders. (3) The delay in recognition meant that 2 Peter had to compete with several later works which falsely claimed to be Petrine (e.g., the *Apocalypse of Peter*). (4) Stylistic differences between 1 and 2 Peter also raised doubts.

Internal Evidence: On the positive side, 2 Peter bears abundant testimony to its apostolic origin. It claims to be by "Simon Peter" (1:1), and 3:1 says, "This is now, beloved, the second letter I am writing to you." The writer refers to the Lord's prediction about the apostle's death in 1:14 (cf. John 21:18,19) and says he was an eyewitness of the transfiguration (1:16-18). As an apostle (1:1), he places himself on an equal level with Paul (3:15). There are also distinctive words that are found in 2 Peter and in Peter's sermons in Acts as well as unusual words and phrases shared by 1 and 2 Peter.

On the negative side, there are a number of troublesome areas that challenge the traditional position: (1) There are differences between the style and vocabulary of 1 and 2 Peter. The Greek of 2 Peter is rough and awkward compared to that of 1 Peter, and there are also differences in formality and in their use of the Old Testament. But these differences are often exaggerated, and they can be explained by Peter's use of Silvanus as his amanuensis for 1 Peter and his own hand for 2 Peter. (2) It is argued that 2 Peter used a passage from Jude to describe false teachers, and that Jude was written after Peter's death. But this is a debated issue, and it is more likely that Jude quoted from Peter (see Jude, Date and Setting). (3) The reference to a collection of Paul's letters (3:15,16) implies a late date for this epistle. But it is not necessary to conclude that all of Paul's letters were in mind here. Peter's contact with Paul and his associates no doubt made him familiar with several Pauline epistles. (4) Some claim that the false teaching in 2 Peter was a form of Gnosticism that emerged after Peter's day, but there is insufficient evidence for this.

The alternative to Petrine authorship is a later forgery done in the name of Peter. Even the claim that 2 Peter was written by a disciple of Peter cannot overcome the problem of misrepresentation. In addition, 2 Peter is clearly superior to any pseudonymous writings. In spite of the external and internal problems, the traditional position that 2 Peter is genuine overcomes more difficulties than any other option.

Date and Setting

Date and Setting—Most scholars regard 3:1 ("This is . . . the second letter I am writing to you") as a reference to 1 Peter. If this is so, Peter had the same readers of Asia Minor in mind (see 1 Peter, Date and Setting), although the more general salutation in 1:1 would also allow for a wider audience. Peter wrote this epistle in response to the spread of heretical teachings which were all the more insidious because they emerged within the churches. These false teachers perverted the doctrine of justification and promoted a rebellious and immoral way of life.

This epistle was written just before the apostle's death (1:14), probably from Rome. His martyrdom took place around A.D. 64-66 (if he were alive in 67 when Paul wrote 2 Timothy during his second Roman imprisonment, it is likely that Paul would have mentioned him).

Theme and Purpose

Theme and Purpose—The basic theme that runs through 2 Peter is the contrast between the knowledge and practice of truth versus falsehood. This epistle was written to expose the dangerous and seductive work of false teachers and to warn believers to be on their guard so that they will not be "carried away by the error of unprincipled men" (3:17). It was also written to exhort the readers to "grow in the grace and knowledge of our Lord and Savior Jesus Christ" (3:18), because this growth into Christian maturity is the best defense against spiritual counterfeits. Another purpose of this letter was to provide a "reminder" (1:12,13; 3:1,2) to the readers of the foundational elements in the Christian life from which they must not waver. This includes the certainty of the Lord's return in power and judgment.

Contribution to the Bible—While 1 Peter dealt with submission to God as the proper response to suffering from without, 2 Peter concentrates on knowledge of the truth as the proper response to error from within. The words "suffering" in 1 Peter and "knowledge" in 2 Peter appear 16 times in various forms. The "knowledge" of 2 Peter involves not only intellectual comprehension but experiential realization as well. It is based on the application of spiritual truth to growth in the life of the believer.

The two epistles of Peter can be contrasted in several ways:

1 PETER	2 PETER
External Opposition	Internal Opposition
Hostility	Heresy
Antagonism	Apostasy
Endurance	Steadfastness
Waiting	Warning
Suffering	Error
Submission	Knowledge
Comfort	Caution
Hope in the Lord's Return	Confidence in the Lord's Return
Holiness	Maturity
"Pain with a Purpose"	"Poison in the Pew"

Peter's scenario from the creation of the present heavens and earth to the dissolution of the universe and creation of the new heavens and earth is one of the most astonishing passages in all of Scripture (3:5-13).

Christ in 2 Peter—Apart from the first verse of his epistle, Peter employs the title *Lord* every time he names the Savior. The Lord Jesus Christ is the source of full knowledge and power for the attainment of spiritual maturity (1:2,3,8; 3:18). Peter recalls the glory of His transfiguration on the holy mountain and anticipates His parousia when the whole world, not just three men on a mountain, will behold His glory.

1 John

"What we have seen and heard we proclaim to you also, that you also may have fellowship with us; and indeed our fellowship is with the Father, and with His Son Jesus Christ."

1 John 1:3

"And now, little children, abide in Him, so that when He appears, we may have confidence and not shrink away from Him in shame at His coming."

1 John 2:28 (Also see 3:1; 4:1; 5:13.)

Focus	The Meaning of Fellowship 1:1 2:27				The Manifestation of Fellowship 2:28 5:21				
D I V I S I O N S	Proclamation of Fellowship (Prologue)	Prerequisites of Fellowship	Product of Fellowship	Perils to Fellowship	Manifestation of Regeneration in Righteousness	Manifestation of Righteousness in Love	Manifestations of the Indwelling God	Method for Loving	Motifs Summarized (Epilogue)
	1:1 1:4	1:5 2:2	2:3 2:11	2:12 2:27	2:28 3:10a	3:10b 3:23	3:24 4:19	4:20 5:17	5:18-21
T O P I C S	The Basis of Fellowship				The Behavior of Fellowship				
	Conditions		Conduct and Conflict		Characteristics			Confirmation	
	Foundation		Fruit		Fulfillment			Faith	
	Abiding in God's Light				Abiding in God's Love 4:21			Abiding in 5:1 God's Life	
Loca-tion	Written in Ephesus								
Time	About A.D. 90								

187

Talk Thru—John wrote his first epistle at a time when apostolic doctrine was being challenged by a proliferation of false teachings. Like 2 Peter and Jude, 1 John has a negative and a positive thrust: it refutes erroneous doctrine and encourages its readership to walk in the knowledge of the truth. John lists the criteria and characteristics of fellowship with God and shows that those who abide in Christ can have confidence and assurance before Him. This simply written but profound work develops the meaning of fellowship in 1:1-2:27 and the manifestation of fellowship in 2:28-5:21.

The Meaning of Fellowship (1:1-2:27): John's prologue (1:1-4) recalls the beginning of apostolic contact with Christ and relates his desire to transmit this apostolic witness to his readers so that they may share the same fellowship with Jesus Christ, the personification of life. This proclamation is followed by a description of the prerequisites of fellowship in 1:5-2:2. Fellowship with a God of light is made possible by the blood of Christ which cleanses the believer and propitiates (satisfies) the Father's righteous demands. Believers must walk in integrity and openness to what the light reveals, with a willingness to confess failures exposed by the light. While no specific instance of sin should be seen as inevitable in a Christian's life, complete sinlessness will not be a reality until we stand before God (cf. 3:2). These verses illustrate the typology of the tabernacle as one moves from east to west: the blood of Christ (brazen altar), cleansing (laver), light (lampstand), fellowship (showbread), confession (altar of incense), and propitiation (mercy seat).

The product of the fellowship in 1:5-2:2 is knowing Him (2:3-11; compare the Upper Room Discourse in John 13-17). This is an experiential knowledge which comes out of a walk of faith and obedience to the commandment to love one another. The believer who manifests God's love in this way is a true disciple who displays the coming light.

The readers' sins have been forgiven and they enjoy fellowship with God. As a result, they "know Him who has been from the beginning" and are strengthened to overcome the temptations of the evil one (2:12-14). The threats to fellowship are both practical (the lusts of the corrupt world system which opposes God, 2:15-17) and doctrinal (the teachings of those who differentiate between Jesus and the Christ, 2:18-23). In contrast to these "antichrists," the readers have the knowledge of the truth and an anointing from the Holy One. Therefore, it would be foolish for them to turn away from the teachings of the apostles to the innovations of the antichrists. The antidote to these heretical teachings is abiding in the apostolic truths that they heard "from the beginning" which are authenticated by the anointing they have received (2:24-27).

The Manifestation of Fellowship (2:28-5:21): The basic theme of 1 John is summarized in 2:28—assurance through abiding in Christ. The next verse introduces the motif of regeneration, and 2:29-3:10a argues that regeneration is manifested in the practice of righteousness. Because we are children of God through faith in Christ, we have a firm hope of being fully conformed to Him when He appears (3:1-3). Our present likeness to Christ places us in a position of incompatibility with sin, because sin is contrary to the person and work of Christ (3:4-6). The concept in 3:6 does not contradict 1:8 because it is saying that the abider, *insofar as he abides*, does not sin. When the believer sins, he does not reflect the regenerate new man, but Satan, the original sinner (3:7-10a).

Regeneration is manifested in righteousness (2:29-3:10a), and righteousness is manifested in love (3:10b-23). The apostle uses the example of Cain to illustrate what love is *not*: hatred is murdering in spirit, and it arises from the worldly sphere of death. John then uses the example of Christ to illustrate what love *is*: love is practiced in self-sacrifice, not mere profession. This practical expression of love results in assurance before God and answered prayers because the believer is walking in obedience to God's commands to believe in Christ and love one another (3:19-23).

In 3:24, John introduces two important motifs which are developed in 4:1-16: the indwelling God, and the Spirit as a mark of this indwelling. The Spirit of God confesses the incarnate Christ and confirms apostolic doctrine (4:1-6). The mutual abiding of the believer in God and God in the believer is manifested in love for others, and this love produces a divine and human fellowship that testifies to and reflects the reality of the incarnation (4:7-16). It also anticipates the perfect fellowship to come and creates a readiness to face the One from whom all love is derived (4:17-19).

John joins the concepts he has presented into a circular

chain of six links that begins with love for the brethren (4:20-5:17): (1) Love for believers is the inseparable product of love for God (4:20-5:1). (2) Love for God arises out of obedience to His commandments (5:2,3). (3) Obedience to God is the result of faith in His Son (5:4,5). (4) This faith is in Jesus, who was the Christ not only at His baptism (the water), but also at His death (the blood; 5:6-8). (5) The divine witness to the person of Christ is worthy of complete belief (5:9-13). (6) This belief produces confident access to God in prayer (5:14-17). Since intercessory prayer is a manifestation of love for others, the chain has come full circle.

The epilogue (5:18-21) summarizes the conclusions of the epistle in a series of three certainties: (1) Sin is a threat to fellowship, and should be regarded as foreign to the believer's position in Christ (compare Romans 6). (2) The believer stands with God against the Satanic world system. (3) The incarnation produces true knowledge and communion with Christ. Since He is "the true God and eternal life," the one who knows Him should avoid the lure of any substitute.

Title—Although the apostle John's name is not found in this book, it was given the title *Ioannou A*, the "First of John."

Author—The external evidence for the authorship of 1 John shows that from the beginning it was universally received without dispute as authoritative. It was used by Polycarp (who knew John in his youth) and Papias in the early second century, and Irenaeus (who knew Polycarp in his youth) specifically attributed it to the apostle John later in that century. All the Greek and Latin church fathers accepted this epistle as Johannine.

The internal evidence supports this universal tradition because the "we" (apostles), "you" (readers), and "they" (false teachers) phraseology places the writer in the sphere of the apostolic eyewitnesses (cf. 1:1-3; 4:14). John's name was well known to the readers, and it was unnecessary for him to mention it. The style and vocabulary of 1 John is so similar to that of the fourth gospel that most scholars acknowledge these books to be by the same hand (see John, Author). Both share many distinctively Johannine phrases, and the characteristics of limited vocabulary and frequent contrast of opposites are also common to them. Even so, some critics have assailed this conclusion on various grounds, but the theological and stylistic differences are not substantial enough to overcome the abundant similarities.

The traditional view is also rejected by those who hold that the fourth gospel and these three epistles were written by John the "elder" or "presbyter," who is to be distinguished from John the apostle. But the only basis for this distinction is Eusebius' interpretation in his *Ecclesiastical History* (323) of a statement by Papias. Eusebius understood the passage to refer to two distinct Johns, but the wording does not require this; the elder John and the apostle John may be one and the same. Even if they were different, there is no evidence for contradicting the consistent acknowledgment by the early church that this book was written by John the apostle.

Date and Setting—In Acts 8:14, John is associated with "the apostles in Jerusalem," and Paul calls him one of the "pillars" of the Jerusalem church in Galatians 2:9. Apart from Revelation 1, the New Testament is silent about his later years, but early Christian tradition uniformly tells us that he left Jerusalem (probably not long before its destruction in 70) and ministered in and around Ephesus. The seven churches in the Roman province of Asia mentioned in Revelation 2 and 3 were evidently a part of this ministry. Although there is no address in 1 John, it is likely that the apostle directed this epistle to the Asian churches that were within the realm of his oversight.

The believers in these congregations were well established in Christian truth, and John wrote to them not as novices but as brethren grounded in apostolic doctrine (2:7,18-27; 3:11). The apostle does not mention his own affairs, but his use of terms like "beloved" and "my little children" gives this letter a personal touch that reveals his close relationship to the original recipients. It was probably written in Ephesus after the gospel of John, but the date cannot be fixed with certainty. No persecution is mentioned, suggesting a date prior to A.D. 95 when persecution broke out in the end of Domitian's reign (81-96).

Advanced in years, John wrote this fatherly epistle out of loving concern for his "children" whose steadfastness in the truth was being threatened by the lure of worldliness and the guile of false teachers. The Gnostic heresy taught that matter is inherently evil, and a divine being could not therefore take on human flesh. This resulted in the distinction between the man Jesus and the spiritual Christ who came upon Jesus at his baptism but departed prior to his crucifixion. Another variation was Docetism (from *dokeo*, to seem), the doctrine that Christ only *seemed* to have a human body. The result in both cases was the same—a flat denial of the incarnation.

The Gnostics also believed that their understanding of the hidden knowledge (*gnosis*) made them a kind of spiritual elite who were above the normal distinctions of right and wrong. This led in most cases to deplorable conduct and complete disregard for Christian ethics.

Theme and Purpose—The major theme of 1 John is fellowship with God. John wanted his readers to have assurance of the indwelling God through their abiding relationship with Him (2:28; 5:13). Belief in Christ should be manifested in the practice of righteousness and love for the brethren which in turn produces joy and confidence before God. John wrote this epistle to encourage this kind of fellowship and to emphasize the importance of holding fast to apostolic doctrine.

First John was also written to refute the destructive teachings of the Gnostics by stressing the reality of the incarnation and the emptiness of profession without practice. These "antichrists" failed the three tests of righteous living, love for the brethren, and belief that Jesus is the Christ, the incarnate God-man.

Contribution to the Bible—The usual characteristics of a letter (salutation, address, greetings, benediction) are absent in 1 John, and some scholars regard it as a transcribed sermon. But John had a definite audience and historical situation in mind, and he composed this work ("I am writing these things to you," 2:1; cf. 1:4; 2:7,8,12-14,21,26; 5:13) with their specific interests in mind. Thus, we can regard 1 John as an epistle written in a sermonic mood.

Like the fourth gospel, John's first epistle is written with disarming simplicity of style and vocabulary. John skillfully uses this simplicity as his vehicle for expressing some of the most profound concepts in all Scripture. Certain ideas like light, love, life, truth, and righteousness are frequently repeated, not monotonously, but as developing motifs that are enriched as the epistle progresses. There is also an abundance of antithetical parallelism: light vs. darkness, truth vs. falsehood, love vs. hatred, love of the world vs. love of the Father, Christ vs. antichrists, children of God vs. children of the devil, righteousness vs. sin, the Spirit of God vs. the spirit of the antichrist, and life vs. death.

First John is characterized by its authoritative declaration of truth and stern denunciation of error, and yet a spirit of love prevails. The structure of the book is subtle, making it difficult to outline, especially because of the way John intertwines motifs. Surpisingly, there are no quotations from the Old Testament, and only one Old Testament incident is mentioned (Cain, 3:12). Finally, John's gospel and first epistle are complementary works in their contents and purposes (compare John 20:30,31 with 1 John 2:28; 5:13).

Christ in 1 John

Christ in 1 John—The present ministry of Christ is portrayed in 1:5-2:2: His blood continually cleanses the believer from all sin, and He is our righteous Advocate before the Father. This epistle lays particular stress on the incarnation of God the Son and the identity of Jesus as the Christ (2:22; 4:2,3), in refutation of Gnostic doctrine. Jesus Christ "came by water and blood" (5:6); He was the same indivisible person from the beginning (His baptism) to the end of His public ministry (His crucifixion).

2 John

"Any one who goes too far and does not abide in the teaching of Christ, does not have God; the one who abides in the teaching, he has both the Father and the Son."

2 John 9 (Also see 6.)

FOCUS	Fellowship with God: Abide		Fellowship with False Teachers: Avoid		
	1	6	7		13
D I V I S I O N S	Abiding in the Truth	Applying God's Love	Admonition Against False Teachers	Avoiding False Teachers	Anticipated Visit
	1　　　　　3	4　　　　　6	7　　　　　9	10　　　11	12　　　13
T O P I C S	Preliminary Thoughts	Practicing the Truth	Protecting the Truth		Parting Thoughts
	Commendation and Commandment		Caution		Conclusion
	Introduction	Injunctions			Intention
	Walking		Watching		
Loca-tion	Written in Ephesus				
Time	About A.D. 90				

195

Talk Thru—This little letter has much in common with 1 John, including a warning about the danger of false teachers who deny the incarnation of Jesus Christ. John encourages the readers to continue walking in love, but exhorts them to be discerning in their expression of love. Truth without love produces autocratic severity, but love without truth leads to blind sentimentality. Walking in love must not be separated from walking in truth (cf. Eph. 4:15, "speaking the truth in love"), and believers must not show hospitality to false teachers who distort the central teaching of Christianity—the person and work of Jesus Christ. After developing the theme of abiding in fellowship with God (1-6), John tells the readers to avoid fellowship with false teachers (7-13).

Fellowship with God: Abide (1-6): The preamble (1-3) centers on the concept of abiding in the truth (mentioned four times in these three verses). The author identifies himself as "the elder" and addresses this letter "to the chosen lady and her children." This designation may refer literally to a specific woman or it may be taken as a figurative reference to a local church (see Date and Setting). In either case, the recipients are loved for their adherence to the truth by "all who know the truth."

The apostle commends the readers for their walk in truth in obedience to God's commandment (4), and reminds them that this commandment entails the practice of love for one another (5,6). The divine command is given in verse 5 and the human response follows in verse 6. This may be familiar ground, but John recognizes the human tendency to forget the basics of Christian experience.

Fellowship with False Teachers: Avoid (7-13): Moving from the basic test of Christian behavior (love for the brethren) to the basic test of Christian belief (the person of Christ), John admonishes the readers to beware of deceivers "who do not acknowledge Jesus Christ as coming in the flesh" (7-9). The apostle is personally concerned for the spiritual welfare of these believers, and he does not want their reward to be diminished by any unfaithfulness to the truth. They must therefore remain unmoved by the innovations of these deceivers and abide in the apostolic teaching of Christ.

In no uncertain terms, the apostle enjoins the readers to deny even the slightest assistance or encouragement to itinerant teachers who promote an erroneous view of Christ (and hence of salvation; 10,11).

This letter closes with John's explanation for its brevity—he anticipates a future visit during which he will be able to "speak face to face" with his readers (12). The meaning of the greeting in verse 13 relates to the interpretation of verse 1.

Title—The "elder" of verse 1 has been traditionally identified with the apostle John, resulting in the Greek title *Ioannou B*, the "Second of John."

Author—Because of the similarity of the contents and circumstances of 2 and 3 John, the authorship of both will be considered here. These letters were not widely circulated at the beginning because of their brevity and their specific address to a small number of people. This limited circulation, combined with the fact that they have few distinctive ideas to add that are not found in 1 John, meant that they were seldom quoted in the patristic writings of the early church. Their place in the canon of New Testament books was disputed for a time, but it is significant that there was no question in the minds of those church fathers who lived closest to the time of John that these two epistles were written by the apostle. The second-century writers Irenaeus and Clement of Alexandria entertained no other view. It was only as the details of their origin were forgotten that doubts arose, but the positive evidence in their favor eventually won them the official recognition of the whole church.

It is obvious that the recipients of 2 and 3 John well knew the author's identity even though he did not use his name. Instead, he designated himself in the first verse of both letters as "the elder." This is no argument against the Johannine authorship of 2 and 3 John because the context of these epistles reveals that his authority was far greater than that of an elder in a local church. The apostle Peter also referred to himself as an elder (1 Pet. 5:1), and John uses the distinguishing term "*the* elder."

The similarity of style, vocabulary, structure, and mood between 2 and 3 John makes it clear that they were written by the same author. In addition, both bear strong resemblances to 1 John (especially 2 John) and to the fourth gospel. Thus, the external and internal evidence lend clear support to the traditional view that these epistles were written by the apostle John.

Date and Setting—There is a problem with the identification of the original readers of this epistle which hinges on the interpretation of "the chosen lady and her children" in verse 1. Some scholars believe the address should be taken literally to refer to a specific woman and her children, while others prefer to take it as a figurative description of a local church. Arguments for the literal view: (1) The "lady" or Kyria is mentioned two times in the singular (1,5), and her children (1,4), house (10), and sister's children (13) are also mentioned. (2) Nothing in the text suggests the use of such an allegory. It is simpler and more natural to accept it at face value. (3) If this referred to a local church, the distinction between the lady and her children would not be meaningful. (4) This figurative designation of a local church is not used elsewhere in Scripture. (5) The identical structures of 3 John 1 (definitely addressed to an individual) and 2 John 1 supports this view. Arguments for the figurative view: (1) The literal view leads to a problem of this woman's name. The "lady Electa" is not acceptable because this would also have to be the name of her sister (13). The "chosen Kyria" is better, but if "lady" is a proper name, the adjective "chosen" should follow rather than precede the name (cf. 3 John 1). In view of verse 13, the woman is probably not named, but this is strangely impersonal (contrast 3 John which names three individuals). (2) Personification was a common practice in ancient times, and it frequently occurs in the Bible. Israel is personified as a wife and a mother in Isaiah 54, and Paul portrays the universal (Eph. 5:25-29) and local church (2 Cor. 11:2,3) as a woman (also see 1 Pet. 5:13). (3) The wide reputation of the "lady and her children" suggested in verse 1 fits a prominent church better than a specific household. (4) The injunction to love one another and to guard against the coming of false teachers is more appropriate to an epistle addressed to a church. (5) The pronouns in verses 8, 10, and 12 are plural.

The evidence is insufficient for a decisive conclusion, but in either case, the readers were well known to John and probably lived in the province of Asia, not far from Ephesus. If the figurative view is taken, "the children of your chosen sister"

(13) refers to the members of a sister church.

In his first epistle, John wrote that a number of false teachers split away from the church ("they went out from us, but they were not really of us," 2:19). Some of these became traveling teachers who depended on the hospitality of individuals while they sought to infiltrate churches with their teachings.

Judging by the content and circumstances of 2 John, it was evidently contemporaneous with 1 John or written slightly later. All three of John's epistles may have been written in Ephesus (see 1 John, Date and Setting).

Theme and Purpose — The basic theme of this brief letter
is steadfastness in the practice and purity of the apostolic doctrine that the readers "have heard from the beginning" (6). John wrote it as a reminder to continue walking in obedience to God's commandment to love one another (practical exhortation, 4-6). He also wrote it as a warning not to associate with or assist teachers who do not acknowledge the truth about Jesus Christ (doctrinal exhortation, 7-11).

It has been suggested that 2 and 3 John were written as covering letters for 1 John to provide a personal word to a church (2 John) and to Gaius (3 John) that would supplement the longer epistle. However, there is no way to be sure.

Contribution to the Bible — All three of John's epistles develop the theme of fellowship. The first focuses on fellowship with God, the second on fellowship with enemies of the truth, and the third on fellowship with proclaimers of the truth.

This letter is the second shortest book in the Bible (3 John is slightly shorter), and it originally fit on a single sheet of papyrus paper. The first six verses are positive in nature, mentioning "truth" five times and "love" four times. The last half of the letter is a negative warning, and these two words are not mentioned at all. If the literal view of "chosen lady" is taken, 2 John is the only biblical book that is addressed to a woman.

Christ in 2 John — John refutes the same error regarding the person of Christ in this epistle as he did in his first epistle.

Again he stresses that "those who do not acknowledge Jesus Christ as coming in the flesh" (7) are deceivers who must be avoided. One must "abide in the teaching of Christ" (9) to have a relationship with God. The doctrine of the person and work of Jesus Christ affects every other area of theology.

3 John

"I have no greater joy than this, to hear of my children walking in the truth. Beloved, you are acting faithfully in whatever you accomplish for the brethren, and especially when they are strangers."

3 John 4,5 (Also see 11.)

Focus	Commendation of Gaius		Condemnation of Diotrephes		
	1 ——— 8		9 ——— 14		
DIVISIONS	Godliness of Gaius	Generosity of Gaius	Rebellion of Diotrephes	Recommendation of Demetrius	Remarks of John
	1 ——— 4	5 ——— 8	9 ——— 11	12	13 ——— 14
TOPICS	Prosperity	Participation	Pride	Praise	Parting
	Fellowship	Faithfulness	Faithless-ness	Faithful-ness	Farewell
	Salutation	Servanthood	Selfishness	Selflessness	
	Gaius		Diotrephes	Demetrius	John
Loca-tion	Written in Ephesus				
Time	About A.D. 90				

Talk Thru—Third John is the shortest book in the Bible, but it is very personal and vivid. It offers a stark contrast between two men who responded in opposite ways to the itinerant teachers who had been sent out by the apostle. The faithful Gaius responded with generosity and hospitality, but the faithless Diotrephes responded with arrogance and opposition. Thus, John wrote this letter to commend Gaius for walking in the truth (1-8) and to condemn Diotrephes for walking in error (9-14).

Commendation of Gaius (1-8): The "elder" writes to one of his beloved "children" whose godly behavior has given the apostle great joy (1-4). Because of the reports John has received about Gaius' adherence to the truth, the apostle can confidently state that he wishes Gaius' temporal journey to reflect his spiritual prosperity.

The "brethren," upon returning to John, informed him of Gaius' faithfulness, love, and generosity on their behalf. The apostle acknowledges these actions and urges Gaius to continue supporting traveling teachers and missionaries who go out "for the sake of the Name" (5-8). These men accept no funds from unbelievers ("the Gentiles," 7) but depend entirely upon the hospitality of faithful Christians like Gaius. He is therefore encouraged to further participate in their ministries.

Condemnation of Diotrephes (9-14): The epistle suddenly shifts to a negative note as John describes a man whose actions are diametrically opposed to those of Gaius (9-11). Diotrephes boldly rejects John's apostolic authority and refuses to receive the itinerant teachers sent out by the apostle. According to Colossians 1:18, only Christ should "have first place" (*proteuon*), but the autocratic Diotrephes "loves to be first" (*philoproteuon*, 3 John 9). John anticipates the need to exercise his divinely given authority by confronting Diotrephes for slandering his emissaries and excommunicating those who wish to receive them. Diotrephes was evidently not unorthodox in his doctrine, but his evil actions indicated a blindness to God in his practice.

By contrast, John gives his full recommendation to Demetrius, another emissary and probably the bearer of this letter to Gaius (12). The closing remarks (13,14) are very similar to those of 2 John as John expresses his hope of a personal visit.

Title—The Greek titles of 1, 2, and 3 John are *Ioannou A, B,* and *G.* The *G* is gamma, the third letter of the Greek alphabet; *Ioannou G* means the "Third of John."

Author—The authorship of 2 and 3 John was considered together because the contents and circumstances of both books are similar (see 2 John, Author). Although the external evidence for 2 and 3 John is limited (there is even less for 3 John than for 2 John), what little there is consistently points to the apostle John. The internal evidence is stronger, and it, too, supports the apostolic origin of both letters.

Date and Setting—The parallels between 2 and 3 John suggest that these epistles were written at about the same time (c. 90). Early Christian writers are unified in their testimony that the headquarters of John's later ministry was in Ephesus, the principal city of the Roman province of Asia (see 1 John, Date and Setting). John evidently commissioned a number of traveling teachers to spread the gospel and solidify the Asian churches, and these teachers were supported by believers who received them into their homes.

Third John was occasioned by the report of some of these emissaries (called "brethren" in this letter) who returned to the apostle and informed him of the hospitality of Gaius and the hostility of Diotrephes. The arrogant Diotrephes seized the reins of an Asian church and vaunted himself as its preeminent authority. He therefore maligned John's authority and rejected the teachers sent out by John, even expelling those in his church who wanted to receive them. This letter, probably carried by Demetrius, another of John's emissaries (12), encourages Gaius to continue supporting such men in spite of Diotrephes' opposition. It also announces John's intention of a personal visit to deal with the situation.

Gaius was a common name in the Roman Empire, and three other men by that name are mentioned in the New Testament: (1) Gaius, one of Paul's traveling companions from Macedonia (Acts 19:29), (2) Gaius of Derbe (Acts 20:4), and (3) Gaius, Paul's host in Corinth, one of the few Corinthians Paul baptized (Rom. 16:23; 1 Cor. 1:14). The Gaius of 3 John evidently lived in Asia, and it is best to distinguish him from these other men.

In verse 9, John alludes to a previous letter that was spurned by Diotrephes. This may be 1 or 2 John, but it is more likely a lost letter, perhaps destroyed by Diotrephes.

Theme and Purpose—The basic theme of this letter is the contrast between the truth and servanthood of Gaius and the error and selfishness of Diotrephes. Moving through 3 John, five specific purposes can be discerned from its contents: (1) to commend Gaius for his adherence to the truth and his hospitality to the emissaries sent out by John (1-6a); (2) to encourage Gaius to continue his support of these brethren (6b-8); (3) to rebuke Diotrephes for his pride and misconduct (9-11); (4) to provide a recommendation for Demetrius (12); and (5) to inform Gaius of John's intention to visit and straighten out the difficulties (10a,13,14).

Contribution to the Bible—This epistle is characteristically Johannine, emphasizing the themes of love, truth, and joy which are so prominent in John's gospel and other epistles. The length, style, and mood of 2 and 3 John are quite similar. Both epistles use similar phraseology and structure:

2 JOHN	3 JOHN
"Love" (4 times)	"Love" (2 times), "beloved" (4 times)
"Truth" (5 times)	"Truth" (6 times)
"The elder . . . whom I love in truth" (1)	"The elder . . . whom I love in truth" (1)
Expresses joy over the report of the readers	Expresses joy over the report of the reader
"Walking in truth" (4)	"Walking in truth" (3,4)
Warns against hospitality to enemies of the truth	Encourages hospitality to teachers of the truth
Commendation followed by rebuke	Commendation followed by rebuke
Condemnation of bad doctrine	Condemnation of bad conduct
Short letter due to planned visit (12)	Short letter due to planned visit (13,14)

While 2 and 3 John do not make any real doctrinal contributions to the Bible that are not found in 1 John, they give important insights into the life and struggles of the church at the close of the apostolic age. Even the churches that were under the care of the apostle John were constantly threatened by unorthodox doctrine and conduct.

In spite of its brevity, 3 John skillfully develops the characters of Gaius and Diotrephes with surprising vividness. This letter gives us a glimpse into the kind of frank and personal correspondence that the apostle John and other early Christian leaders maintained.

Christ in 3 John—Unlike 1 and 2 John, 3 John makes no mention of the name of Jesus Christ. But verse 5 says "they went out for the sake of *the Name*," an indirect reference to our Lord (compare Acts 5:41 where the identical Greek construction is used to refer back to "the name of Jesus" in Acts 5:40). The concept of "truth" runs throughout this letter, and Christ is the source and incarnation of truth, as is obvious from John's other writings.

Jude

"Beloved, while I was making every effort to write you about our common salvation, I felt the necessity to write to you appealing that you contend earnestly for the faith which was once for all delivered to the saints."

Jude 3 (Also see 20,21.)

Focus	Announcement of Apostasy		Anatomy of Apostasy		Antidote to Apostasy	
	1 4		5 16		17 25	
D I V I S I O N S	Designation of Author and Readers	Danger of Apostates	Doom of Apostates Illustrated	Description of Apostates	Duty of Believers	Doxology
	1 2	3 4	5 7	8 16	17 23	24 25
T O P I C S	Emergency		Examples	Exposition	Exhortation	Encouragement
	Purpose of the Letter		Portrait of the False Teachers		Practice of the Truth	
	Occasion		Opposition		Obligations	
	Contention		Condemnation		Counsel	
Location	Place of Writing Unknown					
Time	A.D. 66-80					

Talk Thru—A surprisingly large number of the Pauline and non-Pauline epistles confront the problem of false teachers, and almost all of them allude to it. But Jude goes beyond all other New Testament epistles in its relentless and passionate denunciation of the apostate teachers who have "crept in unnoticed." With the exception of its salutation (1,2) and doxology (24,25), the entire epistle revolves around this alarming problem. Combining the theme of 2 Peter with the style of James, Jude is potent in spite of its brevity. This urgent letter has three major sections: Announcement of Apostasy (1-4), Anatomy of Apostasy (5-16), and Antidote to Apostasy (17-25).

Announcement of Apostasy (1-4): Jude addresses his letter to believers who are called, beloved, and kept, and wishes for them the threefold blessing of mercy, peace, and love (1,2). Grim news about the encroachment of false teachers in the churches impelled Jude to put aside his commentary on salvation to write this timely word of rebuke and warning (3,4). In view of apostates who "turn the grace of our God into licentiousness" and deny Christ, it is crucial that believers "contend earnestly for the faith."

Anatomy of Apostasy (5-16): Jude begins his extended exposé of the apostate teachers by illustrating their ultimate doom with three examples of divine judgment from the Pentateuch (5-7). God impartially judged: (1) those from among His chosen people who refused to believe (5), (2) fallen angels who evidently cohabited with women before the flood (6; cf. Gen. 6:1-4; 2 Pet. 2:4), and (3) the immoral Gentiles described in Genesis 18 and 19 (7).

Like unreasoning animals, these apostates are ruled by the things they revile and destroyed by the things they practice (8-10). Even the archangel Michael is more careful in his dealings with superhuman powers than these arrogant men. Jude focuses more on the teachers of the heresy than on the heresy of the teachers, assuming that his readers would be familiar with the details. He compares these men to three spiritually rebellious men from Genesis (Cain) and Numbers (Balaam, Korah) who incurred the condemnation of God (11). Verses 12 and 13 succinctly summarize their character with five highly descriptive metaphors taken from nature: hidden reefs, airy clouds, uprooted trees, wild waves, and wandering stars. After affirming the judgment of God upon such ungodly men with a quote from the noncanonical book of Enoch (14,15), Jude catalogs some of their practices (16).

Antidote to Apostasy (17-25): This letter has been exposing "these men" (the apostate teachers; 8,10,12,14,16), but now Jude directly addresses his readers ("But you, beloved," 17). He reminds them of the apostolic warning that such men would come (17-19) and encourages them to protect themselves against the onslaught of apostasy (20,21). The readers must become mature in their own faith so that they will be able to rescue those who are enticed or already ensnared by error (22,23). Believers are to show mercy, not belligerence, when contending for the faith. They should hate the heresy but have compassion on those who are victimized.

Jude closes with one of the greatest doxologies in the Bible (24,25). It emphasizes the power of Christ to keep those who trust in Him from being overthrown by error.

Title—The Greek title *Iouda*, "Of Jude," comes from the name *Ioudas* which appears in verse 1. This name, which can be translated Jude or Judas, was popular in the first century because of Judas Maccabaeus (d.160 B.C.), a leader of the Jewish resistance against Syria during the Maccabean revolt.

Author—In spite of its limited subject matter and size, Jude was accepted as authentic and quoted by early church fathers. There may be some older allusions, but undisputed references to this epistle appear in the last quarter of the second century. It was included in the Muratorian Canon (c. 170) and accepted as part of Scripture by early leaders such as Tertullian and Origen. Nevertheless, doubts arose concerning the place of Jude in the canon because of its use of apocryphal books. It was a disputed book in some parts of the church, but it eventually won universal recognition.

A number of critics have attempted to assign a second century date to Jude, thus denying the traditional view of its authorship. This means that Jude was written by some other Jude ("brother of James" in verse 1 is thought to be an addition) or by an unknown forger. It is highly doubtful that a forger would impersonate such an obscure figure as Jude, and the arguments in support of a second-century date are not convincing:

the heresy refuted in Jude is not second-century Gnosticism; the "faith which was once for all delivered to the saints" (3) does not require a post-apostolic time since Paul used such expressions; the "words that were spoken beforehand by the apostles" (17) refers to previous writings but does not demand that the apostles were dead.

The author identifies himself as "a bond-servant of Jesus Christ, and brother of James" (1). This designation, combined with the reference in verse 17 to the apostles, makes it unlikely that this is the apostle Jude, called "Judas the brother of James" in the King James Version of Luke 6:16 and Acts 1:13. The Greek construction is better rendered in most modern translations as "Judas the son of James," so that the apostle Jude does not fit the description in Jude 1. This leaves the traditional view that Jude was one of the Lord's brothers, called Judas in Matthew 13:55 and Mark 6:3 (see James, Author). His older brother James (note his position on the two lists) was the famous leader of the Jerusalem church (Acts 15:13-21) and author of the epistle that bears his name. Like his brothers, Jude did not believe in Jesus before the resurrection (John 7:1-9; Acts 1:14). The only other biblical allusion to him is in 1 Corinthians 9:5 where "the brothers of the Lord" took their wives along on their missionary journeys (the Judas of Acts 15:22,32 may be another reference to him). Extrabiblical tradition adds nothing to our scanty knowledge about Jude.

Date and Setting—Jude's general address does not mark out any particular circle of readers, and there are no geographical restrictions. Nevertheless, Jude was probably thinking of a specific region that was being troubled by false teachers. There is not enough information in the epistle to settle the question of whether his readers were predominantly Jewish or Gentile Christians (there was probably a mixture of both). In any case, the progress of the faith in their region was threatened by a number of apostates who rejected Christ in practice and principle. These proud libertines were especially dangerous because of their deceptive flattery (16) and infiltration of Christian meetings (12). They perverted the grace of God (4) and caused divisions in the church (19).

Jude's description of these heretics is reminiscent of that found in 2 Peter and leads to the issue of the relationship between the two epistles (see 2 Peter, Author). The strong similarity between 2 Peter 2:1-3:4 and Jude 4-18 can hardly be coincidental, but the equally obvious differences rule out the possibility that one is a mere copy of the other. It is also doubtful that both authors independently drew from an unknown third source, so that the two remaining options are that Peter used Jude or Jude used Peter. Both views have their advocates, and a number of arguments have been raised in support of either side. But two arguments for the priority of 2 Peter are so strong that they tip the scales in favor of this position: (1) A comparison of the two books shows that 2 Peter anticipates the future rise of apostate teachers (2 Pet. 2:1,2; 3:3) while Jude records the historical fulfillment of Peter's words (Jude 4,11,12,17,18). (2) Jude directly quotes 2 Peter 3:3 and acknowledges it as a quote from "the apostles" (cf. 1 Tim. 4:1; 2 Tim. 3:1).

Because of the silence of the New Testament and tradition concerning Jude's later years, we cannot know where this epistle was written. Nor is there any way to be certain of its date. Assuming the priority of 2 Peter (64-66), the probable range is A.D. 66-80. (Jude's silence concerning the destruction of Jerusalem does not prove that he wrote this letter before A.D. 70).

Theme and Purpose

—This epistle is intensely concerned with the threat of heretical teachers in the church and the believer's proper response to that threat. The contents reveal two major purposes: (1) to condemn the practices of the ungodly libertines who were infesting the churches and corrupting believers; and (2) to counsel the readers to stand firm, grow in their faith, and contend for the truth. Jude says little about the actual doctrines of these "hidden reefs," but they might have held to an antinomian version of Gnosticism (see 1 John, Date and Setting). The readers are encouraged to reach out to those who have been misled by these men.

Contribution to the Bible

—Like his brother James, Jude used highly descriptive and stinging words to describe those who compromise the truth. Both use considerable nature imagery and a highly succinct style. Both lay strong stress on ethical purity and display loving concern for their readers in spite of the stern approach. Errorists were not to be persecuted but rescued and shown mercy. Though James and Jude were raised in the same household with Jesus, they both humbly refer to themselves as His bond-servants.

One unusual feature of this epistle is its abundant use of triads of thought. Examples can be found in verse 1 (Jude, bond-servant, brother; called, beloved, kept), verse 2 (mercy, peace, love), verses 5-7 (Israelites, angels, Gentiles), verse 11 (Cain, Balaam, Korah), verses 22,23 (some, others, some), and verse 25 (before, now, forever). The letter itself naturally breaks into three divisions (1-4,5-16,17-25).

Jude makes a surprising number of references to Old Testament characters and events in view of its brevity. But many have been troubled by its evident use of two first-century pseudepigraphal books. Jude 9 apparently alludes to the Assumption of Moses, and Jude 14,15 clearly quotes from the Book of Enoch (1:9). But this does not mean that Jude was thereby affirming the authority of these books; he was merely using them to illustrate a point much like Paul when he cited the Greek poets Aratus (Acts 17:28), Menander (1 Cor. 15:33), and Epimenides (Titus 1:12).

Christ in Jude—In contrast to those who stand condemned by their licentiousness and denial of Christ (4), the believer is "kept for Jesus Christ" (1). Jude tells his readers to "keep yourselves in the love of God, waiting anxiously for the mercy of our Lord Jesus Christ to eternal life" (21). But at the same time, the Lord "is able to keep you from stumbling, and to make you stand in the presence of His glory blameless with great joy" (24).

Walk Thru the Non-Pauline Epistles

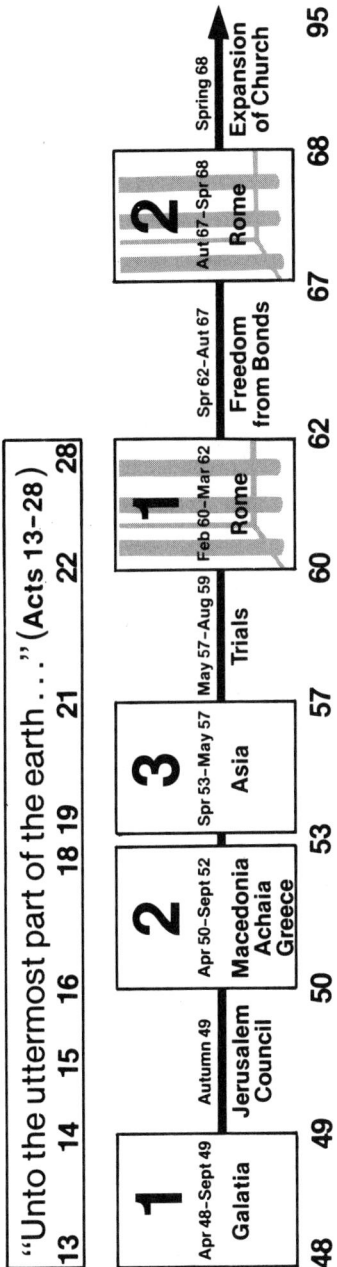

"Unto the uttermost part of the earth . . ." (Acts 13–28)

| 13 | 14 | 15 | 16 | 18 19 | 21 | 22 | 28 |

1 Apr 48–Sept 49 — Galatia

Autumn 49 — Jerusalem Council

2 Apr 50–Sept 52 — Macedonia Achaia Greece

3 Spr 53–May 57 — Asia

May 57–Aug 59 — Trials

1 Feb 60–Mar 62 — Rome

Spr 62–Aut 67 — Freedom from Bonds

2 Aut 67–Spr 68 — Rome

Spring 68 — Expansion of Church

48 49 50 53 57 60 62 67 68 95

James
Place: Jerusalem?
Date: 46-49

1 Peter
Place: Rome
Date: 63-64

2 Peter
Place: Rome?
Date: 64-66

Hebrews
Place: Unknown
Date: 64-68

Jude
Place: Unknown
Date: 66-80

1 John
Place: Ephesus
Date: c. 90

2 John
Place: Ephesus
Date: c. 90

3 John
Place: Ephesus
Date: c. 90

Revelation
Place: Patmos
Date: 95-96

Summary of the Non-Pauline Epistles

Book	No. of Chapters	Author	Key Word	Place Written	Date Written	Recipients
Hebrews	13	Unknown	Milk to Meat	Unknown	64-68	Unstated
James	5	James	Faith Gauge	Jerusalem ?	46-49	The twelve tribes dispersed abroad
1 Peter	5	Peter	Pain with a Purpose	Rome?	63-64	Those who reside as aliens
2 Peter	3	Peter	Poison in the Pew	Rome ?	64-66	Those who have received a faith the same as ours
1 John	5	John	Fellowship Barometer	Ephesus	C. 90	My little children
2 John	1	John	Bolt the Door	Ephesus	C. 90	The chosen lady and her children
3 John	1	John	Open the Door	Ephesus	C. 90	The beloved Gaius
Jude	1	Jude	Fight for the Faith	Unknown	66-80	Those who are the called, beloved in God the Father, and kept for Jesus Christ
Revelation	22	John	Coming Events	Patmos	95-96	The seven churches in Asia

Revelation

"The Revelation of Jesus Christ, which God gave Him to show to His bond-servants, the things which must shortly take place; and He sent and communicated it by His angel to His bond-servant John."   Revelation 1:1

"The kingdom of the world has become the kingdom of our Lord, and of His Christ; and He will reign forever and ever."
Revelation 11:15b (Also see 1:19; 5:13; 22:20.)

FO-CUS	Theophany 1		3	Tribulation 4						18	Triumph 19			22
D I V I S I O N S	Prologue to the Book	Portrait of the Glorious Christ	Pronouncements to the Seven Churches	Juridical Authority of Christ	Judgment of the Seven Seals (Prophetic Parenthesis in 7)	Judgment of the Seven Trumpets (Prophetic Parenthesis in 10-11:14)	Juxtaposed Prophecies	Judgment of the Seven Bowls (Prelude in 15)	Judgment of Babylon	Return of Christ in Glory	Resurrection, Reign of Christ, Final Judgment	Re-creation and the New Jerusalem	Reassurance of the Return of Christ
	1:1-8	1:9 1:20	2 3	4 5	6 8:1	8:2 11	12 14	15 16	17 18	19	20	21 22:5	22:6-21
T O P I C S	"the things which you have seen"	"and the things which are . . ."		"and the things which shall take place after these things" (1:19)									
	Commencement	Churches		Cosmic Conflict					Conquest		Con-summation		
	Heavenly Vision on Earth			Heaven and Earth							New Heaven and New Earth		
	Judge			Judgment							Jubilation		
Location	The Island of Patmos												
Time	A.D. 95-96												

Talk Thru—Just as Genesis is the book of beginnings, Revelation is the book of consummation. In it, the divine program of redemption begun in Genesis 3 is brought to fruition, and the holy name of God is vindicated before all creation. Like no other book, Revelation opens our eyes to the awesome spiritual warfare waged in heaven and earth.

Although there are numerous prophecies in the gospels and epistles, Revelation is the only New Testament book that focuses primarily on prophetic events. It is written in the form of apocalyptic literature (cf. Daniel and Zechariah) by a prophet (10:11; 22:9) and refers to itself as a prophetic book (1:3; 22:7,10,18,19). There are three major movements in this profound unveiling: Theophany (1-3), Tribulation (4-18), and Triumph (19-22).

Theophany (1-3): The prologue to Revelation contains a superscription (1:1-3) before the usual salutation (1:4-8). The Revelation was received by Christ from the Father and communicated by an angel to John. This is the only biblical book that specifically promises a blessing to those who read it (1:3), but it also promises a curse to those who add to or detract from it (22:18,19). The salutation and closing benediction show that it was originally written as an epistle to seven Asian churches.

A rich theological portrait of the triune God (1:4-8) is followed by an overwhelming theophany (visible manifestation of God) in 1:9-20. The omnipotent and omniscient Christ who will subjugate all things under His authority is the central figure in this book. Each of the following messages to the seven churches (2-3) refers back to an aspect of John's vision of Christ and contains a command, a commendation and/or condemnation, a correction, and a challenge. These messages are tailor-made to suit the needs of each of the seven churches, and some expositors have also seen in them a relevance that goes beyond the first-century context. It is possible that they portray some of the general movements in the history of the Christian church.

Tribulation (4-18): John is translated into heaven where he is given a vision of the divine majesty. In it, the Father ("One sitting on the throne") and the Son (The Lion/Lamb) are worshiped by the 24 elders, the four living creatures, and the angelic host because of who they are and what they have done (creation and redemption; 4-5). Christ is declared worthy to judge the earth as the Redeemer of men, and He is about to open the seven seals of the book of judgment.

There are three cycles of seven judgments in chapters 6-16 which consist of seven seals, seven trumpets, and seven bowls. There is a prophetic insert between the sixth and seventh seal and trumpet judgments and an extended insert between the trumpet and bowl judgments. Because of the similarity of the seventh judgment in each series, it is possible that the three sets of judgments take place concurrently or with some overlap so that they all terminate with the return of Christ. An alternate approach views them as three consecutive series of judgments, so that the seventh seal is the seven trumpets and the seventh trumpet is the seven bowls.

The seven seals (6:1-8:1) are generated in large part by the sinfulness of man. They include war, the famine and death that are associated with war, and persecution. The prophetic insert between the sixth and seventh seals (7:1-17) describes the protective sealing of 144,000 "sons of Israel," 12,000 from every tribe. It also looks ahead to the multitudes from every part of the earth "who come out of the great tribulation." The seven trumpets (8:2-11:19) appear to be largely associated with Satanic and demonic activity, judging by the symbolism that is used. The catastrophic events in most of the trumpet judgments result in the destruction of a number of "thirds," and the last three judgments are called "woes." The prophetic interlude between the sixth and seventh trumpets (10:1-11:14) adds more details about the nature of the tribulation period and mentions a fourth set of seven judgments (the "seven peals of thunder") which would have extended it if they had not been withdrawn. Two unnamed witnesses will minister during the last three and one half years of the tribulation (42 months or 1,260 days). At the end of their ministry they will be overcome by the beast, but their resurrection and ascension will confound their enemies.

Chapters 12-14 contain a number of miscellaneous prophecies that are inserted between the trumpet and bowl judgments to give further background on the time of tribulation. The woman of chapter 12 is evidently Israel, her child is Christ, and the dragon is Satan. After he is cast down to earth, Satan will seek to destroy the woman but will not succeed. Chapter 13 gives a graphic description of the antichrist and his false prophet, both empowered by Satan. The first beast is given political, economic, and religious authority, and because of his power and the lying miracles performed by the second beast, he is worshiped as the ruler of the earth. Chapter 14 contains a series of visions including the 144,000 at the end of the tribulation, the fate of those who follow the beast, and the outpouring of the wrath of God.

The seven bowl judgments of chapter 16 are prefaced by a heavenly vision of the power, holiness, and glory of God in chapter 15. This final series of judgments appears to take place just prior to the return of Christ, and it stems from the righteous wrath of God.

Chapters 17 and 18 anticipate the final downfall of the religio-political system of the revived Roman empire. "Babylon" is symbolically used to refer both to a system and to a city. Commentators disagree, but chapter 17 may focus on the false religious aspect of Babylon, while chapter 18 deals with the overthrow of political and commercial Babylon.

Triumph (19-22): Christ Himself is about to return to the earth, and heaven wells up with praise for God. With His triumphant and glorious coming he vindicates His righteousness and all who have been persecuted for His name. The Messianic marriage banquet is ready to take place, and the awesome King of kings appears to overthrow His enemies in one consummating judgment (19). The antichrist and false prophet are thrown into the lake of fire, their followers perish, and Satan is bound for 1,000 years. During this 1,000 year period Christ reigns over the earth with His resurrected saints, but by the end of this millennium, many will have been born who refused to submit their hearts to Christ. Satan will be released for a time and these people will become evident when they are Satanically inspired to wage war with the Lord. But Satan is permanently thrown into the lake of fire, the heavens and earth disappear, and the final great white throne judgment of those who rejected Christ takes place (20).

A new universe is created, this time unspoiled by sin, death, pain, or sorrow. The new Jerusalem, described in 21:9-22:5, is shaped like a gigantic cube, 1,500 miles in length, width, and height (the most holy place in the tabernacle and the temple was also a perfect cube). Its multicolored stones will reflect the glory of God and it will continually be filled with light. But the greatest thing of all is that believers will be in the presence of God "and they shall see His face."

Revelation concludes with an epilogue (22:6-21) which reassures the readers that Christ is "coming quickly" (22:7,12,20) and invites all who wish to drink the free water of eternal life to come to the Alpha and the Omega, the bright morning star.

Title—The title of this book in the Greek text is *Apokalypsis Ioannou*, "Revelation of John." It is also known as the Apocalypse, a transliteration of the word *apokalypsis*, meaning "unveiling," "disclosure," or "revelation." Thus, the book is an unveiling of that which otherwise could not be known. A better title comes from the first verse: *Apokalypsis Iesou Christou*, "Revelation of Jesus Christ." This could be taken as a revelation which came from Christ or as a revelation which is about Christ—both are appropriate. Because of the unified contents of this book, it should not be called "Revelations."

Author—The style, symmetry, and plan of Revelation show that it was written by one author, four times named "John" (1:1,4,9; 22:8; see John, Author). Because of its contents and its address to seven churches, Revelation quickly circulated and became widely known and accepted in the early church. It was frequently mentioned and quoted by second- and third-century Christian writers and received as part of the canon of New Testament books. From the beginning, Revelation was considered an authentic work of the apostle John, the same John who wrote the gospel and three epistles. This was true of Justin Martyr, the Shepherd of Hermas, Melito, Irenaeus, the Muratorian Canon, Tertullian, Clement of Alexandria, Origen, and others.

This view was seldom questioned until the middle of the third century when Dionysius presented several arguments against the apostolic authorship of Revelation. He observed a clear difference in style and thought between Revelation and the books which he accepted as Johannine, and concluded that the Apocalypse must have been penned by a different John. Indeed, the internal evidence does pose some problems for the traditional view: (1) the Greek grammar of Revelation is not on a par with the fourth gospel or the Johannine epistles; (2) there are also differences in vocabulary and expressions used; (3) the theological content of this book differs from John's other writings in emphasis and presentation; (4) John's other writings avoid the use of his name, but it is found four times in this book. While these difficulties exist, two things should be kept in mind: (1) There are a number of remarkable similarities between the Apocalypse and the other books traditionally associated with the apostle John (e.g., the distinctive use of terms like "word," "lamb," and "true," and the careful development of conflicting themes like light and darkness, love and hatred, good and evil). (2) Many of the differences can be explained by the unusual circumstances surrounding this book. The apocalyptic subject matter demands a different treatment, and John received the contents not by reflection but by a series of startling and ecstatic visions. It is also possible that John used an amanuensis who smoothed out the Greek style of his other writings, and that his exile on Patmos prevented the use of such a scribe when he wrote Revelation.

Thus, the internal evidence, while problematic, need not overrule the early and strong external testimony to the apostolic origin of this important book. The author was obviously well known to the recipients in the seven Asian churches, and this fits the unqualified use of the name "John" and the uniform tradition about his ministry in Asia. Alternate suggestions like "John the Elder" or a prophet named John create more problems than they solve.

Date and Setting—John directed this prophetic word to seven selected churches in the Roman province of Asia (1:3,4). The messages to these churches in chapters 2 and 3 begin with Ephesus, the most prominent, and continue in a clockwise direction until Laodicea is reached. It is likely that this book was initially carried along this circular route. While each of these messages had particular significance for these churches, they were also relevant for the church as a whole ("He who has an ear, let him hear what the Spirit says to the churches").

John's effective testimony for Christ led the Roman authorities to exile him on the small, desolate island of Patmos in the Aegean Sea (1:9). This island of volcanic rock was one of several used by the Romans to banish criminals and political offenders.

Revelation was written at a time when Roman hostility to Christianity was erupting into overt persecution (1:9; 2:10,13). Some scholars believe that it should be given an early date during the persecution of Christians under Nero after the A.D. 64 burning of Rome. The Hebrew letters for Nero Caesar (*Neron Kesar*) add up to 666, the number of the beast (13:18), and there was a legend that Nero would reappear in the East after his apparent death (compare Rev. 13:3,12,14). This kind of evidence is weak, and a later date near the end of reign of the emperor Domitian (81-96) is preferable for several reasons: (1) This was the testimony of Irenaeus (disciple of Polycarp who was a disciple of John) and other early Christian writers. (2) John probably did not move from Jerusalem to Ephesus until about A.D. 67, shortly before the Roman destruction of Jerusalem in A.D. 70. The early dating would not give him enough time to have established an ongoing ministry in Asia by the time he wrote this book. (3) The churches of Asia appear to have been in existence for a number of years, long enough for some to reach a point of complacency and decline (cf. 2:4; 3:1,15-18). (4) The deeds of Domitian are more relevant than those of Nero to the themes of the Apocalypse. Worship of deceased emperors had been practiced for years, but Domitian was the first emperor to demand worship while he was alive. This led to a greater clash between the state and the church, especially in Asia, where the worship of Caesar was widely practiced. The persecution under Domitian pointed ahead to the more severe persecutions that would follow.

Thus, it is likely that John wrote this book in A.D. 95-96. The date of his release from Patmos is unknown, but he was probably allowed to return to Ephesus after the reign of Domitian. Passages like 1:11; 22:7,9,10,18,19 suggest that the book was completed before John's release.

Theme and Purpose—The purposes for which Revelation was written depend to some extent on how the book as a whole is interpreted. Because of its complex imagery and symbolism, Revelation is the most difficult biblical book to interpret, and there are four major alternatives: (1) The *symbolic or idealist* view maintains that Revelation is not a predictive prophecy but a symbolic portrait of the cosmic conflict of spiritual principles. In this way the book is divorced from the realm of history and placed exclusively in the realm of ideas. (2) The _preterist_ view (the Latin word _praeter_ means "past") also denies the prophetic aspect of the Apocalypse, limiting it solely to the events of the first century. It is a symbolic description of the Roman persecution of the church, emperor worship, and the divine judgment of Rome. (3) The _historicist_ view approaches Revelation as an allegorical panorama of the history of the (western) church from the first century to the second advent. The lack of objective criteria combined with the changing historical climate from one generation to another has led to a wide range of conflicting interpretations within this school. (4) The _futurist_ view acknowledges the obvious influence that the first-century conflict between Roman power and the church had upon the themes of this book. But it also accepts the bulk of Revelation (chapters 4-22) as an inspired look into the time immediately preceding the second advent (the "tribulation," usually seen as seven years; 4-18), and extending from the return of Christ to the creation of the new cosmos (19-22). According to this view, the Apocalypse centers around the second advent of Christ who will return in power and glory as the Judge of all who rejected His offer of salvation. Futurists attempt to discern the literal meanings behind the symbolism of Revelation whenever this is permitted by the context or by comparison with other Scripture.

Generally speaking, proponents of the first three views are postmillennial or amillennial, while futurists are premillennial. Postmillennialists believe that the spread of the gospel will lead to a golden age of peace on earth followed by the return of Christ; amillennialists believe that the Christian's present heavenly position in Christ is the true "millennium," not an earthly kingdom; and premillennialists believe that the six appearances of "a thousand years" in 20:2-7 are to be taken literally as the duration of the earthly kingdom that Christ will establish between the second advent and the creation of the new universe.

Advocates of all four interpretive approaches to Revelation agree that it was written to assure the recipients of the ultimate triumph of Christ over all who rise up against Him and His saints. The readers were facing dark times of persecution, and even worse times would follow. Therefore they needed to be encouraged to persevere by standing firm in Christ in view of

God's plan for the righteous and the wicked. This plan is especially clear in the stirring words of the epilogue (22:6-21). The book was also written to challenge complacent Christians to stop compromising with the world. According to futurists, Revelation serves the additional purpose of providing a perspective on end-time events that would have meaning and relevance to the spiritual lives of all succeeding generations of Christians.

Contribution to the Bible—Revelation is a unique blend of apocalyptic, prophetic, and epistolary literature. The contents of Revelation are apocalyptic, as can be seen by a comparison with Isaiah 24-27, Ezekiel, Daniel, Joel, and Zechariah, as well as intertestamental apocalypses like the Book of Enoch, the Apocalypse of Baruch, and the Apocalypse of Ezra (2 Esdras 3-14). Such literature is characterized by symbolic language, ecstatic visions, catastrophic judgments, and eschatological material. The theme and message of Revelation are prophetic, according to the book's own claim (1:3; 22:7,10,18,19). The form of Revelation is epistolary, with its salutation (1:4-6), its seven individual letters (chapters 2 and 3), and its closing benediction (22:21).

"Revelation" means an "unveiling" or "disclosure," but many regard its content as veiled or closed because of the heavy symbolism. This leads to the view that the book should not be studied because its undecipherable nature will only lead the student into error. The opposite extreme is the overconfident approach which asserts that every symbolic nuance can be captured. This can lead to unhealthy speculation and "newspaper exegesis." The interpreter should steer a middle course between these extremes by seeking to understand as much as possible while acknowledging that this understanding will be limited. Hundreds of symbolic objects and acts are used in Revelation, but most of these are either explained in the context (e.g., 1:20) or in the rest of the Bible (e.g., the book of Daniel). John's frequent use of comparative descriptions ("like," "as it were") in his attempt to convey visions that are beyond words should be kept in mind. Numerical symbolism also appears frequently; seven, the number of completion or perfection, appears over 50 times (the numbers 4,10, and 12 are also significant). Familiarity with the Old Testament is an important prerequisite to an understanding of many things in Revelation. While there are no direct citations, scholars have found between 250 and 550 allusions to the Hebrew Scriptures in the Apocalypse. For example, note the obvious similarities between the 10 plagues of Exodus 7:14-12:36 and the judgments of Revelation 8 and 16. Another interpretive ingredient in Revelation is the fact that its visions are not always in chronological sequence—they sometimes dart back and forth.

Revelation is characterized by its dramatic interplay between heaven and earth. God is on His throne (4) as the sovereign Ruler of all creation. The earth is the center of the massive spiritual conflict portrayed in Revelation, and it is viewed from a global perspective. Satan gives the beast "authority over every tribe and people and tongue and nation" (13:7), but his power and time are limited (12:12), and he will be permanently judged (20:10). This is a book of divine judgment which culminates at the second advent of Messiah and the later great white throne judgment. God will righteously deal with all evil and vindicate His holy name. It is significant that interspersed between the judgments of this book are songs and declarations of praise for the character and works of God. Revelation abounds with joyful worship for the worthy Lord of creation and redemption (e.g., 4:2-5:14; 7:9-17; 15:2-8; 19:1-7).

This book is more relevant now than ever before, especially in view of modern political, economic, military, technological, and communicative developments. Some of the once mysterious descriptions now have contemporary analogies.

The Apocalypse has been given an appropriate place as the last book in the canon of Scripture because it ties the themes of the Bible together. Just as Genesis is the book of beginnings, Revelation is the book of consummation. There is an especially striking contrast between the first and last three chapters of the Bible:

GENESIS 1-3	REVELATION 20-22
"In the beginning God created the heavens and the earth" (1:1)	"I saw a new heaven and a new earth" (21:1)
"The darkness He called night" (1:5)	"There shall be no night there" (21:25)
"God made the two great lights" (sun and moon; 1:16)	"The city has no need of the sun or of the moon" (21:23)
"In the day that you eat from it you shall surely die" (2:17)	"And there shall no longer be any death" (21:4)
Satan appears as deceiver of mankind (3:1)	Satan disappears forever (20:10)
Shown a garden into which defilement entered (3:6,7)	Shown a city into which defilement will never enter (21:27)
Walk of God with man interrupted (3:8-10)	Walk of God with man resumed (21:3)
Initial triumph of the serpent (3:13)	Ultimate triumph of the Lamb (20:10; 22:3)
"I will greatly multiply your pain" (3:16)	"There shall no longer be any mourning, or crying, or pain" (21:4)
"Cursed is the ground because of you" (3:17)	"There shall no longer be any curse" (22:3)
Man's dominion broken in the fall of the first man, Adam (3:19)	Man's dominion restored in the rule of the new man, Christ (22:5)
First paradise closed (3:23)	New paradise opened (21:25)
Access to the tree of life disinherited in Adam (3:24)	Access to the tree of life reinstated in Christ (22:14)
They were driven from God's presence (3:24)	"They shall see His face" (22:4)

In a very real sense, Revelation 21 and 22 is the new Genesis, but this time there will be no fall. In broadest terms, the Bible gives the story of God's work in creation, redemption, and re-creation, and it centers on the incarnation of the God-man:

A	†	Ω
CREATION	REDEMPTION	NEW CREATION

Christ in Revelation

Christ in Revelation—Revelation has much to say about all three Persons of the Godhead, but it is especially clear in its presentation of the awesome resurrected Christ who has received all authority to judge the earth. He is called Jesus Christ (1:1), the faithful witness, the first-born of the dead, the ruler of the kings of the earth (1:5), the first and the last (1:17), the living One (1:18), the Son of God (2:18), holy and true (3:7), the Amen, the faithful and true witness, the Beginning of the creation of God (3:14), the Lion that is from the tribe of Judah, the Root of David (5:5), the Lamb (5:6), Faithful and True (19:11), The Word of God (19:13), King of kings, Lord of lords (19:16), the Alpha and the Omega (22:13), the bright morning star (22:16), and the Lord Jesus (22:21).

This book is indeed "The Revelation of Jesus Christ" (1:1) since it comes from Him and centers on Him. It begins with a vision of His glory, wisdom, and power (chapter 1), and portrays His authority over the entire church (chapters 2 and 3). He is the Lamb who was slain and declared worthy to open the book of judgment (chapter 5). His righteous wrath is poured out upon the whole earth (chapters 6-18) and He returns in power to judge His enemies and reign as the Lord over all (chapters 19 and 20). He will rule forever over the heavenly city in the presence of all who know Him (chapters 21 and 22).

The Scriptures close with His great promise: "Behold, I am coming quickly" (22:7,12,20). Amen. Come, Lord Jesus.

Integration of the New Testament

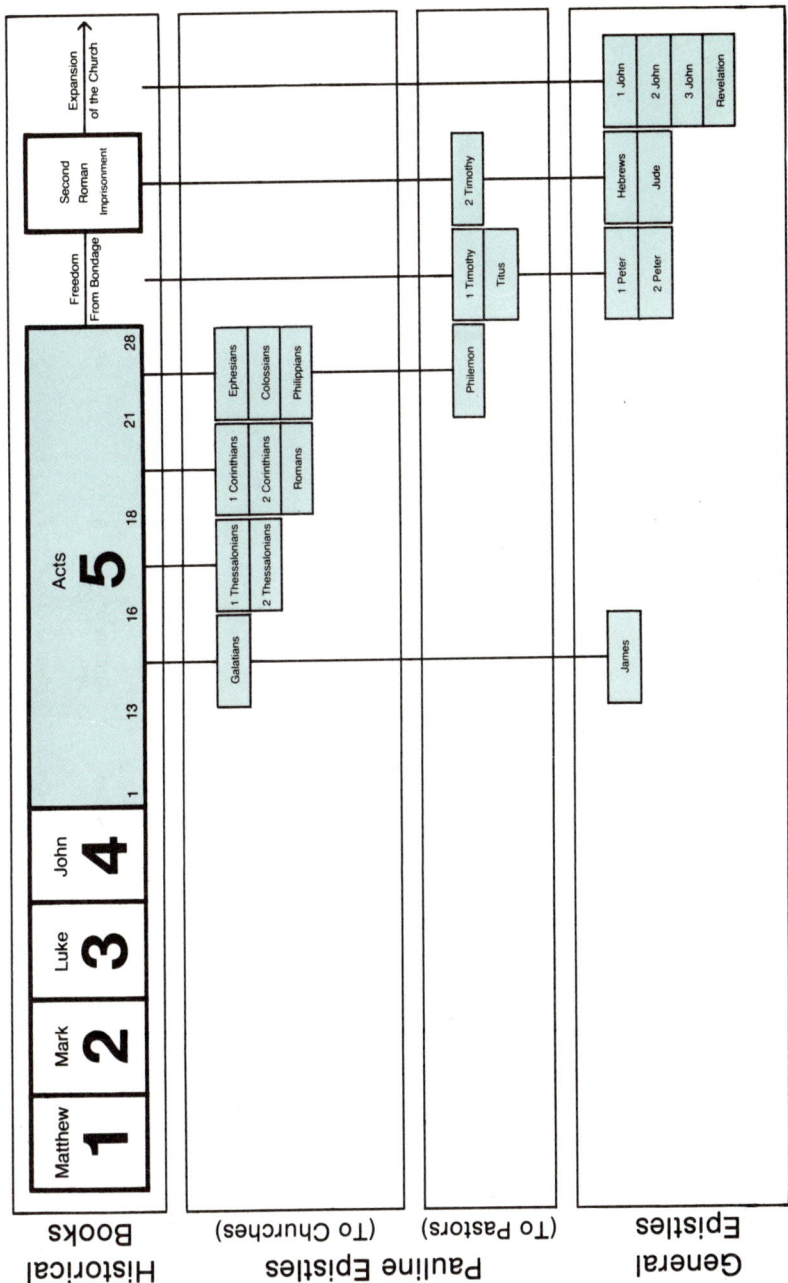

Authors of the New Testament

Name	Nationality	Home Town	Occupation	Relationships	Chapters Written	Verses Written	Books Written
Matthew	Jew	Capernaum	Tax Collector	Apostle of Jesus Christ	28	1,071	Gospel of Matthew
Mark	Jew/Roman	Jerusalem	Missionary	Disciple of Peter	16	678	Gospel of Mark
Luke	Greek	Antioch	Physician	Disciple of Paul	52	2,158	Gospel of Luke Acts
John	Jew	Bethsaida or Capernaum	Fisherman	Apostle of Jesus Christ	50	1,414	Gospel of John 1 John 2 John 3 John Revelation
Paul	Jew	Tarsus	Tentmaker	Apostle of Jesus Christ	87 (100)*	2,033 (2,336)*	Romans 1 Corinthians 2 Corinthians Galatians Ephesians Philippians Colossians Philemon 1 Thessalonians 2 Thessalonians 1 Timothy 2 Timothy Titus (Hebrews?)
James	Jew	Nazareth	Carpenter?	Brother of Jesus Christ	5	108	James
Peter	Jew	Bethsaida	Fisherman	Apostle of Jesus Christ	8	166	1 Peter 2 Peter
Jude	Jew	Nazareth	Carpenter?	Brother of Jesus Christ	1	25	Jude

*Indicates total if Hebrews is assigned to Paul.

The Links of Scripture

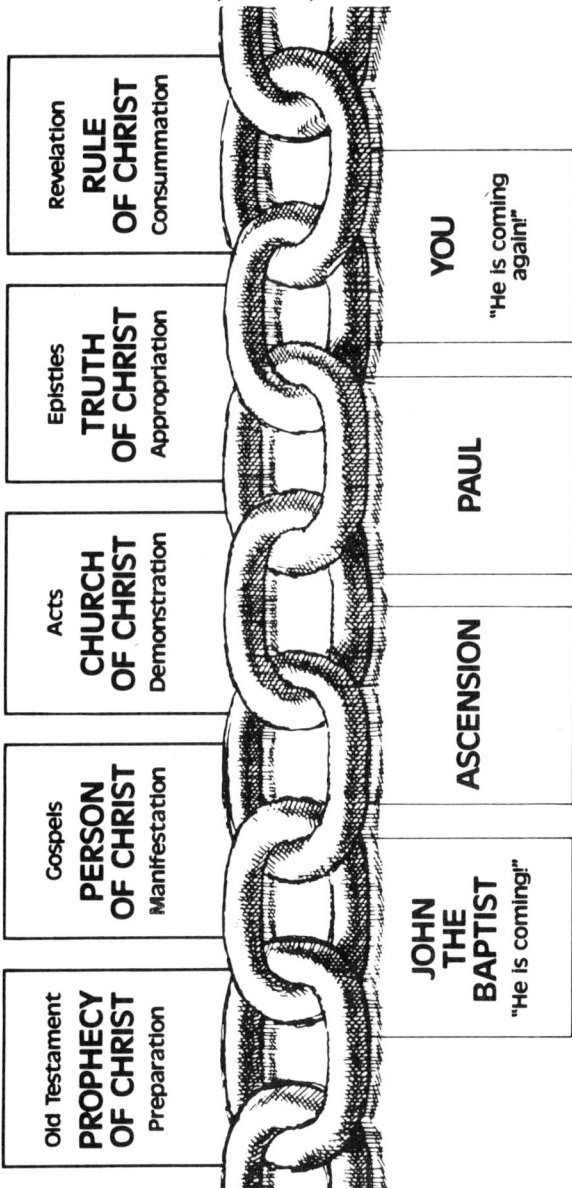

"Even so, come, Lord Jesus"

| Old Testament PROPHECY OF CHRIST Preparation | Gospels PERSON OF CHRIST Manifestation | Acts CHURCH OF CHRIST Demonstration | Epistles TRUTH OF CHRIST Appropriation | Revelation RULE OF CHRIST Consummation |

| JOHN THE BAPTIST "He is coming!" | ASCENSION | PAUL | YOU "He is coming again!" |

"In the beginning God"

229